The Dream Experience

MILTON KRAMER

The Dream Experience

A Systematic Exploration

Routledge
Taylor & Francis Group
New York   London

Routledge is an imprint of the
Taylor & Francis Group, an informa business

Routledge   Routledge
Taylor & Francis Group   Taylor & Francis Group
270 Madison Avenue   2 Park Square
New York, NY 10016   Milton Park, Abingdon
                                         Oxon OX14 4RN

Printed in the United States of America on acid-free paper
10 9 8 7 6 5 4 3 2 1

International Standard Book Number-10: 0-415-95446-0 (Hardcover)
International Standard Book Number-13: 978-0-415-95446-4 (Hardcover)

Library of Congress Cataloging-in-Publication Data

Kramer, Milton, 1929-
    The dream experience : a systematic exploration / Milton Kramer.
        p. cm.
    ISBN 0-415-95446-0 (hb)
    1. Dreams. I. Title.

BF1078.K73 2006
154.6'3--dc22   2006028998

Visit the Taylor & Francis Web site at
http://www.taylorandfrancis.com

and the Routledge Web site at
http://www.routledgementalhealth.com

Contents

The crown of the aged are the children's children
and the glory of children are their parents

Proverbs 17:6

Preface

The "Dream Experience" is intended to provide for the mental health professional a systematic scientific basis for understanding the dream as a psychological event. It will in addition describe a method for examining the dream text to extract a figurative meaning for the reported dream. This understanding of the dream will provide support for utilizing the dream report to confirm and expand the therapist's view of the weltanschauung of the dreamer and facilitate his utilization of the dream in therapy. The research program that I pursued for over four decades provides the basis for my observations and conclusions about dreams and dreaming.

The experience of dreaming has been described in our most ancient texts, e.g., the Beatty Papyrus from Egypt and in the Gilgamesh myth from Mesopotamia. Dreaming is the peculiar accompaniment of sleep during which events occur in which we may participate, simply observe, or just have a feeling they happened that has forever intrigued people. How are we to account for an event that engages us without our being awake and conscious? What can the meaning be of such an unusual event? The earliest explanations were that the dream episode was caused by supernatural forces either benevolent or malevolent. And that the meaning of the dream was to be sought either in dream books in which dream events have fixed interpretations or in more sophisticated texts which take into account the life circumstance and experiences of the dreamer such as that attributed to Artemidorus of Daldis. Professional dream interpreters could be visited in the temples of Aesklepius in Greece or in the streets of Jerusalem. By the 18th century, the supernatural basis for dreaming was replaced by a natural explanation, namely some alteration in the biological functioning of the body, particularly of the brain. W. Robert, a 19th century dream, theorist, suggested that dreaming was the brain disposing of mental waste much as Crick of DNA fame was later to claim as well. The interpretation of dreams remained an exercise of matching the dream events to a fixed meaning in a dream dictionary or linking the dream imagery to some universal symbol.

Dreaming in the modern era has been refocused by two events; one was the psychological description by Freud in 1900 of how the mind creates the dream experience through the dream work mechanisms. The second was the discovery by Aserinsky and Kleitman in 1952 of Rapid Eye Movement (REM) sleep, the biological substrate of much of dreaming. Freud's studies of dreaming provided (1) a theory of the function of the mind; (2) a method, free association, to establish the meaning of dreams; and (3) a treatment technique, psychoanalysis, which captured American psychiatry of the first half of the 20th century and supported a continuing professional interest in dreaming. The discovery of REM sleep, the biological substrate of much of dreaming, attracted the interest of psychiatrists because the promise of such intellectual giants as Freud, Jung, and Hughlings Jackson was that if we understood dreaming, the sane man's psychosis, we would begin to understand psychosis, a major public health problem in the mid-20th century. The ability to collect a number of dream reports from a single night made possible the experimental study of dreaming. Reliable systems to quantify dream content had already been developed and the systematic study of the content of the dream experience from its modest beginning in the last decade of the 19th century was vigorously expanded. New approaches to establish the possible meanings for dreams were undertaken. The series of studies undertaken and discussed in this work explores the proposition that dreams are a legitimate object of scientific study.

This systematic scientific exploration of the dream experience illustrates that the dream report can be legitimately studied scientifically. The dream is an experience extended in time and not the product of the awakening process. There is reason to accept that the dream report is a veridical reflection of the dream experience and not a secondary confabulatory response to being asked: What were you dreaming? It is abundantly clear that dream reports can be recovered from awakenings in the sleep laboratory or spontaneously reported and recorded by subjects in their dream diaries. There are reliable and validated dream content scales that permit the quantification of various aspects of the dream report such as the number of characters in the dream, whether the interaction among the characters was friendly, aggressive, or sexual, where the dream took place and whether there were scene changes in the dream narrative, and what emotions, if any, were expressed in the dream.

The "Dream Experience" will be presented in 13 chapters. Chapter 1 is an introduction that addresses the historical reasons people were interested in dreaming, modern reasons for studying the dream, and the problems in studying subjective processes like dreaming. In chapter 2, the question of whether the dream actually exists or is a product of the awakening experience is addressed. Chapter 3 focuses on whether dreams can be adequately collected in sufficient numbers at particular points in time to permit quantitative study, and in chapter 4, if they can be collected, are there reliable and valid measurement devices that will permit the quantification of variables of interest or will the essence of the dream experience elude our measurement efforts or be destroyed by them.

With the questions that have been raised about the variability of dreaming is there reason to believe that dreaming is an organized enough experience to be the object of scientific study? In chapter 5, I will review the evidence that dream content is signal not noise, that it is regular and not disorganized. Where there are psychological differences at the group level, there are systematic differences in dream content. At the level of the individual, dreams of individuals are different from each other and the dreams of an individual are different night to night.

In a book about dreaming, certain aspects of dreaming need to be addressed: (1) what do most people dream about during so-called normative dreaming? (2) types of dreams that occur frequently and apparently in all cultures, typical dreams; and (3) dreams that reoccur to a dreamer across time, the repetitive dream. Chapter 6 will encompass these special types of dream experiences: normative dreaming, typical dreams, and repetitive dreams.

Chapter 7 will review work on psychopathologic dreams, nightmares, and on dreams in psychopathologic states such as schizophrenia and depression. Nightmares reflect integrative disturbances that may be short-lived or chronic while the dreams of the mentally ill reflect their cognitively and emotionally altered mental condition.

Circumstances and events that have been shown to influence dream content are discussed in chapter 8. Dream content is responsive to the emotional experiences of the previous day, to new and continuing novel situations, to interpersonal situations, and to hearing familiar names during sleep. Chapter 9 describes the relationship between waking and dreaming thought from a state and trait point of view and shows that waking emotion and dream content are related. Dreams appear to be more reactive to prior wakefulness than proactive to subsequent wakefulness while emotions in dreams are more proactive than reactive. Dreams have the necessary orderliness to support the possibility they are meaningful, and in chapter 10, a methodology, dream translation, is described and examples of its application to dream samples are provided to assist the reader in applying the method.

A frequently asked question is: Does the dream serve any adaptive purpose? Chapter 11 reviews theories of dream function pointing out that function may relate to how the dream is constructed or to what dreaming does. Freud has offered the view that dreaming serves a sleep protective function. Solms has confirmed this in showing that brain-injured subjects who report the loss of dreaming also report more interrupted sleep. I have concluded from the research I have done that dreaming is a selective affective regulator, sort of an emotional thermostat that changes affect across the night. The significance of changing affect across the night is that how you feel on arising in the morning is a major determinant of your psychomotor functioning.

Selected theories that describe a biological substrate for dreaming are reviewed in chapter 12 and critiques are provided related to biological theories of dreaming in general and each of the theories in particular. Chapter 13 is a summary and concluding chapter addressing the regularity of dreaming, the basis that provides for the possibility that dreams are meaningful, the approach to extracting meaning that suggests that dreaming reflects the dreamers affectively determined worldview, and the recognition that biological approaches do not adequately address the syntactic, semantic, or pragmatic aspects of dreaming. An analogy of dreaming to delirium was questionable in the 19th century and remains so today.

Acknowledgments

I look back with pleasure and sadness as I remember the wonderful people who were so crucial to my 46 years of productive work in the field of dream research and sleep disorders medicine. My thoughts traverse a "Sentimental Journey" filled with the generosity of so many people who provided the environment, opportunity, and support for my endeavors. Life and careers are with people and it is to a group of teachers that I want to begin to express my gratitude. The intellectual environment and experiences at the College of Medicine of the University of Illinois in Chicago laid the foundation for my interest in research. I worked in the kidney pharmacology laboratory of the late Ted Sherrod, M.D., who made the observation that if you don't publish within five years of graduation you're unlikely to ever publish. The late Douglas Goldman, M.D., who was medical director of what was then Longview State Hospital in Cincinnati facilitated my first project that resulted in a publication in 1958, only four years after graduation. Yes Ted, I was counting.

I trained in psychiatry in a remarkable department with a remarkable chairman, Maurice Levine, M.D., who provided an intellectual atmosphere of unusual depth and breath. It was to Cincinnati that I returned after two years in the military with wife and three children to begin working at the VA hospital under Hal Hiatt, M.D., who was encouraging, supportive, and a dear friend who remains in my heart and mind. Roy Whitman, M.D., who had one of the first grants from NIMH to do dream studies, collecting dreams by awakening subjects from REM sleep, offered me the opportunity to join his research group and we worked together until 1967. It was with Roy that I began my work in dreaming that continues to this day and is the basis for this book. My friend Jerry Baum, M.D., who was associate chief of staff for research at the VA provided logistic support for me to open a sleep/dream laboratory and the Veteran's Administration provided grant support for my work from 1962 until 1984.

I closed my laboratory in Cincinnati in 1982 following the death of Dr. Levine and the retirement of Hal Hiatt and joined Ed Draper's department at the University of Mississippi in Jackson opening the first Division of Sleep in a medical school. I opened a laboratory at the VA hospital as well with Ed's support. The encouragement Ed offered and the support I got from the administration allowed my research to continue.

I returned to Cincinnati in 1984 to open a clinical sleep program at Bethesda Hospital, continuing my clinical work in sleep medicine and my research in dreams and dreaming. The hospital director, Tom Willburn, encouraged my work by providing space, staff, and funding. In 1999, I moved to New York City into retirement with clinical appointments at NYU and Albert Einstein College of Medicine and to a position as Director of Psychiatric Research at the Maimonides Medical Center in Brooklyn where my current chief, Marvin Lipkowitz, M.D., has fostered my continuing to teach and do research.

The course in Dream Translation, which to a large extent is the basis for this book, was developed while I was on the faculty at the Universities of Cincinnati and Mississippi. I continue to teach the course at Albert Einstein in New York and to my residents at Maimonides. I have enjoyed the opportunity the American Psychiatric Association has provided in allowing me to teach Dream Translation at the Annual Meeting for the past eight years. I am grateful to the residents and colleagues who have attended these presentations and provided such valuable feed back.

The colleagues I have met through the Association for the Psychophysiological Study of Sleep now the Sleep Research Society and American Academy of Sleep Medicine and the Association for the Study of Dreams now the International Association for the Study of Dreams have made the journey a wonderful and fulfilling experience. In particular, those dream researchers came to a conference in Cincinnati in 1967 funded by NIMH and remain friends to this day. When I look at the published proceedings of the 1967 conference, "Dream Psychology and the new Biology of Dreaming," I return to a time of beginning when we were all young and the departed have returned.

I want to thank a number of authors and publishers who have granted me permission to reproduce material from their work. Stephen LaBerge kindly granted me permission to quote a lucid dream of his from his book "Lucid Dreaming." The quotations from Freud's "The Interpretation of

Dreams" are with the permission of Basic Books Publishers. The dream material from my paper "Patterns of Dreaming" is with the permission of the publishers of the *Journal of Nervous and Mental Disease*. Alan Hobson, Ed Pace-Schott and Bob Stickgold were accepting, if not in complete agreement, with my paraphrase of their work. Tom Roth agreed to allow citations from our paper "Dream Translation" to be used. I am grateful to you all.

The colleagues, professional and technical, who traveled with me at various times in my "Sentimental Journey" have contributed to my education both personal and professional and I am grateful to you all. The best is truly saved for last, my life partner, Fradie, who tolerated and encouraged but never compromised, who provided us with the joys of the children, Ruthie, Danny, Mary, and Sammy, their spouses Asher, Judy, Jerry, and Roberta and the children's children, Avishai, Yael, Nadav, Ilona, Hannah, Josh, and Max. The dream fulfilled is the family we have.

Milton Kramer

CHAPTER 1

Introduction

A. The Historical Interest in Dreaming

The traditional interest in dreaming is to be found in the folk beliefs of dreamers who apparently were intrigued by their nocturnal experiences and sought an explanation for them (Lincoln, 1935). In most circumstances beyond their control, the ancients invoked a supernatural explanation. It was believed, in many traditions, that the will of God, or of the Gods, was revealed through dreams. The interpretations offered by the Biblical Joseph to the Pharaoh that explained the meaning of the seven fat kine (cows) followed by the seven lean kine led to his release from prison and elevation to high office. Joseph attributed the dream interpretation not to his skills but that God had interpreted the dreams (Hertz, 1976). The revelations of the Prophet Mohammed, recorded in the Koran, came to him in dreams where he was visited by the Angel Gabriel who spoke to him of God's will (Dawood & Wyatt, 1991). The early church fathers became concerned about their congregants viewing all dreaming as a message from God (Sanford, 1968). They worried that the Devil might use the dream experience to mislead the believer. They recognized a distinction between dreams from above, from God, and dreams from below, from the Devil that could lead the dreamer astray (Van de Castle, 1994). To avoid the dangers of being misled by evil forces, the church fathers early on turned against dream interpretation and dream interpreters and vigorously discouraged any attention to the dream and especially to experiencing the dream as a revelation (Kelsey, 1968).

People through the ages have looked to the dream experience as a possible predictor of future events. In an unpredictable world filled with capricious Gods, foreknowledge then becomes a highly desirable commodity and premonitory dreaming a way to obtain such knowledge. Alexander the Great had laid siege to Tyre but was undecided about moving against the city. He had a dream of a Satyr. His court magician interpreted this by dividing the word Satyr and concluding that the meaning was Tyre is yours (Hughes, 1984; Kelsey, 1968). This interpretation apparently strengthened Alexander's resolve and he attacked and conquered the city.

There was a possible premonitory dream that preceded the horrible air disaster that was the crash of an American Airlines DC-10 at Chicago's O'Hare International Airport on May 26, 1979 in which 275 passengers were killed. David Booth, a 23-year-old office manager in Cincinnati, Ohio had the same nightmare for 10 nights in a row. He heard the sound of large engines failing then he saw an American Airlines passenger plane swerve and roll in the air and crash into the ground in a red fire. David was deeply troubled by what he had experienced. "There never was any doubt to me that something was going to happen. It wasn't like a dream. It was like I was standing there watching the whole thing." On May 22, 1979, he called a psychiatrist at the University of Cincinnati, American Airlines, and the Federal Aviation Administration (FAA) office at the Cincinnati airport. The FAA took him seriously but couldn't match the site to his description. The FAA felt the description of the crash bore a striking resemblance to what David had described. Was it pre-cognitive or coincidence? For some the question is an open one.

The belief in the curative and revelatory nature of dreaming was accepted and utilized by the Greek physicians who were members of the Asklepian cult (Meier, 1966). Asklepios was the Greek God of healing and his temples were places people came to be healed. Early on in the history of the Asklepian temples, the patient came to the temple and slept there, generally in the open, and had a dream experience that was healing. The temple grounds had many testimonials from patients who had been healed. Later on in the history of the temples, the practice changed, some have said degenerated. The patient came to the temple and slept, often with the aid of a potion, and the temple priest-physician moved among the sleepers in costume. On awakening, the patient reported his dream to the priest who interpreted the healing prescription that the God had communicated through the dream. Dependence on the expert for interpretation occurs early in the history of the effort to understand the import of the dream experience.

The 2nd century work on dream interpretation entitled *Oneirocritica* by Artemidorus of Daldis (White, 1990) provides a more sophisticated approach on which to base an interpretation of dreams than the simple and arbitrary substitutions of the dream books of the ancients. Artemidorus advised that the life circumstances of the dreamer be taken into account in guiding the interpretation including the identity, gender, age, marital status, financial status, ethnicity, health, and occupation, among other things. He believed in the premonitory nature of dreaming and used the outcome of his interpretations to underpin his interpretive approach. He warned to be cautious to separate dreams that can be taken at face value and those that are to be understood allegorically. Artemidorus recommended particular attention be paid to dreams with no obvious motivating force. He observed that dreams are often only a continuation of the day's activities and he believed that dreams are often prompted by bodily needs or recent psychologically significant events. Recurrent dreams were to be regarded as especially significant. Artemidorus exemplified an insightful and valuable approach that went beyond what was usual for his time and is in concert with a modern view of dreaming.

It was in the 18th century with the beginning of the Enlightenment that the shift began to occur in the West from supernatural to naturalistic explanations in our understanding of the world and of man in that world. We might expect that the explanation for the dream experience and what the experience means, if anything, would have a more naturalistic and less supernatural explanation. This was indeed the case and the dream experience came to be seen as a consequence of physiologic changes in the dreamer. Nevertheless a segment of the population maintained a belief in a supernatural explanation of dreaming. My colleagues and I undertook to survey a statistically representative sample of adults in a mid-American city, Cincinnati (Kramer, Winget, & Whitman, 1971). In addition to asking each participant for a dream report, they were asked whether they believed that dreams could be premonitory and predict future events. Some 5% of our respondents stated that dreams could foretell future events. Perhaps in a country that has been described as the most religious in the Western world that some 1.5 million of our fellow citizens may express a belief in the supernatural should not be a surprise.

Does the belief in the premonitory nature of dreaming manifest itself in other ways? It has been said that the major work on dreaming that has captured the public's imagination and has re-awakened and sustained an interest in dreams is Freud's magnum opus *The Interpretation of Dreams* (Freud, 1955). Freud had an interest in the occult, but he rejected the notion that the dream in a supernatural manner could predict the future. Books such as *Aunt Sally's Policy Players Dream Book* (Yronwode, 2003) and others like it reflect the general public's interest in looking to dreams for information about what will happen in the future. Beginning in the 1890s in the black communities in the United States, a lottery-like illegal gambling game developed called "Policy." The bets could be quite small, pennies, and the pay offs were 10 times the bet. The choice of the number to bet by the policy player often was chosen from a dream book such as Aunt Sally's. The player would select the image from a dream he had and search the dream book for the number that was linked to his dream image. There has been some interesting speculation about the basis for the relationship between a number and a dream image. For example, the interlocking nature of 6 and 9 has been offered as the basis for relating 69 to sexual activity in dreams. Policy and particular numbers and images became so commonplace that they appeared in blues songs in the 1920s and 1930s. Illegal gambling expanded over time into the white community and control shifted to organized crime; the game was now called "the numbers." Pay-offs were linked to numbers that appeared in the public domain such as the number of shares traded on a designated stock exchange and this helped maintain a belief in the honesty of the winning number. Interest in and the use of dream books that provided number equivalents for dream images remained high. I wonder if players in the legalized state run lotteries of today turn to current versions of Aunt Sally's book. The ancient Egyptians used dream dictionaries with fixed symbols, e.g., the Beatty Papyrus III and the lottery player of today may well continue the same behavior. We have gone from the Beatty Papyrus (Van de Castle, 1994) to Aunt Sally's over three to four millennia.

The other work that has sustained an interest in dreaming, as was noted earlier, was Freud's *The Interpretation of Dreams*. It was written in the last decade of the 19th century and published in 1900. It was barely noticed when it first appeared and took eight years to sell out its first printing (Kramer, 1994). This was in contrast to the work of Darwin (Darwin, 2003)—*The Origin of Species by Means of Natural Selection,* published in 1859, whichh was an immediate best seller. Freud always felt that the dream book was his major work. Psychoanalysis went on to capture the popular imagination and became the preferred treatment for emotional distress, especially in the United States. Interest in understanding the forces in the unconscious, in the motives outside of our awareness that were the "true determinants" of our behavior and revealed what we really thought and believed, were eagerly sought. Freud had expressed the view that "The interpretation of dreams is the royal road to a knowledge of the unconscious activities of the mind." This led psychoanalysts and later psychotherapists to encourage the reporting of dreams by their patients and to attempt through the use of the "free associations" of their patients to undo the dream work that created the disguise of the manifest dream that the patient experienced and reported. The therapist then could reconstruct the latent dream thoughts, the source of the manifest dream, that reflected the true feelings and motivations of the dreamer. Carl Jung (Jung, 1964a,b), an early disciple, collaborator, and finally a defector from Freud, in his Analytic Psychology, saw the dream experience as essentially a compensation for the exaggerated waking maladaptive traits of the dreamer. He recognized in the dreams characters, actions, and symbols were expressions of both individual and universal aspects of the human condition (Jung, 1974; Jung, 1984). The dream for Jung was revealing of the dreamer's psyche and the task of the therapist was to grasp the meaning that was being expressed. Techniques such as the use of active imagination, amplification, and symbol interpretation were used in the search for the meaning of the dream. The value of this increased self-knowledge, this message to the dreamer from his unconscious, would be to enhance the development of the individuation process within the individual to become more self-actualizing. Alfred Adler (Adler, 1956; Schulman, 1969), an early disciple and the first major defector from Freud and psychoanalysis, in his Individual Psychology, saw the dream experience as providing the emotional motor power to support the dreamer's striving toward his fictive life goal. As the individual came to terms with the need for superiority in order to enhance his life style and solved his waking problems with courage and social interest, the need to seek fictive and simplified solutions in dreams would diminish and dreaming would decrease if not cease entirely.

A fascination with and a firm belief in the revelatory and healing nature of dream exploration resides currently in two relatively small groups of people. One is involved with the Association for Research and Enlightenment in Virginia Beach, Virginia, that has built their beliefs on the work of the spiritual healer and mystic Edgar Cayce (Cayce & Cayce, 1971). The other group has a "new age" orientation and may be seen as growing out of the ideas and themes that flowed from Esalen. This "new age" group has developed ideas around dream sharing, the intrinsic truthfulness of dreams, and the healing nature of the dream experience (Ullman & Zimmerman, 1979). Those involved with leading and participating in "dream sharing groups," so-called dream workers who generally are nonprofessionals, have come together with scientific researchers into the dreaming experience and formed the International Association for the Study of Dreaming.

The three major schools of depth psychotherapy, Psychoanalysis, Analytic Psychology, and Individual Psychology, in the first third of the 20th century placed a priority on the exploration of the dream experience in order to enhance an understanding of the dreamer. It is to be expected that psychotherapists would focus their attention on the dream reports of their patients and attempt to unravel the dream as it would facilitate an understanding and alleviation of the distress their patients were experiencing. Unfortunately, the basis for relating the dream experience to other aspects of the dreamer's life was not on very sound ground (Fisher & Greenberg, 1977). The method for establishing meaning was left to the individual judgment of the therapist and patient. No systematic examination of the reliability of such judgments was undertaken. The linkage of the understanding gained from dream interpretation to other aspects of the patient's psychic life was described only in an anecdotal manner. The therapists' dream interpretive endeavor needed to be supported by reliability and validity studies as well as demonstrations of the linkage between sleeping and waking consciousness that would show the connection between the two. Otherwise the undertaking of dream exploration and interpretation would remain an arbitrary and idiosyncratic process even if an imaginative, entertaining and, at times, a helpful one.

B. The Dream Has Not Been Considered an Appropriate Topic for Scientific Study

There has long been a distrust of studying subjective states scientifically. Psychologists struggled for years to escape from the introspective approach championed by Titchener (Millon, 2004) The focus moved from a first person data source to a third person one, from a study of subjective states to the study of objective states that were not dependent on the vagaries of the experimental subjects' reporting. The view of the behaviorist psychologist Watson (Millon, 2004) that the proper data for study was solely the directly observable became the only acceptable scientific position. The paradigmatic experiment was to study the relationship between a stimulus given to a subject and the resultant response and to ignore any processes that might have occurred in the "black box" between stimulus and response in the mind of the subject. This paradigm would, of course, preclude a scientific study of the dream experience. Those interested in dreaming reported clinical anecdotes of dreams told by a patient in therapy or, in rare instances, a study of the dream content of a group of people. It was only when a highly regarded academic psychologist, Calvin Hall, turned his attention to dreaming and provided a method for quantifying the dream report (Hall & Van de Castle, 1966) that a scientific approach to the dream experience became possible.

The study of the mind was enlivened with the development of the cognitive sciences that were stimulated by the introduction of computers and the concepts related to artificial intelligence. Cognitive science (Gardner, 1985) is a collaborative approach involving psychologists, philosophers, linguists, neuroscientists, computer specialists, and anthropologists. The focus of these endeavors is directed at understanding waking consciousness, particularly rational thought, and did not include studies of emotion or dreaming in their working agenda. Concomitantly, with this study of the mind and as a result of the discovery of various brain imaging devices, neuroscientists focused on brain localization studies linking various areas of the brain to observable behaviors. The view taken by those scientists who studied brain function was and continues to be that the important level of description for such an undertaking is biological rather than psychological. Patricia Churchland, a neurophilosopher, describes consciousness, of which dreaming is an example, as having its reality rooted in its neurobiology (Churchland, 2002). The view that consciousness is rooted in biology is captured in more specific terms by the neuroscientist Joseph LeDoux (LeDoux, 2002) when he says, "you are your synapses." He proposes "a synaptic explanation of the self." For many of these neuroscientists, the mind became epiphenomenal to the more fundamental brain processes (Hobson, 1988). *Traume sind Schaume*—mind, at best, became the foam on the beer that is the brain.

Some neuroscientists who became interested in consciousness were dismissive in their approach to the dreamer's memory of the dream experience. Crick, a Nobel Prize winner for his work on the structure of DNA, saw the dream experience as a reflection of the process by which the brain rid itself of superfluous memories (Crick & Mitchison, 1983). This process was analogized by him to an offline clearance of data from a computer's memory system to avoid an overload breakdown. He was of the opinion that dreaming dumped thoughts from the brain and thereby avoided the overloading of the brain's memory capacity. This view of memory storage as similar to a storage facility with a fixed capacity does not square with our understanding of brain function.

Robert, in the 19th century (Freud, 1955), expressed a similar view of dream function, which Freud called the "excretion theory" of dreams, similar to that proposed by Crick. Robert describes dreams as "a somatic process of excretion of which we become aware in our mental reaction to it. ... A man deprived of the capacity for dreaming would in the course of time become mentally deranged, because a great mass of uncompleted unworked-out thoughts and superficial impressions would accumulate in his brain and would be bound by their bulk to smother the thoughts which should be assimilated into his memory as completed wholes. Dreams serve as a safety-valve for the overburdened brain. They possess the power to heal and relieve." The interference with or the loss of the function of dreaming in the Robert/Crick scenario leads to a "locked brain" as interference with the gastrointestinal function of motility leads to "locked bowels." The dream deprivation experience of the New York disc jockey Peter Tripp who stayed awake for 201 hours in a glass booth in Times Square as a publicity stunt and experienced a psychotic breakdown during which he hallucinated and had persecutory delusions seemed to confirm the dangers of the loss of dreaming. Apparently Mr. Tripp had had a previous psychotic episode and the stress of the extended sleep deprivation appeared to trigger a reactivation of his disturbed mental state (Dement, 1974). Koranyi and Lehman had shown in a group of hospitalized, withdrawn, chronically ill schizophrenic patients that sleep deprivation reactivated their acute symptoms (Koranyi & Lehmann, 1960). As his science fair project in 1964, a 17-year-old high-school student, Randy Gardner, deprived himself of sleep and the accompanying dreams for 264 hours and did not become psychotic but showed impaired cognitive function and illusions. Some have challenged the rather benign description of the effect of the lengthy sleep deprivation on Randy and insist that he had transient psychotic symptoms (Ross, 1965).

The loss of the dreaming experience that is reported with certain types of localized brain lesions has as a consequence reports of disturbed sleep continuity not mental derangement (Solms, 1997). The disruption of sleep with the loss of dreaming is in keeping with Freud's view of dreaming as having a sleep protective function and does not fit the waste product model that is implicit in the Robert/Crick theories of dreaming which may be seen as dismissive of dreaming as an experience.

The study of the dream experience is the study of the dream report that is a first person, subjective report as was noted earlier. Science, in studying human behavior, has insisted on focusing on external observables as its object of study, what are termed third person reports. Even in studying cognitive processes when two alleged internal mind processes are compared what is measured is the time it may take to complete a task. For example, comparing on a mental map how long it takes using your mind's eye to go from New York to Chicago compared to New York to Los Angeles, the latter takes longer and the time difference is roughly proportional to the mileage differences (Kosslyn, 1980). The reluctance or refusal to study first person reports of experience, such as a dream, relates to a concern about the introspective ability of the subject to attend to and recall inner experiences and the willingness of subjects to report such potentially revealing and embarrassing thoughts as may occur in dreams. Given the vagaries of memory in the waking state such as are caused by transience, blocking, misattribution, suggestibility, and bias raises doubt about the dream report being a valid reflection of the dream as experienced (Schacter, 2001). I would suggest that science is not determined by what is studied but is a method of study. It has been advocated by Daniel Dennett (Dennett, 2005) that reports of conscious experience while awake utilizing the techniques and approaches of so-called third person scientific approaches are a legitimate approach to consciousness and I would suggest that as dreaming is a form of consciousness that there can be as scientific an approach to study-ing dream reports as studying reports of waking consciousness.

C. Why Study the Dream Experience?

I have already discussed several reasons why people have been interested in the dream experience and might want to study dreaming more closely. These include the belief that dreaming is a mode that God chooses to com-municate with people, the dream from above (Sanford, 1968). Another reason that serves to have dreamers pay attention to their dreams is the belief that dreaming has the capacity to predict the future, premonitory dreaming (Kramer, Winget, & Whitman, 1971). And, that attention to the dream experience may reveal significant aspects of the psychology of the dreamer, the revelatory nature of dreaming.

Those scientists interested in studying the mind are attracted to study-ing the dream report because it provides the opportunity to study an output of the mind in "pure culture," relatively less constrained, less influ-enced by outside forces (Foulkes, 1978). For some investigators the study of the dream is seen as a window on the functioning of the brain, on the processes which determine the dream experience (Hartmann, 1984).

The discovery of REM sleep, which was considered to be the biologi-cal substrate of dreaming, has opened the possibility of collecting large numbers of dream reports at a given point in time so that experimen-tal dream research becomes possible (Cartwright, 1972). The tools were already available to quantify the content of the dream experience. The Hall-Van de Castle dream content system, mentioned earlier, was one such quantification system (Hall & Van de Castle, 1966). The book I published with Carolyn Winget, *Dimensions of Dreams* (Winget & Kramer, 1979), is a compendium of many such quantification systems. It has been said that science begins with quantification. Being able to gather a large number of dreams and to measure them opens the possibility that investigators can engage in the scientific study of dreams.

We had been led to believe by such psychiatric and neurological greats as Sigmund Freud (Freud, 1955), Carl Jung (Jung, 1964b), and Hughlings Jackson (Jackson, 1958) that the study of dreams, the so called "sane man's psychosis," would unlock the mysteries of psychosis. Mental illness was considered a major public health problem at the time, 1952, when REM sleep, the alleged biological substrate for dreaming and perhaps of psycho-sis, was identified. Perhaps one-tenth of the hospital beds in the United States were occupied by patients with psychotic illnesses. Psychiatrists were attracted to studying the dreaming process in the laboratory as it might enrich their understanding of how to more effectively use dreams in therapy and shed light on the psychotic process. I believe we learned a great deal about dreaming in our studies of dreams, but unfortunately less about psychosis and we did not unlock the mystery of psychosis. Julius Axelrod, the Nobel Prize winner, pointed out that in supporting the beginning studies of nor-epinephrine in depression, we would learn a lot about nor-epinephrine even if we didn't learn all we would have liked about depression.

The discovery of REM sleep with its often replicated strong correlation to dreaming opened the possibility of resolving the mind-body problem that had preoccupied religionists, philosophers, and scientists since Descartes' formulation of the intrinsic difference between bodily states and mental states in the 16th century (Descartes, 1912). Descartes' dualistic theory of the nature of man deeply troubled those scientists who in the 18th century resolved to explain biology with the same mechanistic modalities or forces that were used elsewhere in sciences such as in physics and chemistry. Their materialist approaches led to rejecting the vitalist explanation for the difference between animate and inanimate things and to reject teleological explanations for bodily activities (Millon, 2004). It was hoped that the formerly unbridgeable could be united now that we were armed with the REM/dream correlation (Hobson, Pace-Schott, & Stickgold, 2000).

In the modern era, two major theories have addressed the biological basis of dreaming claiming to a greater or lesser degree to have resolved the Cartesian division. The earlier so-called AIM State model of dreaming is an expanded version of his activation-synthesis theory proposed by Allan Hobson and his colleagues (Hobson, Pace-Schott, & Stickgold, 2000). The other biological dream theory is the neuropsychological brain lesion theory of dreaming offered by Mark Solms (Solms, 1997). All biological theories of dreaming are unable to provide the transduction rules to go from neurons firing in the brain to the conscious experience of dreaming (Kramer, 2003). They are reductive in trying to explain psychology by biology. They focus only on the syntax (form), not the semantics (content, meaning) or pragmatics (function) of dreaming. They may posit the brain chemistry of dreaming, which is not directly measurable in humans. And they do not account for the narrative aspects of dreaming. The biological theories of dreaming will be discussed later (Kramer, 2000).

Correlation lets us stand on one or the other shore of the Cartesian divide and perhaps view the other side. Predictive validity might allow us to set foot on the bridge to begin the crossing, although some philosophers, called "Mysterians" by Owen Flannigan (Dennett, 2005), doubt we have found or will ever find the bridge over the divide (McGuinn, 1999). Our view of the nature of the world so commits us to reject the Cartesian duality of mind and brain that many have taken to talking about mind by always linking it to the biological underpinning in the brain and expressing the linkage in writing as the mind/brain.

Questions remain, beyond those related to memory variables and using third person methods to study first person reports, as to whether the dream report is so idiosyncratic, ineffable, and variable that it cannot be the object of legitimate scientific investigation (Hall & Van de Castle, 1966). These concerns relate to the reliability of the measurement process in studying dream reports. Do two judges examining the content of the same dream report render the same judgment and how often are they able to do this? In a study of 14 men who slept for 20 consecutive nights in the sleep laboratory and were awakened from each of the first four REM periods of the nights, 820 dream reports were collected from 1,086 awakenings as there were 34 missed first REM periods (Kramer & Roth, 1979). The dream recall percentage of 76% is a fairly typical laboratory REM awakening recall rate. These dream reports had been recorded, transcribed, and coded, and they were scored independently by two raters using the Hall-Van de Castle dream content scoring system for three content categories: characters, activities, and descriptive elements. Characters are people, animals, and creatures in the dreams; activities include physical and verbal activities; and movement and descriptive elements are modifiers in the dream report such as size, color and intensity. The percentage agreement for dream by dream scoring by the judges for each content category was 91% for characters, 93% for activities, and 89% for descriptive elements with an overall percentage agreement of 91% (Kramer & Roth, 1979). The reliability level indicates that reproducible judgments can be made about what is present in a dream report. Important psychological differences can be established with this rate of recovery of dream reports in the laboratory, e.g., gender differences (male-female), illness/normal differences (sick-well), age differences (young-old), and differences between mental illnesses (schizophrenia-depression) (Kramer, 1982).

The question still remains as to whether the aspects of dreaming covered by the Hall-Van de Castle system capture the aspect of the dream experience in which the dreamer or investigator may be interested. We showed that one could express a scale developed to quantify masochism in the dream reports of depressed subjects into combinations of various Hall scales and obtain similar results to what Beck and his colleagues found using their ad hoc masochism scale (Kramer, Trinder, Whitman, & Baldridge, 1969). *Dimensions of Dreams* is a compendium of dream content scales with available reliability and validity information to encourage a quantitative approach to dream studies with the use of known and tested rather than improvised and untested measurement instruments (Winget & Kramer, 1979).

The stability and variability of the dream report is of interest to the psychotherapist who utilizes dream reports in therapy and to the scientist studying consciousness as it sheds light on how the mind works. For the clinician, the finding that the average night-to-night correlation across three content areas—characters, activities, and descriptive elements—is .46 supports his using the dream to contribute to psycho-diagnostic statements about the dreamer/patient (Kramer & Roth, 1979). It also indicates that 79% of the variability in dream content remains unexplained allowing for considerable individuality. Support is given to the practice of examining dream reports for how they reflect the evaluative responses to external events in the dreamer's life. The dream was found to reflect both state, short term (Kramer, Roth, Arand, & Bonnet, 1981) and trait, long term (Kramer, Roth, & Palmer, 1976) aspects of the dreamer's psychology.

For the scientist interested in examining dreams, we have shown that the dream experience can be adequately collected from 76% of REM awakenings and reliably quantified with a 91% reliability (Kramer & Roth, 1979). If dream content is not stable to some degree, dreaming would be random, i.e., "noise" in the system not signal, and would be of no interest clinically or scientifically. If it were not variable, it would not have sufficient flexibility to reflect or become involved with ongoing changes in the dreamer's life. The average of the three content categories overall is 9 [± 3] per night with a first and second week overall average and standard deviation of 8 [± 8] contents. The average night-to-night correlation of .46 reflects stability in the system as it accounts for 21% of the variability between one night's dream contents and the next. This leaves 79% of the night to night content variability unexplained by the previous night's content and opens the possibility that the content is responsive to the events which occurred since the previous night's dreaming such as those of the day before the second night's dreaming as the correlations are between successive nights of dreaming. The average magnitude of dream contents (9) and their 95% range (3 to 15) offer sufficient variability to potentially reflect responsiveness in the dream experience.

This aspect of our work shows that some degree of adaptation occurs across the 20 nights of dream collection. The mean content and standard deviations for week two is the same as for week one, 8 [± 8] and the night-to-night correlations increase from a mean of .22 in week one to a mean of .50 in week two. More dramatically, the night one to night two correlation is .05, the night 10 to 11 is .30 and the night 19 to 20 is .80. Adaptation to the sleep lab experience, which is quite preempting, may be taking place. The low first-to-second night correlation compared to the higher night

10-to-11 correlation and even higher night 19-to-20 night correlation suggests a first night or beginning effect on content analogous to what often happens in physiologic sleep studies (Agnew, Webb, & Williams, 1966).

A comparison of these results with comparable data from physiological studies of sleep may be enlightening (Roth, Kramer, & Roehrs, 1977). The reliability of sleep stage scoring is generally somewhat less than the reliability of scoring dream content. The stability of sleep stages from night to night depends on whether the percentages or the minutes in each stage are correlated. The overall average night-to-night correlation of sleep stages using time data is .28 and using percentages, which decreases variability, is .44. Certainly the night-to-night correlations in the sleep physiology percentage data set is comparable to the overall dream content correlation of .46 suggesting similar stability and variability in the physiology and psychology of sleep. A scientist may prefer to study the physiology of sleep (e.g., sleep stages) or the psychology of sleep (e.g., the dream experience) because of personal taste or interest but clearly not because one is science and the other art.

D. Possible Confusions in Studying Dreaming in the Modern (REM) Era

The experience of dreaming is most commonly described in verbal terms as it is an attempt to express the event that the dreamer has undergone during sleep. For example, a significantly depressed dreamer may report a dream experience as "I dreamed Rose, my mother, was feeding her son, my brother Jack." In a study of depressed dreamers in or out of the sleep/dream laboratory, one could probe further for more or specific content such as feeling tone, if any, in the dream, the presence of others in the dream, the location of the experience, and for the beginning or ending of the dream experience beyond what had been reported. The results of both a laboratory (Kramer, 1966) and nonlaboratory (Kramer, Baldridge, Whitman, Ornstein, & Smith, 1969) study of dreaming in the depressed found that the character type unique to the dreams of the depressed were characters described by their family role; in the example just described, it would be the mother role and the son role. If an effort was made at the time of collecting the dream report to test for connections to the dream images to establish the possible sources of the images and/or the possible meaning of the dream, the dream collector may have inquired of the dreamer whether the dream images reminded the dreamer of anything and, more specifically, if the dreamer was reminded of events of a time prior to the dream particularly to the immediately previous day. The inquiry could have gone on subsequent to the time of experiencing the dream as is sometimes done in psychotherapy. The efforts described are all psychological in nature and are examples of applying third person scientific strategies, categorization by character type in the dream illustration, to first person data, the dream report.

The discovery of REM sleep led to an intense focus on the physiological aspects of many processes in sleep as well as dreaming. An assumption developed that all dreaming occurred only during REM. This led to studies of dreaming that reported not the content of the dream experience but the amount of time spent in REM sleep which substitutes a physiological measurement for a psychological one. The dream experience is not bound to REM sleep as there are dream reports from awakenings that are done out of non-REM sleep (Foulkes, 1966) and even from relaxed wakefulness (Foulkes & Fleisher, 1975; Kripke & Sonnenshein, 1978). Reporting the time in REM sleep cannot substitute for dream reports when studying the dream experience or as Nelson (Winget & Kramer, 1979) did when he reported the amount, not the content, of dreaming.

It is often not clear in a psychological study of dreaming whether the intent is to study the process of dreaming or to use dreams to illuminate some other problem. The study of gender differences in dream reports may serve to suggest that the dream experience is shaped by the gender of the dreamer and lead the investigator to search for other demographic factors that may serve to influence the content of dreams. Or, if the interest is in gender differences per se then the nature of the differences, such as the larger number of color references and friendly social interactions in women's dreams, becomes the focus as it may shed light on the cognitive or experiential differences between the genders. In the former approach, the study intent is to study dreaming; in the latter approach, the intent to study gender differences. Each approach may have a different hypothesis and the results would be weighted differently if they were predicted as primary end points by the hypothesis or were secondary end points or post hoc findings.

The study of mental or cognitive processes has to a large degree focused on the form of such processes, what might be thought of as the grammar or syntax of such processes. The work of Chomsky (Chomsky, 1968, 1980) is a case in point. This places a high emphasis on rationality in studying thought and in studying consciousness of which dreaming is an example. In studies of dreaming, we are particularly drawn to the nonsyntactical aspects of cognition, to the semantic or meaning aspects of dreaming consciousness, and to the pragmatic or functional aspects of dreaming. There has developed a growing awareness that studies of cognition must include an investigation of the emotional aspects of consciousness (Nussbaum, 2001) with Damascio (Damascio, 1999) pointing out that rationality demands an evaluative or affective concomitant. Theories of the dream experience must focus on the content of the dream report not just its form and must include an explanation of the dream's relationship to affect and include an exploration of the possible function of dreaming. Limiting dream studies to the neurophysiology or chemistry of REM sleep reflects a misleading reductionism that confuses biology with psychology (Kramer, 2000). With apologies to Emerson, "A foolish biological reductionism is the hobgoblin of an adequate explanation."

The enthusiasm that accompanied the discovery of REM sleep and its relationship to dreaming has spawned a large number of assumptions about the dream experience that do not reflect the empirical data on dreaming despite the recognition that a specific brain function for SWS (Slow Wave Sleep) and REM (Rapid Eye Movement) sleep have remained elusive. Some of these questionable assumptions include that the dreams of REM sleep: (1) are generally vivid and full of emotion, (2) often have the release of childhood memories into dreams, and (3) are the totality of dreaming, i.e., while not all REM sleep includes dreaming, no dreaming occurs outside of REM sleep. These unsupported or frankly incorrect assumptions about the empirical data on dreaming serve only to impede the study of the dream experience.

E. Summary

There has been a long history of interest in the dream experience as it reveals the will of God, becomes a potential source of information about the future, facilitates the choice of the number to choose in playing the lottery, or yields insights into the concerns of the dreamer. The study of the dream experience has been thought to be outside the realm of scientific inquiry but, with the introduction of the cognitive approach to studying mental process and the suggestion that first person experiences such as waking and dreaming consciousness could be studied with third person scientific methods, the study of dreaming has been legitimized to some degree. The interest in studying the dream relates to it being an example of relatively pure, uncontaminated mind function, which, if carefully studied, might unlock the mystery of psychosis. Confusions have occurred between studying the dream experience psychologically or neuro-physiologically, or in focusing the syntax of the dream to the exclusion of its semantic and pragmatic aspects. The dream experience is an orderly not random experience that shows both a regularity and variability such that it may have meaning and be capable of participating in adaptive processes.

CHAPTER 2

Do Dreams Exist?

A. Introduction

The existence of the dreaming experience is implicit in a work that intends to explore the structure, function, and meaning of dreams. To question whether dreams actually occur during sleep and are experienced as an event extended in time seems a gratuitous undertaking. It has already been pointed out that some of the earliest written records (Van de Castle, 1994), the Beatty Papyrus from Egypt and the Gilgamesh legend from Mesopotamia, refer directly to dreaming, as does the Old and New Testament, the Koran, the Indian sacred texts, the Buddhist legends about the dreams of the Buddha's mother, and the revelation that came to Joseph Smith, the founder of Mormonism. In the philosophical world from ancient Greece, Aristotle and Plato, to Emanuel Kant in the 18th century, the experiential nature of dreaming has been accepted (Freud, 1955). In the scientific world, the commitment to the idea of the existence of the experience of dreaming is universal, confirmed in the work of Freud and the many predecessors he cites going back to the Greek physicians such as Hippocrates and the priests of the Asklepian temples (Meier, 1966). The extensive laboratory study of dreaming was initiated by Aserinsky, Kleitman, and Dement in the 1950s with their observations of a portion of sleep with rapid synchronous eye movements, the so-called REM sleep, during which dreaming was thought to occur (Aserinsky & Kleitman, 1953; Dement & Wolpert, 1958). In the 21st century, Reiser (Reiser, 2001), a noted psychobiologic researcher proposed "…a preliminary psychobiologic concept of the dream process…."

In the light of such overwhelming acceptance, who has raised question about the existence of dreaming?

The dream experience as it is the report of an inner, subjective first person experience has been dismissed at least as an object of serious examination by those who hold that only third person events can be the object of scientific examination. Certainly behaviorists such as Skinner (Skinner, 1974) would hold such a view. This is not a denial of the process of dreaming but of our ability to study it within the rubric of science. Dennett (Dennett, 2005) has provided a rather compelling argument that first person experiences once they are articulated can be studied with the third person methods that are part of the scientific endeavor. Cognitive scientists (Gardner, 1985; Kosslyn, 1980) have devised interesting and replicable techniques to study first person states during waking.

B. Dreaming Is the Report of Dreaming

1. Malcolm-Erickson

Dreaming is viewed as a type of consciousness that occurs during sleep. There are those philosophers of mind (Nagel, 2002; O'Shaughnessy, 2002) who hold the view that consciousness only occurs when a person is in the waking state and, under that definition, dreaming is not a state of consciousness under the special conditions of sleep and, if not entirely denied, is at least in some sort of limbo without any conceptual mooring. In an effort perhaps to rescue the dream experience from a definitional limbo, it has been argued by Malcolm (Malcolm, 1959), a highly influential philosopher of mind, in his seminal monograph *Dreaming,* published in 1959, that the dream exists but not as an event that occurred during sleep and was extended in time but rather that dreaming has as its criterion the dream report. Erickson (Erickson, 1954,17) takes a similar position in regard to what the definition of a dream may be when he says that "A dream is the verbal report of a series of remembered images, mostly visual, which are usually endowed with affect." Malcolm's position stirred an extensive discussion among philosophers (Dennett, 1977; Dunlop, 1977) and dream researchers (Dement & Wolpert, 1958; Kramer, Winget, & Roth, 1975) of the essence of the dream experience, if it existed at all and whether it occurred during sleep and, if so, if it was extended in time. For example, Dennett, a philosopher, suggested a "cassette theory" of dreaming in which stored memories of narratives are activated during the awakening process and provide the illusion of the dream experience occurring during sleep and being extended in time. The hypothesis that dreaming occurs during the transition from sleep to wakefulness has been termed the "Goblot Hypothesis" (Freud, 1955).

Rejecting the dream report because it is not considered a legitimate object for scientific study or not accepting dreaming as an experience during sleep that is extended in time and as a form or type of consciousness does question or directly deny the reality of the subjective experience of dreaming itself. Malcolm (Malcolm, 1959) discusses the possibility that reports of dreaming during sleep are based fundamentally on children in a culture learning how to respond to the question "What were you dreaming?" Or, children being told when they awaken from sleep frightened at night, "That was only a dream." You are in effect taught to label what you recall during waking from sleep a dream. Wittgenstein (Malcolm, 1959) calls labeling something a dream a language game we learned as children.

We must acknowledge that despite the popular, biological, and philosophical acceptance of the dream as an experience extended in time there are those who deny the dream state as an experience during sleep that is extended in time and with a consciousness identical to or similar to other forms of consciousness. It is necessary to explore the critique offered by Malcolm and some others (Dunlop, 1977) before we begin our systematic exploration of the dream experience.

Malcolm (Malcolm, 1959, 4) questions the "received opinion ... that dreams are the activity of the mind during sleep." He points out that for Descartes a dream "...consists of thoughts, feelings, and impressions that one has when asleep." And further that Descartes noted "there are no certain indications by which we may clearly distinguish wakefulness from sleep." This view is identical with the view of Cheng Tzu (Bartlett, 1980) who was not sure if he was a man dreaming he was a butterfly or a butterfly dreaming he was a man. If to dream is to be mentally active while asleep as reflected in one being able to recall the content of the dream, the dream must be a conscious experience.

It is clear, according to Malcolm (Malcolm, 1959), that if the dreamer could assert he was asleep while asleep that would be a self-contradiction. Saying that one is asleep cannot ever be correct and it is not a possible judgment, namely whether I am asleep. I can't wonder if I am asleep while sleeping. Others can judge by behavior whether I am asleep. Being asleep is to be without awareness, in a horizontal position, and immobile and such states as somnambulism, hypnotic trance, and nightmares go beyond the usual concept of being soundly asleep. However lucid dreaming, which has been well documented in the laboratory by LaBerge (LaBerge, Nagel, Taylor, Dement, & Zarcone, 1981a; LaBerge, Nagel, Taylor, Dement, & Zarcone, 1981b), is not addressed and would be a direct empirical contradiction of Malcolm's description of what sleep is like as is the recognition that sleep across the night is not a unitary state.

Aristotle states that one could be asleep and awake at the same time (Freud, 1955). This inter-penetrability of the two states is rejected by

Malcolm but accepted by most sleep researchers as reflected in there being no universal definition of sleep that permits a complete separation of the two. Kleitman, the father of modern sleep research, says that it is as hard to say a person awakened at a certain moment as it is to determine the exact time of falling asleep (Kleitman, 1963). If one can hear an external noise during sleep that is incorporated into the dream report, this would suggest for Malcolm (Malcolm, 1959) that the dreamer was not soundly asleep as would being restless or moaning while asleep. As we cannot make the judgment of being asleep when we are asleep, Malcolm concludes we can't make any judgments while asleep and, therefore, as there is no way of verifying the judgment was made during sleep, the assertion is not verifiable. No physiological measurement can be used to support the statement that an event occurred during sleep because the appropriate waking correlate of that event type appeared during sleep. As the correlation in question only has been shown to be operative during waking, we would be assuming the correlation also was operative during sleep. This position of a state dependent correlation (Overton, 1973) can occur in certain learning recall experiments. The objection Malcolm makes, if correct, would raise serious question in the study of brain activity during sleep in which brain area functions established during waking are assumed to continue during sleep (Hobson, Pace-Schott, & Stickgold, 2000), e.g., the assumption that if the limbic system is active during sleep then an emotional process is operative or if the dorso-lateral prefrontal cortex is not active during REM sleep then executive functions of the brain are not active. If the argument made by Malcolm that judgments cannot be said to occur during sleep is viable, then statements about thinking, reasoning, imagining, images, feeling, and so forth in sleep, i.e., dream consciousness, become unverifiable and questions about it are unintelligible.

The criterion for having a dream for Malcolm (Malcolm, 1959) is awakening from sleep and telling a dream. It is not having awakened from a particular stage of sleep (e.g., REM sleep; Dement & Wolpert, 1958; Roffwarg, Dement, Muzio, & Fisher, 1962). Telling a dream in no way commits the dream reporter to any notion that the dream was extended in time or occurred during the prior period of sound sleep. In most dream studies, what is examined or measured is the dream report, which is generally considered a reasonable reflection of the dream experience. Malcolm maintains that the dream report is the basis for calling something a dream. He quotes Wittgenstein that an inner process stands in need of an outward criterion, i.e., telling a dream. Malcolm is not trying to say what dreaming may be. Criterion is not essence but rather it is occurrence and that you tell the dream is the criterion that dreaming occurred.

The idea that dreaming is linked inextricably to the waking report of the dream makes questions about the location of the dream in physical time have no sense for Malcolm (Malcolm, 1959). With the dream report criterion for dreaming, searching for a relationship to so-called physiological concomitance during sleep is meaningless. The same is true for long and short dreams as what is being measured is whether the subject can guess the length of the prior REM period 5 vs. 15 minutes (Dement & Wolpert, 1958). Malcolm feels the authors are substituting REM time for a dream report as a criterion for dreaming and radically altering the concept of dreaming.

As we can't verify that the dream is an occurrence in its own right, we are left with the dream report. Events such as judging, reasoning, feeling, and imagining can't take place in dreams. We can't tell if the dream took place during sleep as we can't verify it. Telling a dream is telling a story. This would contradict the psychoanalytic view of dreaming as Freud (Freud, 1955) reported a dream of one word, actually a neologism, "autodidasker" and proceeded to analyze it. The word was made up of two parts author and autodidact, i.e., self-taught, and lead via associations to two German-Jewish socialist politicians Lasker and Lassalle who died from relations with women, one from syphilis and the other in a duel, and this touched on the concern parents have about what will happen to their male children when they grow up.

I think many have seen the dream as a story (Foulkes, 1999), so Malcolm has agreement on his observation that telling a dream is telling a story. You don't prove you had a dream as it's more like imagining something. You don't raise the issue of veracity in response to a person reporting something he imagines and labels as such and, similarly, you don't question the truth of a dream report.

Some might say that Malcolm's main idea is refuted by the continuity between dream contents, emotions and sensations, and post-sleep reports during wakefulness (Kramer & Brik, 2002; Kramer, Roth, Arand, & Bonnet, 1981; Kramer, Roth, & Palmer, 1976). But the report, according to Malcolm, already has the elements in it in wakefulness for the so-called continuity. The content identity in dream reports and wakefulness is inherent in the language.

There is the high probability that one can tell whether one is awake or asleep by the coherence and predictability of the events experienced. If events are highly coherent and predictable, the more likely it is you are awake (Malcolm, 1959). Descartes (Descartes, 1912) posed the straw man of dream/wake indeterminacy to reject it with his espousing the coherence test for wakefulness. The coherence principle permits only the affirming I am awake, as when one is asleep no such affirmation is possible. Malcolm believes the principle is worthless as we could dream coherence and not be awake. Malcolm does not doubt the existence of dreams, he just takes the position that it cannot be shown to have occurred during sleep nor that it is an experience extended in time.

Malcolm (Malcolm, 1959) notes in his concluding chapter that he has rejected a large part of Freud's dream theory (Freud, 1955). He has rejected that during sleep one could have a hallucination or try to satisfy some mental stimulus. He has no conflict with the clinical work with dreams that focuses exclusively on the dream report.

2. The Goblot Theory of Hall and Raskin

Hall and Raskin (Hall & Raskin, 1980), in an unpublished monograph, offer an alternative that has as its starting point the possibility that dreaming does not occur during sleep in agreement with what Malcolm has said. Maury's famous guillotine dream of 1878 (Freud, 1955) in which, after being sentenced by the revolutionary tribunal, he is led to the guillotine and beheaded and at that point he awakens with the bedstead having collapsed and struck his neck like the blade. This gave rise to discussions about how so much material could be compressed into such a short period of time between the stimulus and awakening.

Hall and Raskin (Hall & Raskin, 1980) have built on the suggestion offered by Goblot, 1895, (Freud, 1955) that dreaming occurs during the process of awakening from sleep. Dreaming, it was held by Binz, 1878, (Freud, 1955), was a response to stimuli experienced during awakening. Freud saw Goblot's ideas as "an attractive conjecture" but rejected the idea because there were dreams without awakening and dreams that we were dreaming, lucid dreams. Freud saw the dream preparation process, the dream work, starting during the day and taking all night and then going off in a moment. Hall and Raskin's major objection to Freud's dream development is that the dream work goes on all night. The version of the Goblot hypothesis that they propose is that dreams, i.e., post-sleep reports, are constructed between the time of awakening from sleep until the report is given. Their hypothesis offers a theory of how and why post-sleep reports are constructed which Goblot's did not. In the Freudian dream theory (Freud, 1955), we dream to protect sleep, the why, and our motive, the what, is to seek satisfaction of unfulfilled childhood wishes and it is these wishes that determine the images we select to obtain satisfaction. In the Goblot theory of Hall and Raskin (Hall & Raskin, 1980), the wish that guides cognition, the why, is the wish to wake up to resume the cognitive continuity of waking life but from a circadian point of view this doesn't fit as time of awakening is clock fixed. The post-sleep report is a record of how the obstacles of disorientation, confusion, and misperceptions impaired sensory, cognitive, and motor functions, the what, were overcome to reestablish waking consciousness. This description of dream formation is like the pre-sleep state dreams that Silberer (Silberer, 1951) has described which reflect in dream images the immediate preoccupations of the dreamer on falling asleep. Hall and Raskin are similarly describing the dream's registration of the events occurring on awakening.

Hall and Raskin (Hall & Raskin, 1980) point out that the chief task in waking up is the reestablishment of cognitive structures and processes that were lost during going to sleep, to reengage with the world of consciousness and resume conscious continuity. This process may take as long as 25 minutes, but they estimate the time from the beginning of awaking to the end of reporting the dream as usually being 5 minutes long. They postulate that the cognitive activity during waking up is probably moving in a direction opposite of what occurred in falling asleep, i.e., from confusion to clarity, disorientation to orientation, random, fragmented, disorganized, impaired thinking to organized conceptual thinking. This is the kind of thinking Hobson (Hobson, 1988) feels occurs in dream reports but for him it is during sleep. The post-sleep reports are verbal descriptions of the cognitive processing of stimuli acting on us while waking up. The sources of these stimuli are from the immediate surroundings, features of the place and circumstance into which we are awakening, e.g., the bedroom, the bed, the bed clothes, others in the bed, the furniture, and light, time, and temperature; bodily stimuli which include bodily states such as hunger, thirst, and cold, as well as a full bladder and muscle cramps and skin sensations. Memory also makes a contribution but it is not clear whether this is directly in response to stimuli, external or bodily, or whether memory can be tapped independently of these stimuli sources. The stimulus stirs associations from memory stores. The basis for stimulus choice or dominance, saliency, may be a function of intensity, frequency, or some other factor. Stimuli may predominate in sequence or stir a collage-like response in evoking a post-sleep report response.

During the awakening process, the mind is favorable to misperceiving, and, as the dream images in dreams are usually reported in narrative form, the nature of the narrative could influence the misperception as well. In the 1,000 dream reports that were the basis for the Hall-van de Castle dream content norms (Hall & Van de Castle, 1966), some 31% of over 5,000 objects found in the reports are related to the external surroundings one awakes into or to the common bodily states that are often associated with awakening. Hall and Raskin (Hall & Raskin, 1980) suggest that the large percentage of objects related to the external world one awakens in and to bodily states common on awakening lend support to their theory that these external sources and bodily states are the sources of the content of post-sleep reports. They see sleep as a sort of torpor, a time of energy conservation and would suggest we view cognitive activity during sleep in the same manner, as a time of reduced cognitive activity. They review a number of laboratory dream studies and comment on their compatibility with the Goblot hypothesis. They point out that there are very few correlations between REM sleep physiologic variables and post-sleep reports; such is the case to this day (Pivik, 2000), many years after the description of REM sleep. It is as if the mind and the body were dissociated, a position that in a materialistic world is not a reasonable one. Even if there were mind-body correlates, they would not affect the Goblot hypothesis because the physiological variables would be stimuli during the awakening process. Given the assumption that the awakening process is the reverse of the falling asleep process, there is a study of falling asleep which is of considerable interest (Vogel, Foulkes, & Trosman, 1966). It shows that as the falling asleep process based on sleep variables, EEG and eye movements, proceeds, the recovery of hallucinated dramatic content goes from 31% awake and alert, to 43% alert but drowsy, to 76% drifting off to sleep, to 71% in light sleep. If indeed awakening is a reverse process to falling asleep, then there would be as much dream-like cognitive activity in post-sleep reports as in REM awakenings and dream-like material in one third of waking reports, an interesting but surprising finding. This result would be very confirming of the Goblot hypothesis. Unfortunately, this study of falling asleep has not been replicated and the awakening study has never been done. The study of awakening has been of little interest to sleep researchers and studying dreams in relation to sleep physiology of even less interest to dream researchers.

C. Dreaming Occurs During Sleep-Lucid Dreaming

There are views of the dream experience that find it a world that can be seen as on par in many ways with the waking world. Dreaming is described as a valid experience that is said to exist during sleep and is extended in time. This is the position taken by Gordon Globus (Globus, 1987) and interestingly described in his book *Dream Life, Wake Life: The Human Condition Through Dreams.*

1. Freud

The premier work on dreaming is *The Interpretation of Dreams* (Freud, 1955). It provides, in addition to a theory of dream formation and interpretation, an incredibly complete and detailed description of the dream experience itself. It is always illuminating to examine this work to see what is said about any aspect of dreaming. Freud notes that the dreamer may report that during dreaming he said that "This is only a dream" clearly noting the dreamer's awareness that the experience he is having is a dream. Functionally, for Freud, this awareness of dreaming while dreaming occurs at a point of distress in the dream narrative and serves to reassure the dreamer and detract from the validity of what has transpired. If the dream continues after the reassurance, the dream represents what the dreamer wishes. Usually the dreamer awakens after the awareness of dreaming occurs. Noting that "This is only a dream" was seen by Freud as part of the secondary revision aspect of the dream work that Freud ultimately attributed to the mechanisms of waking criticism and not as intrinsic to the dream work. In order to be processed by the dream work, the content, "This is only a dream," had to have representation in the latent dream thoughts, the source material on which the dream work operated to create the dream report. Further, Freud observes that some people are aware while sleeping that they are dreaming and are able to direct their dreams and to even change the ending of their dreams. In his concluding chapter, Freud notes that "…throughout our whole sleeping state we know just as certainly that we are dreaming as we know that we are asleep" (Freud, 1955b, 571). All dreams for Freud are, in effect, lucid dreams.

Freud has unequivocally placed dreaming within sleep and has claimed that the dream report is a valid report of that experience. In particular, he has noted that some dreamers recognize explicitly that they are dreaming while dreaming and are even able to alter the outcome of their dream experience. Unfortunately, dream reporting after the fact, i.e., after waking, does not confirm that the experience occurred during sleep as both Malcolm (Malcolm, 1959) and Hall and Raskin (Hall & Raskin, 1980) have pointed out. What is needed is concomitant confirmation from a dreamer that he is dreaming when we have clear evidence that the dreamer is asleep. This would also provide evidence that consciousness in some sense and to some degree occurs during sleep and is not restricted to wakefulness.

2. LaBerge

Stephen LaBerge and his colleagues have provided such evidence (LaBerge, 1977; LaBerge, Nagel, Taylor, Dement, & Zarcone, 1981; LaBerge, Nagel, Taylor, Dement, & Zarcone, 1981). They reported that subjects who had previously experienced lucid dreaming were able while asleep in the sleep laboratory and appropriately electronically monitored to signal that they were aware they were dreaming. The signaling was done by having the dreamer move his eyes back and forth very rapidly. The eye-muscles are one of the few groups of voluntary muscles that are not paralyzed during REM sleep so they were utilized for signaling. The study involved seven subjects, five men and two women, who slept for a total of 52 nights with a range for the 7 subjects of 3 to 23 nights. The subjects reported 50 lucid dreams following awakening from various stages of sleep with 48 being from REM sleep. REM sleep continued from five to 450 seconds and averaged 60 seconds after the signaling took place. The subjects who had been requested to signal when they became aware they were dreaming reported signaling from 45 of these lucid dreams and a judge was able to verify the epoch with the signaling 41 times on the basis of the correspondence between reported and observed signals. REM sleep apparently provides the necessary high level of cerebral activation for lucid dreaming to occur. Time estimation for short periods, 10 seconds, during lucid dreaming is similar to that found in subjects while awake supporting the view that the dream is an experience extended in time and that time experienced in dreams and time experienced awake may be similar if not identical. The descriptions of long extensive experiences during dreaming such as Mohammed's Night Journey from Arabia to Jerusalem on a celestial horse, meeting other prophets, and his ascent through the seven heavens recorded in the Koran do not support an identity of dream time and wake time (Dawood & Wyatt, 1991). Time in such experiences may reflect a report of an experience rather than the experience itself.

Freud (Freud, 1955) suggested that many, although not all, the experiences that one is aware of dreaming while dreaming seem to occur in dreams in response to a threat experience in the dream and end generally in an awakening. Many of the dream reports found in Stephen LaBerge's *Lucid Dreaming* (LaBerge, 1977, 91) seem to fit this dream type:

> I was walking along a gradually ascending mountain path with a friend. As far as the eye could see, the only thing moving was the silent mist that veiled the majestic peaks in mystery. But suddenly we found ourselves before a narrow bridge that precariously spanned a chasm. When I looked down into the bottomless abyss beneath the bridge, I became dizzy with fear and could not bring myself to proceed. At this, my companion said, "You know Stephen, you don't *have* to go this way. You can go back the way we came." But then the thought crossed my mind that if I became lucid, I would have no reason to fear the height. A few seconds of reflection were enough for me to realize that indeed I *was* dreaming. My confidence was restored and I was able to cross the bridge and awaken.

The dreamer was fearful, became lucid, things changed, and shortly the dreamer awakened. This dream type correspondence is encouraging as it suggests that the phenomenology described by Freud is similar to the dreams that LaBerge has been describing. Awakenings in the laboratory study of lucid dreaming averaged one minute after the onset of lucidity, a short time, as Freud had observed about such dreams. "… Throughout our whole sleeping state we know just as certainly that we are dreaming as we know that we are asleep." Is there any evidence to support such an extreme position? Gackenbach (Gackenbach, 1984), in a review of the work on the incidence of lucid dreaming, concludes that 58% of the population has experienced a lucid dream at least once in their lifetime, while 21% report having such dreams at least once a month. Individuals who keep dream diaries were found to have about 13% of their diary dream reports that were judged to be lucid. Lucidity, the awareness of dreaming while dreaming, is not a universal experience but certainly not an unusual one and that lends support to the position that dreaming occurs during sleep. Gackenbach has shown that individuals can be taught to become lucid dreamers, which lends further credence that lucidity provides to the view that dreaming occurs during sleep.

Whether the dream experience exists is of general interest to people as almost everyone reports having dreams. Whether dreaming is experiential or a report is essential for anyone who considers doing or has done research in dreaming and to the understanding of conscious states. The essence of the object of the study of dreams is, to some degree, defined by what dreaming is considered to be. That is whether dreaming is an experience during sleep or just a report given on awakening from sleep, as Malcolm (Malcolm, 1959) has maintained, or is dreaming an event that occurs not during sleep but in the arousal process from sleep as Hall and Raskin (Hall & Raskin, 1980) have suggested. LaBerge (LaBerge & Rheingold, 1990) has confirmed what Aristotle first described in the 4th century B.C., that dreaming occurs during sleep and that the sleeper can become aware of the experience of dreaming while dreaming.

D. Dream Development and Content Incorporation During Sleep

My own interest in the nature of dreaming was expressed in a series of studies in which my laboratory was involved. We compared the report of a dream to a report of a nightmare and the report of the nightmare to a confabulated nightmare (Taub, Kramer, Arand, & Jacobs, 1978). In another study, we awakened subjects from various times into a REM period and obtained a report of their dreaming just prior to being awakened and plotted various dimensions or aspects of the report to see whether the dream report had a developmental course (Kramer, Czaya, Arand, & Roth, 1974; Kramer, Roth, & Czaya, 1975). We also attempted to influence the content of the dream experience by inserting people into the process while the dreamer was in REM sleep (Kramer, Kinney, & Scharf, 1983). An examination of the results of these studies may contribute to the conviction that the dream experience does exist, occurs during sleep, and is extended in time.

The intent of the first study (Taub, Kramer, Arand, & Jacobs, 1978) was to compare a dream report to a nightmare report and then to compare the nightmare report to a report of what subjects thought a nightmare was like. Forty-two university students, 12 men and 30 women, who reported experiencing a nightmare once per month, were invited to participate. They were asked to write down a dream they had at night after an uninterrupted night's sleep and the next nightmare they had. The nightmare was defined as a frightening dream that awakened them. Another group of university students matched in age and gender with the first was asked to write down an imaginary nightmare not using any material from any dream or nightmare they may have had. All the reports were coded and blindly content analyzed using the Hall-Van de Castle dream content analysis scales (Hall & Van de Castle, 1966).

Although similar on many dimensions, the significant differences between the recalled dream and nightmare were that the dreams had more friendly interactions, less apprehension as the most frequent emotion, and fewer misfortunes as the most frequent theme than nightmares. Nightmares had more aggressive interactions, physical activity, color, castration anxiety, and institutional-residential-vocational settings. The content differences clearly reflect two different types of reports. They appear to be capturing two different categories of experience. It is possible that in the language game of dream reporting described by Malcolm (Malcolm, 1959) that we learned to associate different reports in relationship to the two labels, dreams and nightmares. We will address this question further when we compare the content of spontaneous nightmare reports to confabulated ones. Can we envision that these content differences are related to the awakening process? They do not reflect an aspect of the immediate surround in which the dreamer may have awakened that Hall and Raskin (Hall & Raskin, 1980) used to support their view that dreaming occurs during awakening from sleep. In a study of dream content themes (Kramer, Schoen, & Kinney, 1984) comparing vivid dreamers to dreamers with frequent nightmares, we found no difference in themes and speculated that the anxiety which the nightmare dreamers reported might have been a reaction to the dream rather than intrinsic to the dream experience itself.

The nightmare dreams (Taub, Kramer, Arand, & Jacobs, 1978), when compared to the confabulated nightmares, showed significant differences that indicated they were distinct phenomena. Confabulated nightmares were higher in aggression, movement activity, intensity, misfortune, indoor settings, and color and lower in friendliness. They were reported in fewer words: a mean of 89 words for confabulated nightmares, 193 for nightmares and 209 for dreams. It is difficult to imagine how the child is taught in the word game of dream reporting that dreams and nightmares are of approximately the same length and approximately twice as long as a confabulated nightmare. The confabulated nightmare appears to reflect an idealized concept of a nightmare, more intense than the actual experience.

It had been found that the later into the night a REM period dream report was obtained, the more dream-like the report, e.g., more vivid, active, dramatic, and emotional (Foulkes, 1966; Verdone, 1965). The reports only sampled two time points, early and late, which limited the descriptive possibilities. We attempted to capture reports both total and immediately prior to awakening from six time points across the REM period (Kramer, Roth, & Czaya, 1975). We had four college age men who were good dream recallers sleep in the sleep laboratory for three nonconsecutive nights for eight weeks. Each subject was awakened twice a night, once during the second and once during the fourth REM period. Awakenings were on a random schedule at 0.5, 2.5, 5, 10, 20, or 30 minutes into the REM period. The subjects were asked to report (1) what they recalled from the 10 seconds before being awakened, and (2) from the entire dream, and (3) to complete a Dream Intensity Questionnaire (D.I.Q.) which asked them to rate each of 12 questions on a 6-point scale for the last 10 seconds of dreaming. The parameters rated were recall, activity, emotion, anxiety, clarity, pleasantness, fright, violence-hostility, dramatic quality, distortion, relationship to personal life, and logic. A significant effect of time was found for four variables of the D.I.Q.: recall, emotion, anxiety, and pleasantness. The trend analysis on the four significant variables showed they were all linear and, in addition, emotion showed a quadratic or stepwise relationship. Across all 12 variables, the effect of time was significant with 10 minutes being different from 5 minutes; 20 minutes was not different from 10 minutes but 30 minutes was different than 20 minutes. It is essentially the intensity of an affective dimension that changes, increasing across the time periods. The overall pattern of change was an increase in intensity from 5 to 10 minutes, then a plateau from 10 to 20 minutes and a further increase from 20 to 30 minutes. This pattern is the same whether rated by the dreamer, an external judge, or a content analysis of the dream reports (Kramer, Czaya, Arand, & Roth, 1974).

There is a developmental course in reported dream content intensity, particularly in the affective aspects of the dream report, across the REM period. This would support the position that the dream is an experience that occurs during sleep and is extended in time. The plateau from 10 to 20 minutes argues for changes in an internal process rather than the changes simply being a function of the amount of time in REM that the dreamer has experienced which would more likely have only a linear trend as the studies of content collected from two points during the REM period have shown. The 20 minute pattern echoes a possible correlation of dream content intensity with a 20 minute cycle of eye movement activity that Azerinsky (Aserinsky, 1971) has described and we have replicated (Johnson, Kramer, Bonnet, Roth, & Jansen, 1980). The increase in affective intensity across the REM period may well bear some relationship to the functional role that has been suggested for dreaming in the Selective Mood Regulatory Theory of dream function (Kramer, 1993) in which the dream experience serves as an "emotional thermostat" to reset the dreamer's mood from its altered and elevated level before sleep at night to a more central and decreased intensity position in the morning.

If the dream experience does occur during sleep and is extended in time, can we provide a stimulus during REM sleep, when dreaming is likely going on, and have that stimulus incorporated into the dream experience and reported in the dream report obtained on awakening? We selected for incorporation the name of a person (Kramer, Kinney, & Scharf, 1983). We chose to try to have a person incorporated because who appears in dream reports is central to the effect the dream experience has on the waking affect of the dreamer. We did two experiments using nine good dream recallers in the first and seven in the second. All subjects before sleeping in the laboratory for three nights generated and tape recorded in their own voice a list of 20 highly familiar names: H names, of family, friends, and present living companions, and 20 low familiarity names, L names, that did not belong to anyone they knew or had known and would have few or no associations for the subjects. During each REM period, one stimulus name was presented one time to the subject through an earpiece. Each subject had a total of three H and three L names presented.

In neither experiment did recall for the dream in general or recall of hearing the stimulus word differ as a function of the meaning of the stimulus word, i.e., recall of hearing the stimulus word. Incorporation was a function of meaning with the familiar name (H) being incorporated more often than the unfamiliar name (L) at a significant level. Incorporation for the H presentation was 59% in Experiment 1, 39% in Experiment 2, and only 11% for the L presentation in Experiment 1 and 5% in Experiment 2. The nature of the incorporation was most often representational, i.e., the person appears as themselves, 56% of the time in Experiment 1 and 87% of the time in Experiment 2.

The incorporation rate for the familiar name was 30% higher than the rate of the subject hearing the name presentation in both experiments. This rate difference would argue against the incorporation being explained by the dreamer awakening, hearing the name, and then going back to sleep, resuming dreaming, and including the person associated with the name in the dream report. Rather this degree of incorporation suggests that a level of awareness, of consciousness, with the capacity to make discriminations, familiar from unfamiliar names, exists at least during REM sleep. It argues for a dreaming process that is extended in time. The mother who awakens selectively to the cry of her sleeping infant and the father to the ring of the telephone may well be making similar discriminations. Being awake and being asleep are interpenetrable states (Kleitman, 1963). And, as sleep was permitted to continue after the stimulus for up to 10 minutes, it makes the incorporation as unlikely to have taken place during the awakening process.

I would conclude that dreaming is a process in which the dreamer is engaged in experiences that are, to some degree, extended in time, and with a degree of consciousness during which awareness and discriminations can be made. Dreaming has a developmental course and that being awake and asleep and dreaming are not mutually exclusive states. The content of dreaming can be altered by stimuli presented concurrently with dreaming.

CHAPTER 3

The Recall and Collection of Dreams

A. The Remembering of Dreams: An Historical Review

It is apparent that the study of dreaming is dependent on the recall and reporting of the dream experience. There is the general recognition that remembering dreams is often a difficult if not impossible task. The dream is often so ephemeral as to be beyond capturing, beyond remembering. Freud (Freud, 1955, 43) observed that "It is a proverbial fact that dreams melt away in the morning…we can observe, too,… a dream which was still lively in the morning will melt away…in the course of the day." Freud also recognized that a dream might persist in memory for days or years, although this was very much less common.

Freud was of the opinion that the review of dream forgetting provided by Strumpell in 1871 was the most thorough at the time. Strumpell (Freud, 1955) recognized dream forgetting to be a complex phenomenon with multiple causes. It was acknowledged that the forces that would influence remembering events in waking life would also operate to influence the recall of dreams.

Strumpell enumerated eight factors that influenced the recall or forgetting of dreams but no single one was sufficient to explain all recall or forgetting. The first factor was the *intensity* of the dream experience, which included its vividness as well as its dramatic nature and emotionality, although, in later studies, these aspects of the dream experience have been treated separately. The second recall factor noted was that of single versus *repeated events*, with the latter being more likely to be recalled. The dream experience is, generally, a single event and that weighed against its recall. The exception might be dreams, which are reexperienced, such as have been said to occur in traumatic states. Dreams according to Freud (Freud, 1955) are lacking in intelligibility and orderliness. The *disconnected* and disorderly nature of the dream experience is the third factor that makes it harder to remember them. Words that are arranged in an order, connected, and have meaning are easier to remember.

The transition from sleep to wakefulness results in our attention being engaged by our waking consciousness and the dream experience, which is not anchored in the thoughts and sequences of waking life, fades from our mind (Whitman, 1963). It is the *distraction* that waking provides that is the fourth factor contributing to our forgetting of dreams. Those individuals who have little or no *interest* in their dreams are more likely not to recall them. It is a mental experience that has no value for them. The fifth factor affecting recallability can be countered by becoming interested in dreaming with a resultant increase in dream recall. Yet for many who have an interest in dreams, the struggle with trying to hold on to last night's dream is a difficult battle and one that is too often lost. Interest in dreaming is probably a minor factor in determining dream recall. There is the recognition that the two states—wakefulness and dreaming consciousness—are distinct states and that an event experienced in one state is difficult to recapture in the other. The experiences and their recall are said to be *state dependent* (Overton, 1973). This sixth factor, state dependency, may well influence recall as has been the case with material learned under a medication altered state of consciousness only being retrievable if the drug induced state is re-created. The very nature of the ideational material in the dream experience may be such that it is not able to be represented or expressed in the waking state. Subjects who have memorized the dream reports of poor dream recallers have greater difficulty in recalling them in contrast to those from good recallers and this difference may reflect the problem in representation that makes retention more difficult.

The last two factors affecting the recall of dreams touch on other issues related to dreaming. One is the experience that a dream, not recalled on awakening, may be recalled later in the day. The recall appears to be triggered by some thought or event usually related to the dream narrative. This priming-like effect has certainly been described in the study of remembering while awake. The second of the additional factors is the possibility that recalling a fragment of a dream may lead to filling out the dream narrative and make it more connected than it was. This may be seen as a type of *confabulation* analogous to what some patients with brain injuries do in responding to questions with fabricated answers. The filling out of the narrative is what Freud (Freud, 1955) described early in his theory building as secondary revision, which was included as a dream work mechanism and later was seen as a response to the product of the dream work.

Freud's (Freud, 1955) addition to our understanding of dream remembering or perhaps better dream forgetting was his introduction of the concept of censorship or *repression*. This process is attributed to the effort of dreamers not to have their sleep disrupted by troubling, disturbing thoughts or feelings. To accomplish this protection of the continuity of sleep such unacceptable thoughts, the latent dream thoughts, are subject to a process of re-working by the dream work. The dream work mechanisms of condensation, displacement, representability, and symbolization find ways to express the satisfaction of the unacceptable desires in the disturbing latent dream thoughts in a disguised manner. The satisfaction of the unacceptable wish/desire in the dream experience in a form that is not disturbing to the dreamer's sensibility allows sleep to continue undisturbed.

B. Experimental Studies of Factors Affecting Dream Recall

It is necessary, before reviewing our studies of factors that may influence dream recall, to obtain some estimate of the rate of dream recall and to recognize that dream recall is not an inevitable outcome of awakening from sleep. College students estimate that on the average they have two to three dreams a week, some 15% of them report they never recall dreaming, and 5% report having more than one dream a night (Belicki, 1986). We studied the frequency of dream recall in a representative group of adults in the city of Cincinnati (Kramer, Winget, & Whitman, 1971). Sixty-one percent of the participants were able to report a recent dream. This compares favorably with the 58% rate of dream reporting of eight patients in psychoanalysis with an analyst known to have a high interest in dreams. In our population study, we noted a very clear effect of gender on dream reporting with women being more likely to report a dream than men, 65% compared to 53%, and a more complex, non-linear relationship to age, however, as younger subjects, 21–34, had a higher dream recall rate than older subjects, 65+ (Webb & Kersey, 1967). The discovery of REM sleep revitalized an interest in the study of dreaming as it provided the possibility to increase the recovery rate of dreaming. It has been found in 16 studies that an awakening from REM sleep is likely to yield a dream report from 60% to 89% of the time with a median of 74% (Snyder, 1969). In two laboratory studies, involving REM awakenings from 54 subjects, we had dream recall rates of 76% (Kramer & Roth, 1979) and 74.2% (Kramer, Roth, Arand, & Bonnet, 1981). The females and males had the same number of dream reports. It is necessary and reassuring that we were able to obtain a sufficiently high rate of recall to approximate the generally accepted 74% median REM recall rate and that we were performing similarly across our studies.

We all have some four to six REM periods a night from which a dream report can be recovered some 74% of the time. Yet even in a circumstance of high interest in dream reporting, such as in psychoanalysis, a dream report occurs only 58% of the time (Kramer, Whitman, Baldridge, & Lansky, 1964). This is approximately the rate of morning dream recall per day, 50%, that Webb and Kersey (1967) have reported generally occurs, and is not dissimilar to the frequency of 61% we found in our population study (Kramer, Winget, & Whitman, 1971). Subjects are able to recall three to five dreams if awakened at night, but, at best, report only one every other day in a psychoanalytic treatment (Kramer, Whitman, Baldridge, & Lansky, 1964).

A person has three to five dreams a night and recalls 75% of them in the laboratory, yet in the morning people only recall one dream every other day. What accounts for the selection process? In our study "Which Dream Does the Patient Tell?" (Whitman, Kramer, & Baldridge, 1963b), we compared the dreams reported at night to the experimenter from REM awakenings to those reported to the psychiatrist the next day. We had two subjects, a male hospitalized psychiatric patient who had a personality disorder and a female graduate student from a nearby university who was shy and introverted. They each slept in the laboratory two nights a week for 8 weeks. They were awakened from each REM period after 5 minutes and reported their dream to a male experimenter at night. The subjects saw the male psychiatrist alternately either 1 hour after sleeping in the laboratory or 24 hours after to report their dreams.

The male patient had 46 REM periods and 34 dream reports, while the female subject had 60 REM periods and 54 dream reports. The patient reported seven of the 34 dreams to the psychiatrist and three additional ones not told to the experimenter, while the female subject reported 41 of the night dreams to the psychiatrist and an additional seven she didn't report to the experimenter. Major changes or deletions were three times more common than complete forgetting. The male patient retold dreams to the psychiatrist that highlighted his capabilities as a man, while the dreams he omitted dealt primarily with homosexual impulses. On night 11, he retold to the psychiatrist this dream, "This girl had her dog trained so well she was afraid to let anyone near it. It was gone and I was helping her look for it." Theme: Takes the role of an adequate masculine figure helping a woman. From the same night, the following dream was told to the experimenter but not to the psychiatrist, "I was with a buddy of mine. We went on a tour of a big factory...new automobiles being built. When I came out of the factory it wasn't a buddy of mine anymore—it was Jack

Benny." Theme: Closeness to a man. From night 16, he reported "...about being out with another woman." Theme: Involved with a woman other than his wife. From the same night, he did not tell the psychiatrist the following dream. "Some fellow giving me a tattoo." Theme: A man being penetrated rhythmically by another man.

Dreams that demonstrate masculinity or imply heterosexuality are retold to the psychiatrist and homosexually oriented dreams are left out as they might diminish the self-esteem of the dreamer in the eyes of the psychiatrist.

The female subject frequently omitted telling dreams to the psychiatrist that were thinly disguised critical or sexual references. From night five, she did not tell the psychiatrist the following dream: "Asking for an appointment. He was only in two days a week. It was a doctor. I was wearing a bathing suit and was real embarrassed." Theme: Resentment about the infrequency of appointments and also sexual exhibitionistic wishes. Hostile and sexual dreams about the experimenter were told to the psychiatrist but not to the experimenter. From night three, she reported, "A boy was lost; he didn't know anything. I said the little dog knows more than he does." Theme: Associations clearly suggested her competitive depreciation of the experimenter. From night four, she told the psychiatrist but not the experimenter, "I was embarrassed because I didn't want to sleep close together (with a male)." Theme: Sexual feelings of wanting to sleep close to the experimenter. Most striking were the 15 dream scenes expressing her fears of psychiatry not told to the psychiatrist. She dreamt on night seven, "...I remember thinking his method wasn't good. It might cause depression in the patient." Theme: Suggests possible harm from treatment.

The fidelity with which the subjects retold their dreams despite the large number of dreams that dropped out or the changes that were made suggests that ordinary forgetting was playing a minor role. The number of dreams not told to the psychiatrist 1 hour after sleeping in the laboratory or 24 hours later was essentially the same, 11 versus 12. The dreams omitted were slightly less likely to come from the first half of the night, 10, in the last half, 13. Dreams that might diminish the dream listener's estimate of the dreamer are those that are selectively not reported. The position of the dream in the night appeared to be a minimally determining factor.

The possible selective effect of the interpersonal situation on dream reporting in the laboratory was examined further by varying the gender match of the subject and the experimenter (Fox, Kramer, Baldridge, Whitman, & Ornstein, 1968). We had a male college student and a female nurse each sleep for seven nights in the laboratory with either a male psychiatrist or female technician doing the dream collection. On the first, second, fourth, and seventh nights, the subject and experimenter were of the same sex while they were of opposite sex on the other three nights. We found that recall was 6–7% higher for both subjects with the male experimenter. Crowds and groups appeared in dreams more often when the pair was of opposite sexes, as did characters of unstated sex. Both subjects had more anxiety with the female experimenter. Hostility was lower for the male subject with the male experimenter and dependency and sexuality were lower in the female subject's dreams reported to the male experimenter. The female subject, in reporting to the male psychiatrist, saw the doctor in her dreams as need fulfilling with the intravenous fluids in the dreams flowing nicely; with the female experimenter, the intravenous was not connected in one dream and in another had run dry. The male subject reported to the male-doctor experimenter dreams in which he was performing before others with a feeling of satisfaction, conducting an orchestra, playing a concert, or taking a test on complicated machinery before two doctors. The themes changed across time as the female subject began to complain in her dreams with the female technician about the doctor not being available. With the female experimenter, the male subject reported dreams in which the subject was or could be hurt. Later he complained that an older woman was interfering with his efforts at love making with a younger woman. In both subjects, references to the experimental situation in the first three nights and the last three nights were present in 68% of the dream reports. There is a clear differential experience for the subjects related to the person (sex) of the experimenter and to the interpersonal situation in the laboratory. Psychological adaptation to being in the laboratory essentially does not seem to take place but the dream content appears to evolve across time as it might in psychotherapy.

Cartwright (Cartwright & Kasniak, 1991) compared the dream reports from heterosexual male medical students to those of a group of male "Gay Rights" activists following their being shown an explicitly erotic heterosexual film. The MMPI of the two groups differed only in that the homosexual group was somewhat more anxious and feminine. The homosexual subjects were sexually aroused and attributed it to their focusing on the male in the erotic film scenes. The medical students showed a dream recall decrease of 14% from their baseline while the homosexual group decreased only 2.5%. The medical students may feel that expressing sexual fantasies in dreams to their professors may not be appropriate and that led to a decrease in dream reporting. The homosexual subjects felt that expressing their sexuality was an appropriate and expected behavior. The content of the dreams reported reflected the different identity definition of the two groups, the heterosexual subjects identified the role of the major dream character as a student or student doctor while the homosexual subjects identified a friend as the role of the major dream character. A sexual identity role definition was two and a half times more common for the homosexual subjects than the heterosexual. The dream interactions of the heterosexual subjects were less intimate after the film with both male and female characters. The homosexual subjects moved toward greater intimacy and closer relations especially when reporting to the male experimenter. The dreams were influenced by the experimental situation and were in keeping with what the subjects felt would be approved behavior in the situation of the laboratory. This position is supportive of our work (Whitman, Kramer, & Baldridge, 1963a, 1963b; Whitman, Kramer, Ornstein, & Baldridge, 1970) in that the interpersonal situation in the laboratory is a determinant of dream content and reporting as it reflects the world view of the dreamer.

If adaptation took place in laboratory reported dreams, then the likelihood of the dreams being responsive to the interpersonal situation in the laboratory would be decreased. Dream content adaptation in the laboratory as reflected in representations of the laboratory in the dreams was described by Dement (Dement, Kahn, & Roffwarg, 1965) as occurring across the night from 46% for the first REM period to 16% for the sixth and from night one to night two from 25% to 7%. Whitman (Whitman, Pierce, Maas, & Baldridge, 1962) saw no change in anxiety across four nights of dream collection. We looked at laboratory representation across seven nights of dreaming in two subjects comparing the first three nights of dreaming to the last three and found 68% of dreams in both halves had a laboratory reference (Fox, Kramer, Baldridge, Whitman, & Ornstein, 1968). We looked for laboratory references in the laboratory dreams of 14 subjects who slept for 20 consecutive nights in the laboratory and had dreams collected from each REM period (Piccione, Thomas, Roth, & Kramer, 1976). The percentage of laboratory incorporation varied from a low of 2.05% on night five to a high of 44.3% on night 10. There was no significant decrease in incorporation of the laboratory in the subject's dream reports. Incorporation was about 35% for night one which was also the average of all the other nights. When we compared the average of nights one to five to subsequent five night blocks, we found no difference in incorporation rates. We correlated three dream contents: characters, activities, and descriptive elements from night to night across 20 nights (Kramer & Roth, 1979). The mean correlation for each of the contents was not significant in the first week and all three were significant in the second week, but the week two correlations were not statistically different from the week one correlations. The overall correlation for nights one to two was .05, for nights 10 to 11 was .30, and for nights 19 to 20 was .80. The last correlation was significant. We were able to establish some evidence for dream content adaptation across 20 nights of laboratory dream collection. This limited degree of adaptation suggests that the dream may well be responsive to the interpersonal situation in the laboratory for over 2 weeks.

Our interest in psycho-dynamically determined dream selectivity was expanded in our reviewing the many uses of the dream in clinical psychiatry (Whitman, Kramer, Ornstein, & Baldridge, 1970). For example, at the time of the approaching termination of treatment, a patient reported a dream in which railroad tracks that had run parallel were in the distance beginning to diverge. The disparate results from several different studies of the morning dream reports of patients who are schizophrenic may be partially determined by the state of the illness at the time, but the nature of the relationship between the dreamer and the dream collector may have been a factor as well in accounting for the differences in the dreams reported.

It seemed possible that if the meaning of the content of the dream experience was potentially determining of whether the dream was recalled, an examination of the work relating personality attributes of dreamers to their ability to recall dreams might be illuminating. Methodological differences in these studies have precluded drawing any generalizable conclusions (Cohen, 1974). Our intent was to study the same group of subjects using both laboratory and dream diary methods so we could see if we got similar or different results based on the method of dream collection. We, therefore, studied 24 college students who slept for 3 nonconsecutive nights in the laboratory and were awakened from each REM period for dream collection (Schwartz, Kramer, Palmer, & Roth, 1973). The same subjects completed a dream diary for 2 weeks 1 month prior to sleeping in the laboratory. Measures of the most common personality dimensions that have been reported to co-vary with dream recall namely anxiety, repression, ego strength, and field independence were obtained. The first three were MMPI scales (Hathaway & McKinley, 1943), and the fourth was derived from the Group Embedded Figures Test (Witkin, Oltman, Raskin, & Karp, 1971). We separately correlated the recall percentage obtained from REM awakenings and from the dream diaries with the scores on each personality variable. Only one of the eight correlations reached statistical significance and that was in the wrong direction, i.e., repression showed a positive correlation (.44) with recall. This study begins to raise question about the central role of meaning as a determinant of dream recall. Hartmann, in the continuing search for personality correlates of dream recall, has suggested that people with the personality characteristic he labeled "thin boundaries" have increased dream recall. Unfortunately, the amount of variance in dream recall explained by a person's score on a boundary questionnaire was only 16% (Hartmann, 1989). When dream length was controlled, the relationships between dream content and boundary scores was no longer significant (Hartmann, Rosen, & Rand, 1998). A series of studies on normal subjects (Trinder & Kramer, 1971) called attention to formal, i.e., dream length, dramatic intensity, and position in the night, rather than psychodynamic aspects of the dream report that appeared to determine whether the night reported dream was recalled in the morning.

We collected in the laboratory the dream reports from each REM period of 14 hospitalized schizophrenic patients for a total of 68 nights (Trinder & Kramer, 1971). Our intent was to see if the formal aspects of the dream that were reported as determining dream recall in the morning were operative as well in a psychiatrically ill population. The position of the dream report in the night influenced whether it was recalled in the morning. We obtained a *recency* effect, i.e., the last dream report was more likely to be recalled than an earlier one. A *primacy* effect was found as well, i.e., the first report was recalled more often than the second. The serial position of the dream report in the night's dreams was a determinant of morning recall. *Long* dream reports were more likely to be recalled than short ones. The fewer the dreams on a given night that were reported, the more likely the recall in the morning, an *interference* effect. *Dramatically intense,* i.e., salient, dreams were more likely to be recalled than nondramatic dreams. The formal aspects of dream content were essentially independent in determining the morning dream report recalled except in the case of the primacy effect where long and intense dreams occurred more at the first than second position.

We then examined the recall of dreaming across the REM period. It had already been reported by Foulkes (Foulkes, 1966) and Verdone (Verdone, 1965) that dreams recovered from REM periods later in the night compared to those recovered earlier in the night were more vivid, active, dramatic, and emotional. These reports did not allow for an examination of recall and content development, if any, across the REM period. As I described in chapter 2 (Kramer, Czaya, Arand, & Roth, 1974; Kramer, Roth, & Czaya, 1975), we examined dream reports from six time points across the REM period. We found that that there were significant effects of time for recall, emotion, anxiety, and pleasantness. We found content intensity at 5 minutes was less than at 10 minutes, but the intensity at 10 minutes was not different than at 20, while intensity at 20 minutes was less than at 30 minutes. This pattern of development of dream content intensity is consonant with the cyclic distribution of eye movements across a REM period described by Aserinsky (Aserinsky, 1971) that we confirmed (Johnson, Kramer, Bonnet, Roth, & Jansen, 1980) and with the observation that REM density is associated with dream intensity and emotionality (Molinari & Foulkes, 1969).

These results (Kramer, Czaya, Arand, & Roth, 1974; Kramer, Roth, & Czaya, 1975) provided a significant challenge to our previous position

(Whitman, Kramer, & Baldridge, 1963b; Whitman, Kramer, Ornstein, & Baldridge, 1970) that dream reporting was selective and based on the psychodynamic meaning of the dream and the nature of the relationship between the dreamer and the dream collector and illustrated the repressive mechanism described by Freud. Certainly both dynamic and nondynamic factors could be operative in determining the dream selected for reporting. To explore the possibility of dynamic selectivity further, we compared the content of the Schizophrenic patients' night reported dreams to those reported in the morning across the 12 major content categories of the Hall-Van de Castle dream content scoring system and found essentially no differences comparing night-collected dreams to morning reports of the nights' dreams (Trinder & Kramer, 1971). Item frequencies were higher across all scales in the morning but the differences were not statistically significant. The percentages of groups in the dreams were significantly higher at night and individual characters were significantly higher in morning reports. This difference echoed our study of the effect of gender differences between dreamer and dream collector in which crowds appeared more commonly in dreams when the pair was heterosexual, i.e., female dreamer and male experimenter, and was interpreted as a defense against sexual temptation (Fox, Kramer, Baldridge, Whitman, & Ornstein, 1968).

Domhoff has argued that morning dreams are representative of the nights' dreams partially because content differences among the dreams of a night have not been demonstrated (Domhoff, 1969). In exploring this issue of content differences among dreams of the night, we found word count differences and content differences among the REM periods across the night for the 22 subjects who slept for 20 consecutive nights. This strongly suggests that there would be psychodynamic differences depending on which dream was reported in the morning (Kramer, McQuarrie, & Bonnet, 1981). However, despite our studies suggesting that dream content is psycho-dynamically sensitive and that the dreams of the night show differences in content related to the position of the dream in the night, the formal characteristics of dreaming need to be given significant weight in explaining which dream is reported in the morning in addition to the dynamic factors that may also be operating. These studies call into question how representative of the night's dreaming the morning recalled dream may be.

Freud (Freud, 1955) called attention to the evanescent nature of the dream experience that makes it difficult to retain the dream in memory and to recall it either immediately on awakening or later in the day. It has been suggested that the state people are in while asleep and dreaming is fundamentally different than the state they are in after awakening (Snyder, 1963). The dream is experienced in one state and is being recalled in another. The difficulty may be similar to what Overton (Overton, 1973) has described, namely that material learned in one state, e.g., while under the influence of drugs, may be more easily recovered later during that drug induced state than when drug free. He has discussed this issue of *state dependent* remembering as applied to dream recall as accounting for some of the difficulty in remembering dreams. Certainly the connectedness of thematic content during the waking state before and after sleeping is greater than among the intervening dreams while in the sleeping state (Kramer, Moshiri, & Scharf, 1982). The cognitive organizational difference between waking and dreaming suggests two different states of consciousness.

It has often been observed that individuals who have poor dream recall report an increase in dream recall when they are placed in a situation that encourages the recall of dreams such as entering dynamic psychotherapy or sleeping in a sleep lab to have dreams collected. Does an *interest* in dreams lead to a greater recall of the dream experience? College students who volunteered to sleep in a sleep lab for dream collection indicated on a questionnaire a greater interest in dreams and believe that they have more dreams compared to students who chose not to volunteer (Roth, Kramer, & Trinder, 1972). However, in keeping a dream diary for 21 days, the non-volunteers with less interest in dreams reported one third more mornings with a dream report, 12 compared to 9. Apparently having an interest in dreams does not necessarily lead to an increase in dream recall. When poor sleepers are compared to good sleepers, it is the poor sleepers who report a greater interest in dreams (Arand, Kramer, Czaya, & Roth, 1972). The poor sleepers in their two-week dream diaries had one third more mornings with a dream report than the good sleepers, 10.6 compared to 7.7. The poor sleepers reported more awakenings during the night than the good sleepers, and awakening after a dream experience increases the likelihood of recalling the dream. The opportunity to rehearse the dream while awake may be an alternative explanation to an interest in dreams as to why the poor sleepers report more dreams than the good sleepers. The universal experience of wanting to remember a dream and having it slip away does not lend much credence to an interest in dreams enhancing dream recall. This view is supported by our studies of recall in laboratory volunteers and in poor sleepers.

The competing interests that emerge as we move from sleep to wakefulness require that we direct our attentional energies toward the demands of wakefulness (Whitman, 1963). We have already pointed out an interference or distraction effect in that the recall of a specific dream in the morning decreases as there are more dreams reported in the same night (Trinder & Kramer, 1971). The effect of two dream reports on a night decreases the probability of recall 40%; five dream reports on a night decreases the probability of the recall of a particular dream 64%. Goodenough (Goodenough, Lewis, Shapiro, Jaret, & Sleser, 1965) has shown that abrupt arousal from sleep increases the likelihood of a dream report being obtained probably because it decreases the likely of the dreamer's attention on awakening turning to other matters.

We have not examined directly whether the degree of disconnectedness or disorganization among dream reports contributes to recall. We did find that a commonality among dream content themes of a night was less frequent than between wakefulness themes although the latter were further apart in time as they were collected before and after sleep (Kramer, Moshiri, & Scharf, 1982). Dream themes are more diverse than waking themes and potentially more disconnected. When Barber (Barber, 1969) presented subjects with dream reports that varied in the degree of disorganization, she failed to find recall differences related to the degree of disorganization. However, she did find that the dream reports of poor dream recallers were harder even for good recallers to remember. Something intrinsic to the dream report contributes to whether it can be recalled but not its state of disorganization. The formal characteristics of dream length and dramatic intensity, which contribute importantly to whether a dream is recalled, also may be seen as an intrinsic quality of the dream report and although acting independently they are highly correlated, $r = .72$.

The factor of repeated events contributing to better recall in general focuses attention on the fact that it may be harder to recall dreams because they generally are not repeated events. It has been suggested however that recurrent dreams may provide a focus to highlight the core concerns of the dreamer from both a trait and state perspective. (Cartwright, 1979; Domhoff, 1993; Whitman, Kramer, Ornstein, & Baldridge, 1970). Recurrent dreams are said to occur among nightmare suffers (Kramer, Schoen, & Kinney, 1984) and patients with Post Traumatic Stress Disorder (PTSD) (Kramer, Schoen, & Kinney, 1984). The content themes of the nightmare sufferer are the same as a control group of good dream recallers with a high interest in their dreams. The content theme frequency of the two groups correlates .87 (Kramer, Schoen, & Kinney, 1984). The patient with nightmares is, in general, an average dream recaller. However, the nightmare sufferer is more responsive and aroused in response to nightmares than the control group. The patients with PTSD have dreams about the traumatic event about half time but rarely have exactly the same dream. The nightmare sufferer puts the focus on the dream, not the response to the dream. The PTSD patient appears to selectively recall the dream related to the trauma, although it is not the only dream, it may be the most salient, the most dramatically intense.

Freud (Freud, 1955) addressed two issues related to dream recall: repression and confabulation. Our studies of the formal characteristics affecting recall, content development across the REM period (Kramer, Czaya, Arand, & Roth, 1974; Kramer, Roth, & Czaya, 1975), and the lack of a correlation between personality attributes and dream recall (Schwartz, Kramer, Palmer, & Roth, 1973) do not support a primary repression explanation accounting for dream recall. Freud's (Freud, 1955) concept of secondary revision, the preconscious reworking of the dream, however, is bolstered by our observation that the fragmented dream report obtained at night is presented the following morning in an expanded and better organized narrative form (Whitman, Kramer, & Baldridge, 1963b). The recall of dreams later in the day, which many people report, probably reflects inadvertent priming by an experience related to the dream occurring later in the day (Stickgold, Scott, Rittenhouse, & Hobson, 1999).

We have put our primary focus, when discussing laboratory dream collection, on those dream reports collected from REM sleep. Dream recall percentages from non-REM sleep range from 7% to 75% depending on the standard for rating the report as a dream, the non-REM stage of sleep from which the subject is awakened, how long after eye movements have occurred, the time of night of the awakening, and the expectations of the experimenters in regard to the possibility of recovering mental content (Herman, Ellman, & Roffwarg, 1978). We wondered what affect the prior stage of sleep might have on immediate recall and long-term recall, as the stage 4 is considered deeper sleep than the stage 2. We had 14 subjects sleep in the sleep lab for five nights and tested their ability to learn and remember words short- and long-term after awakening from stage 2 and stage 4 sleep (Bonnet, Alter, & Kramer, 1981). This was done on one occasion immediately after being awakened from each stage of sleep, 2 and 4, and in addition being awakened twice from stage 4. The latter two stage 4 awakenings had subjects engaged with an unrelated task for 8 minutes before learning. The other time, the subject was awake and occupied for 8 minutes on an unrelated task after learning. Fewer words were recalled both in short- and long-term recall after being awakened from stage 4, the deepest stage of sleep. Both short-term and long-term recall was better when the memory task occurred 8 minutes after being awake. Being awake for 8 minutes after learning did not improve morning recall. The decrements in rehearsal or immediate consolidation after arousal from sleep are related to the prior depth of sleep and can be decreased by keeping the subject awake for 8 minutes before learning; the subject is probably more aroused and alert when learning takes place. The concept of a carryover effect from the prior sleep stage into waking was demonstrated by Fiss and colleagues (Fiss, Klein, & Bokert, 1966) in showing that the quality of responses to T.A.T. cards is different depending if one performs following being awakened from REM or non-REM sleep. The post-REM sleep T.A.T. stories are more dream-like than those after non-REM awakenings.

We studied the effect of dementia and age on dream recall in the laboratory (Kramer & Roth, 1975). Kahn and Fisher (Kahn & Fisher, 1969) had already reported that older subjects, 70–87, showed only a 43.5% dream recall rate when awakened from REM sleep. We found that mildly demented middle-aged men showed a decrement in dream recall reporting dreams from only 57% of REM awakenings, and the severely demented men of the same age from only 35%. Severely demented aged patients recalled dreams from only 8% of awakenings. Dementia and aging both negatively affect dream recall and if both are present the affect is additive.

A large number of factors influence the recall of dreaming. We have reviewed primarily those in which we have been involved. The formal aspects of recall, particularly dream length and dramatic intensity, emerge as of prime importance with content related factors being of secondary importance in selecting or determining which dream is recalled. Intrinsic properties of the dream experience, i.e., the length of time into the REM period and the time of night of the dream collection, and the state of the brain, i.e., the stage of sleep prior to awakening and/or the degree of brain damage, will affect recall as well. Demographic factors such as the sex of the dreamer or his age are also contributory. Processes of rehearsal, consolidation, and level of arousal play a role as well. An extensive listing of issues that may affect dream recall is to be found in Shafton's book, the *Dream Reader* (Shafton, 1995).

C. An Assessment of Dream Recall Theories and an Arousal-Retrieval Theory of Dream Recall

Goodenough (Goodenough, 1978) assesses the status of the field of dream recall in a review in 1978. The article is republished in 1991 (Ellman & Antrobus, 1991) without, according to the editors, any need to be updated. He has reviewed the issues and research related to the problems associated with accounting for the limitations on dream recall. He points out that the research on dream forgetting can be divided into two categories based on whether the recall problems are related (1) to the content of the dream, or (2) to some aspect of sleep that alters or impairs memory function and makes it difficult to recall experiences from sleep. He divides dream forgetting into either content-centered or memory process-centered theories. He points out that as even nondream events occurring during sleep are hard to recall the next day, content centered theories are less likely to account for failure to recall events during sleep than memory process theories which potentially have greater generalizability. It should be recognized that both factors might be operative in many circumstances.

Goodenough (Goodenough, 1978) reviews the evidence for the most important content-centered theory categories (including dream salience, dream disorganization, dream kinesthesia, disinterest in dreams, and repression). He concludes that dream salience is an important factor in accounting for which dreams are likely to be recalled. The more salient dreams are associated with REM periods with increased eye movements, i.e., increased REM density, and more rapid and irregular respiration. He notes that dream salience does not address why dreams are hard to recall but rather why one dream is recalled rather than another. The disorganized nature of the dream report does not, he believes, contribute significantly to problems in dream recall. Dream movement at awakening decreases recall and may be understood as a specific example of distraction which has been shown at awakening to reduce dream remembering. Changing the motivation to recall dreams can increase dream recall but may have only a limited role. An interest in dreams per se may not have an increased dream recall frequency associated with it. Repression may play a role in some instances of dream forgetting but, like salience, does not explain why in general dreams are so hard to recall.

The review by Goodenough (Goodenough, 1978) of the memory process-centered theories of dream recall includes classical memory phenomena, state dependent learning, and impairment in memory trace consolidation. Alterations in memory processing in sleep would potentially affect recalling both dream and nondream events occurring during sleep and therefore offers a potentially more comprehensive explanation for the difficulty of recalling events from sleep. The acquisition of information during sleep is impaired. The classical memory effects seen in serial learning tasks, e.g., primacy, recency, saliency, and such, are found for dream recall following awakenings from sleep, but this does not contribute to understanding why the recall of sleep experiences is more difficult than waking recall. Explanations related to state dependent recall in which experiences that occurred in one state can only be recalled in that state are attractive in explaining why it is difficult to recall events from sleep while awake but are not adequately supported by research results. Impairment of memory trace consolidation in sleep assumes that an experience is held in short-term memory for some period of time and is then moved to more permanent long-term memory. The consolidation process takes time and, perhaps, a particular set of conditions, for it to take place. It was found that dream recovery after a REM period was dependent on an awakening right after the period; the further one got from the end of the REM period, the lower the recall rate. In addition, the amount of time awake was positively related to later recall and this was thought to be related to consolidation of the dream and to rehearsal. However, the level of alertness at the time of reporting the dream appears to have more to do with later recall than with how long the dreamer is awake. Consolidation appears to occur in seconds after reporting. The more aroused the subject at the time of reporting, the longer it will take to return to sleep, which would explain the longer time awake-consolidation relationship as a consequence of the arousal level. It has been suggested by Foulkes (Foulkes, 1966) that the recovery problem may be in retrieval of the dream from long-term memory not in the consolidation of the dream.

Goodenough and Koulack (Goodenough & Koulack, 1976) offer an *arousal retrieval hypothesis* to account for the recall of dreams. They assume that a cognitive processing of the dream in short-term memory occurs in preparation for transfer to long-term memory. If the subject is insufficiently aroused, this cognitive process of coding, reorganizing, and labeling of the memory is inadequate and transfer to long-term memory is impaired or does not occur. In addition, retrieval of the memory, if it is transferred, is more difficult or impossible. Distractions on awakening would interfere with the cognitive processing and transfer to long-term memory. As it is apparent that it is difficult to recall any experience that occurs during sleep, content-based recall theories are less likely than memory-based theories to account for recall.

D. Factors Affecting Dream Content to be Considered in Collecting Dreams

We do not collect or study the dream experience even in laboratory studies but, rather, the verbal report of that experience as both Malcolm (Malcolm, 1959) and Erickson (Erickson, 1954) acknowledge. There are a number of factors alone and in combination that may influence the dream report (Kramer, Winget, & Roth, 1975). These include the following: (1) the place in which the dream is experienced, (2) the method of awakening the dreamer, (3) the context of the interpersonal situation in which the dream report is given, (4) the style of the collection interview, (5) the time of night and stage of sleep from which the sleeper is awakened, (6) the method of recording the dream report, and (7) the type of subject from whom the dream is collected.

Dream reports collected in *different settings* have clear content differences (Domhoff, 1969). Sleeping at home or in the laboratory results in changes in the content of dream reports. Laboratory collected dreams have been said to be less intense and less vivid than those collected at home. When the circumstances were equated, no differences were found in vivid fantasy (Weisz & Foulkes, 1970), although home dreams were more aggressive. The laboratory situation may continue to appear in dreams for 3 weeks without significant adaptation taking place (Piccione, Thomas, Roth, & Kramer, 1976). And male and female subjects have different fantasies about sleeping in the laboratory. Men have fantasies of being exploited and women of being raped (Whitman, Pierce, Maas, & Baldridge, 1962).

The *method of awakening* the dreamer, fast or slow, alters the frequency of dream recall. The faster the awakening, the less the distraction and the more likely a dream report is obtained. It is not clear if the nature of the awakening stimuli, e.g., tactile versus auditory, makes a difference, although frequency of incorporation into the dream is stimulus dependent (Dement & Wolpert, 1958; Kramer, Kinney, & Scharf, 1983).

The real or imagined *interpersonal situation* in which the dream report is collected will influence what is reported and what is withheld (Whitman, Kramer, & Baldridge, 1963a, 1963b) (Cartwright & Kasniak, 1991; Fox, Kramer, Baldridge, Whitman, & Ornstein, 1968). Factors such as the familiarity between the dreamer and dream collector, as well as the sex and status of the collector in relation to the dreamer, influence what will be reported and to whom. Variations in the interpersonal relationship between dream reporter and collector make establishing a baseline problematic.

The *method and technique* of the collection interview can alter the reported dream. Asking "What were you dreaming?" may obtain different results from "What was going through your mind before you were awakened?" (Lewis, Goodenough, Shapiro, & Sleser, 1966). Given the subtleties of the relationship and the demand characteristics of the situation, safeguards are necessary to prevent the interviewer obtaining from the subject what he wants to find.

The time of night and stage of sleep from which the dreamer is awakened will influence the probability (Trinder & Kramer, 1971), quantity (Kramer, McQuarie, Bonnet, 1980), and quality of the recall (Trinder & Kramer, 1971). Differences between early and late REM periods (Cartwright & Kasniak, 1991), short and long REM periods, and interrupted and uninterrupted periods have all been reported (Trinder & Kramer, 1971). The content recovered depends on how far into the REM period the dreamer was when awakened (Kramer, Roth, & Czaya, 1975).

The *method of recording* the dream will inevitably alter the report obtained. Verbal reporting leads to longer and more poorly organized dream reports while writing the report leads to better organized and shorter reports. The former is limited by the verbal facility of dreamers and the latter by their written facility (Taub, Kramer, Arand, & Jacobs, 1978; Whitman, Kramer, & Baldridge, 1963b).

Subject variables have been shown to influence the probability of recall, i.e., dream reporters compared to dream nonreporters (Goodenough, 1978). Both personality and physiological differences have been found to co-vary with recall frequency. Volunteer subjects have a different recall frequency than nonvolunteers (Roth, Kramer, & Trinder, 1972) as do poor sleepers compared to good sleepers (Arand, Kramer, Czaya, & Roth, 1972).

We have provided a brief historical review of the issues in dream recall to set the stage for presenting a representative sample of experimental studies of the factors affecting dream recall. A summary of the assessment of dream recall theories, both dream content-based and memory process-oriented was included. The arousal-retrieval theory of dream recall (Goodenough & Koulack, 1976) was chosen for description as it encompasses the literature on dream recall most adequately. Factors affecting dream content that need to be considered in collecting dreams was presented as a prelude to our work on quantifying dreams that follows in chapter 4.

The Measurement of Dreams

A. Introduction

The essence of every scientific enterprise is the ability to reliably and validly measure the object of interest. Lord Kelvin (Strauss, 1968, 482b), in the 19th century, expressed this view: "When you cannot measure it, when you cannot express it in numbers,... you have scarcely in your thoughts, advanced to the stage of science, whatever the matter may be." Martin Fischer (Strauss, 1968, 482b) expressed a similar sentiment in the 20th century: "Quibbling over qualitative differences is always an evidence of sophistry. Vital distinctions are always quantitative."

Attention to quantification is essential if the study of the content of dreaming is to be scientific. Unfortunately, attention to issues of quantification has been relatively neglected in the study of dreaming. This has been especially the case in studies of the content of dreaming. The pioneer effort of Hall and Van de Castle in developing a descriptive system for quantifying what appears in dream reports is a model for such efforts. The observation of the correlation of REM sleep and dreaming (Aserinsky & Kleitman, 1953; Dement & Wolpert, 1958) led to an upsurge in research not just in the physiology of sleep but in the psychology of dreaming as well. This effort in studying the physiology of sleep was given a great impetus in 1968 by the development of a common quantification system, *"A manual of standardized terminology, technique and scoring system for sleep stages of human subjects"* (Rechtschaffen & Kales, 1968). An effort, in 1970, at the 10th annual meeting of the Association for the Psycho-physiological Study of Sleep, to consider the standardization of the quantification of dreams to improve communication among investigators was attempted but it was felt to be premature. In retrospect, it was an unfortunate decision. It was recommended at that time that a compilation of scoring systems be undertaken. Carolyn Winget and I undertook the task building on the work of Calvin Hall and Robert Van de Castle. In the resultant publication, *Dimensions of Dreams* (Winget & Kramer, 1979), we called attention to the collection and quantification problems in dream research and provided a brief summary and an evaluation of 132 dream content scales noting their great redundancy. Domhoff (Domhoff, 1996), many years later, again reviewed the problems in developing new dream content scales. He pointed out the weaknesses of many scales, noting their redundancy with existing scales and argued that the content of interest in such studies could be expressed by combining several of the better known and more widely used Hall-Van de Castle scales allowing for improved communication between investigators, as well as the development of a relatable body of knowledge. In the same work, Domhoff provided a detailed review of the dream content literature with a particular focus on the studies that used the Hall-Van de Castle scales. The focus of attention in the more recent content analysis literature is not on the development of dream content scoring systems but on automating the measurement of verbal systems (Gottschalk, 1999). It is worthwhile to review a number of specific issues as they relate to the measurement of dream content. This will provide a context for the position that the proper development of new scoring systems is a considerable undertaking and that the scoring of dream content requires considerable care and attention.

B. Should the Dream Report Be Measured?

It has been too readily assumed that *the dream is ineffable,* that it cannot be measured, or that any effort at quantifying it will so distort the essence of the dream as to render the resulting measurement trivial if not meaningless. This is a view of quantification that has its defenders, such as Loren Eisely (Strauss, 1968,482b) who said, "...the physicists made extended use of mathematical techniques and still were hopelessly wrong and, it must be added, arrogantly wrong." Dwight Ingle (Strauss, 1968, 483a) echoed the sentiment when he observed that "Science cannot be equated to measurement...." These negative opinions about quantification have the unintended consequence of supporting those who consider that the essence of the dream experience is ineffable and therefore not amenable to capture, study, and measurement. The conviction that there is an ineffable aspect of the dream experience has an appealing mystical aura that has been fed by the various religious traditions in their belief that the deity spoke to the believer through dreams (Van de Castle, 1994). Jung (Jung, 1964b) has attributed special knowledge and function to the dream experience in providing corrections for various psychological excesses as well as expressing the understanding people have obtained across the millennia in the collective unconscious. Ullman (Ullman & Zimmerman, 1979) sees the dream experience as containing a truthfulness that surpasses our conscious self-knowledge. Freud (Freud, 1955,525) spoke of the core or navel of the dream experience toward which the associations led but beyond which which the associations could not be followed. Some modern philosophers of mind are of the opinion that experience has a crucial qualitative aspect, the so-called qualia, which renders the experience irreducible to brain states (Searles, 1992); others do not find that to be the case (Dennett, 2005).

The major reluctance to engaging seriously in quantifying the content of the reported dream, the so-called manifest dream, stems from the position so vigorously enunciated by Freud (Freud, 1955). He held the view that focusing on the manifest dream was an impediment to establishing the meaning of the dream contained in the latent dream thoughts. Attention to the manifest dream report served to distract from the search, through the use of the patient's free associations, for the latent dream thoughts that were the starting point for the dream and which the manifest dream served to disguise. It was the latent dream thoughts that could be inserted into the ongoing waking life of the dreamer. The work of Erickson (Erickson, 1954) and Spanjaard (Spanjaard, 1969) within the psychoanalytic community facilitated the legitimacy of examining the manifest content of dreams. Freud (Freud, 1955,506) in a footnote in the *Interpretation of Dreams* expressed disappointment that his followers so slavishly followed the dictum to ignore the meaningless manifest and search only for the latent content of dreams. It was the early involvement of highly regarded analysts such as the late Charles Fisher in New York (Fisher, 1965) and Roy Whitman in Cincinnati (Kramer, Winget, & Roth, 1975; Whitman, Pierce, & Maas, 1960), both of whom led research groups that collected dreams in the sleep laboratory, that supported the legitimacy in the psychoanalytic community of the quantitative examination of the manifest content of dreams, at least for research purposes.

C. Issues in Measuring the Dream Report

The verbal dream report is what is usually collected for study and becomes the text for measurement, for quantification, in psychological dream studies. There are several issues that need to be clarified in regard to measuring the text of the dream reports. These measurement issues are related to

(1) the verbal nature of the dream report, (2) the definition of the scoreable dream report text, (3) the effect of dream report length on the type of measurement made, (4) the methods of quantifying dream content; and (5) the reliability and validity of the measurement (Kramer, 1982; Kramer, Winget, & Roth, 1975; Winget & Kramer, 1979).

1. The Verbal Nature of the Dream Report

The verbal nature of the dream report raises two issues that are immediately germane in discussing measuring dream reports. The first issue is that the dream report obtained is potentially so influenced by the verbal fluency of the subject that any content differences obtained, within and between subjects, may be explainable on the basis of the verbal fluency of the subjects. There has been only limited direct comparison of verbal behavior awake describing an experience to the verbal behavior of the same subject describing a dream. We obtained dream reports of subjects from an epidemiological study reporting a dream and the same subjects' reporting an early memory. The dream report and the early memory report were essentially of identical length, averaging 22 words in each type of report (Kramer, Winget, & Whitman, 1971). Systematic study of verbal fluency comparing laboratory collected dreams to other verbal productions of the same subject would serve to clarify the possible confounding role of verbal fluency in our measurement of dream reports. The second issue related to the verbal nature of the dream report is whether the content or form of the verbal dream report is different from other comparable verbal reports. Comparable reports would be those obtained from other narrative fantasy productions such as are obtained from the responses elicited from TAT cards (Kramer, Roth, & Palmer, 1976), from verbal samples (Kramer, Roth, Arand, & Bonnet, 1981), or from early memory reports (Kramer, Ornstein, Whitman, & Baldridge, 1967; Kramer, Winget, & Whitman, 1971). We summarized the results of 28 studies that compared nonlaboratory collected dream reports to various psychological tests (Winget & Kramer, 1979). These studies, each with highly different designs, not surprisingly, reported inconsistent results in relating dreams to other psychological tests. When we looked at a number of different informational sources, e.g., a subject's history, laboratory collected dream reports, and psychological testing reports, and used a 100-item Q-sort technique to describe the patient, done independently by judges from each data source, significant relationships were found across the various data sources (Kramer, Roth, Clark, & Trinder, 1972). In regard to the form of the dream report, we noted that the dream report collected at night from a REM awakening was much more fragmentary than the same dream reported the next morning or the following day (Whitman, Kramer, & Baldridge, 1963). This observation calls attention to the possibility that the narrative structure of the dream report may reflect a secondary organizing of the more fragmented dream experience related to what Freud (Freud, 1955) described as secondary revision. Thematically, the verbal productions before and after sleeping in the sleep laboratory, although further apart in time, were more related to one another than the themes of the intervening dream reports collected from each intervening REM period (Kramer, Moshiri, & Scharf, 1982).

It has become clear that the assumed uniqueness of the dream report as a verbal report remains to be demonstrated. Freud postulated the special nature of the dream in expressing the view that "The interpretation of dreams is the royal road to a knowledge of the unconscious activities of the mind." Endless illustrations, anecdotal evidence, that fill *The Interpretation of Dreams* are not a demonstration, and are not scientific evidence. The uniqueness of the dream experience remains an open question.

2. The Text to be Measured

The text that is finally measured, the verbal dream report, has been described as somewhere on the continuum between all of the subjects' response to the question "What were you dreaming" or "What had been going through your mind before I awakened you" in a sleep laboratory study or to the instructions given in a post-sleep dream recall study in which the report is usually written out by the subject. The writing out of dream reports presents its own special concerns related to the writing skills of the subject and the difficulty in writing in a disorganized manner. The need to write in an organized and concise manner dominates our written productions; the exceptions do test the rule, as in James Joyce's *Finnegan's Wake* or William Faulkner's *The Sound and the Fury*.

The verbal dream report text subjected to measurement is some distilled version of the answer to the question that the dream collector has posed to the dreamer. The repetitions, contrasts with real life, exclusionary comments, associational remarks, and gratuitous comments and explanations are generally removed. It is apparent then that the final measured dream report text depends very much on the assumptions made about the dream experience one is attempting to measure. All of the reported dream would be considered as the basis for developing a dream interpretation in an analytic treatment. To illustrate the effect of including the associations as part of the dream report, we did a study (Kramer & Glucksman, 2006) of affect in dream reports in analytic treatment. We found affect was present in 58% of the manifest dream reports, but, if the associations to the dream report were included, then affect was found in 96% of the dream reports and associations. The hypothesis that dreams are driven by affect, a commonly held view, is weakened if the dream is conceptualized as represented only by the manifest dream report, but supported if the associations are included. The assumptions we made about the dream experience influenced the definition of the text utilized for scoring and changed the result of the study to a significant degree.

3. The Length of the Dream Report

The length of the dream report will affect the result of the measurement made; generally, the longer the dream report, the greater the possibility that a scoreable item will occur. How then are dream reports of different lengths to be equated? Solutions offered are to limit dream reports that are studied to a certain length or to express a scoreable item in terms of another item so ratios are compared between samples rather than absolute amounts. The setting of word length limits has the unfortunate consequence of choosing only to study certain types of dreams, which, in turn, limits the generalizations that are possible. Freud (Freud, 1955) reported a one-word dream of his own "Autodidasker," which he subjected extensively to analysis; a 48-word dream, "The Dream of the Botanical Monograph" (Foulkes, 1978); and the "Dream of Irma's Injection" with 369 words (Kramer, 1999, 2000). The use of ratios may be useful if the question being asked is related to the ratios chosen and the dream is long enough so items of both aspects of the ratio appear. For example, to look at the ratio of aggressive interactions to friendly ones in a male/female comparison in dreams of some length might be an understandable choice, while comparing the ratio of physical activities to sadness in psychotically depressed and schizophrenic patients less so, particularly if the items have a low frequency of appearance. The dividing of scoreable item frequencies by the length of the dream to achieve comparability has been suggested, but this assumes a fixed relationship between item frequency and length which does not seem to be the case (Trinder, Kramer, Riechers, & Fishbein, 1970).

The process of quantifying the content of the manifest dream report text presents some major technical issues. A usable measuring scheme should (1) state the underlying assumptions in regard to the item or concept that the device attempts to measure, (2) give well-defined anchoring points, (3) list inclusive and exclusive examples for each scale point, (4) indicate the unit that is to be coded, (5) specify the contextual unit to be used in making scoring decisions, and (6) provide a summarizing unit for deriving a total score. Many of the scales that we reviewed in *Dimensions of the Dream* do not meet these criteria (Winget & Kramer, 1979). The other major issue in the quantifying of the dream report text has to do with the question of how to deal with the problem of the intensity dimension in the scaling process. Nominal scales, also called category scales, have been developed that simply sort the content of the dream into various classes or categories of items. An intensity dimension can be approximated by reporting the increases or decreases in the various classes of items based on such a nominal scale. A dream with six people may be considered as more "peopled" than one with only two people. If one undertakes to do an equal interval scale that attempts to establish the amount of difference among related items, one runs the risk of certain absurdities. For example, if one develops a 4-point heterosexual equal interval scale in which scale point 1 is the presence of a heterosexual pair and scale point 4 is sexual intercourse, the absurdity of four instances of heterosexual pairs equaling one instance of intercourse emerges. Unfortunately, attention to this interval scaling problem has been generally neglected (Domhoff, 1996; Hall & Van de Castle, 1966).

4. The Reliability of Measurement

The reliability of dream content measurement, i.e., the reproducibility of measurement is an issue of considerable interest and concern. The reproducibility of a white blood count, for example, needs to be known and, hopefully, found to be in an acceptable range if a decision about a surgical intervention is to be based to a significant degree on the blood count. The assumption that once a scorer is trained to use a scale, the ratings on a dream content scale remain stable is unlikely to be the case and repeated training needs to be done. When scoring a large sample of dream reports, reliability testing should be done on all or at least a sample of the dream reports at the beginning, middle, and end of scoring the set of dreams (Kramer, Roth, & Palmer, 1976). Drift is common in all human judgment systems and scoring dream reports is no exception. The level of agreement of two independent judges is the method most commonly used to express the reliability of a scoring undertaking. The effect of using percentages to express reliability and the inflation of reliability if the category being scored is rarely present because the scorers are agreeing on absence of the item is discussed by Hall and Van de Castle (Hall & Van de Castle, 1966). Reliability, accuracy of measurement, sets the upper limit on a study's validity.

5. The Validity of Measurement

The validity of the dream content scoring of a dream report text is, in principal, established as validity would be in any other psychological circumstance. The scoring system should have face or content validity, i.e., the scale content should be appropriate to the concept being measured. The scale should show construct validity, i.e., the scale should be measuring the right construct, the scale items should be related to each other, and the scale should do what it was intended to do (e.g., angry people should have higher anger scores). The scales should show criterion or predictive validity, i.e., the scales should predict outcomes or consequences. The Hall-Van de Castle (Hall & Van de Castle, 1966) category, or nominal scale for aggression, has eight classifications that include acts that lead to (1) the death of a character, (2) physical harm to a person, (3) chasing, capturing, or physically coercing another, (4) theft or destruction of possessions of a person, (5) a serious threat or accusation (6) rejection, exploitation, control, or verbal coercion of a character, (7) verbal or expressive activities like shouting, or (8) covert hostility feeling. The first four are physical aggressions and the last four are nonphysical. The scale demonstrates face or content validity and construct validity as the appropriate range of items is covered. The predictive validity has been repeatedly demonstrated. The Hall-Van de Castle character scale demonstrates face validity in the extent of the types of characters that can be scored; has construct validity in that it delineates types of people by gender, age, familiarity, occupational, social, and family roles; and has construct validity as applying it has shown that the character type special to schizophrenic patients is the stranger and in the depressed it's a family member role, i.e., a brother, a mother, and so forth (Beck, 1967; Kramer, Baldridge, Whitman, Ornstein, & Smith, 1969; Kramer & Roth, 1973; Langs, 1966). The Beck Masochism scale demonstrated criterion or predictive validity as it found an increased frequency of masochism in depressed patients (Beck, 1967).

D. Application of Dream Content Scoring

1. The Hall-Van de Castle Dream Content Scoring System

The quantitative dream content scoring system that has been most extensively used is that developed by Hall and Van de Castle (Hall & Van de Castle, 1966). This is intended as an empirical system without an explicit theoretical orientation. The aspects of the dream report that can be scored by their system include characters, social interactions, activities, striving, i.e., success and failure, environmental press, i.e., misfortunes and good fortunes, emotions, physical surroundings, and descriptive elements. The system was developed on written samples of home collected dream reports from college students. The normative information on dream content they offer comes from nonlaboratory dream reports of 100 male and 100 female college students ages 19–25 each of whom provided 12 to 16 dream reports from which five dream reports each of between 50 and 300 words were selected to develop the norms. The reliabilities we found scoring 418 dream reports of 50 to 300 words from 26 male and 39 female college students were very similar to what was reported by Hall and Van de Castle.

We found the proportional distribution of character scoring on 34 aspects of character were almost identical for our scoring and that of Hall and Van de Castle (e.g., the proportion of total human characters of all characters in the dream reports for male subjects reported in the Hall and Van de Castle norms was .939 and we found .942). Dream characters known to the dreamer for female subjects in the Hall-Van de Castle norms were .368 and we found .359. Particularly striking was the fact that they found 2.6 characters per dream and we found 2.4 (Riechers, Kramer, & Trinder, 1970). We extended the application of the system to laboratory collected dream reports of under 50 words and found similar levels of reliability between two judges, who had no prior consultation, to that reported by Hall and Van de Castle on the character, social interactions, activities, and emotions scales. We found agreement for the presence of a dream character to be 83%, with agreement for number, sex, identity, and age being between 92% and 98% (Sandler, Kramer, Fishbein, & Trinder, 1969; Sandler, Kramer, Trinder, & Fishbein, 1970).

It becomes apparent that a system such as described by Hall and Van de Castle in 1966 could have been a starting point for a common measurement system such as was established for measuring the physiology of sleep (Rechtschaffen & Kales, 1968) with the consequence of encouraging a common metric to foster communication among investigators. Any weakness in the Hall and Van de Castle system such as the relative limitation on identifying emotions in dream reports could be overcome by using an additional carefully constructed system such as the Gottschalk-Gleser Content Analysis Scales (Gottschalk, Winget, & Gleser, 1969). The approach of using complementary scoring systems to measure dream content reports is analogous to the use of different staining techniques used in examining various aspects of the nervous system. The Nissl stain, for example, is used to highlight cell bodies, while the Golgi stain is used to examine axons or dendrites (cell fibers).

2. Comparing Dream Content Scoring Systems for Hostility

One of the objections mentioned earlier to the quantification of dream reports is that the essence of the experience would be lost. Hauri (Hauri, 1975) conducted a study in which a series of dreams was scored utilizing a number of different scaling systems for hostility. The scoring was done, generally, by the author of the particular system. He found two things of particular interest. One result was that the average correlation among the various scoring systems was .50 and statistically significant, suggesting considerable overlap or redundancy among the systems. However, as 75% of the differences, i.e., variations among the systems was not accounted for and may not all have been error of measurement, then different aspects of the concept of hostility may not have been captured and the dream report is not reduced to any single numerical value and its essence is potentially preserved.

3. Applying Measurement to a Clinical Observation

In a clinical case report, Drs. Miller and Buckley describe the manifest dream content change that occurs to a patient as he goes through three manic-depressives cycles. We undertook a systematic examination of the dream reports utilizing essentially aspects of the Hall-Van de Castle system or Beck's Masochism scale to see if we could confirm the impressions of the authors (Kramer, Brunner, & Trinder, 1971). We were able to confirm, using the emotions scale of the Hall-Van de Castle, that there was a greater incidence of happy emotions when the patient was depressed (0.54/dream) than when he was manic (0.25/dream). The converse was not true; all the sadness scoreable in the dream reports (0.39/dream) came from the depressed phase. The contention of the authors that conflict was more prominent in the manic phase was not supported as there were fewer aggressive social interactions (0.15/dream) and more friendly interactions (0.25/dream) in the manic phase. The patient, as we already noted, had more emotion, happy or sad, when depressed than when manic. The delusion the patient reported awake while manic only occurred in his dreams when he was depressed as they reported. The presence of recurrent dreams either of a "big object" or of "not being prepared" at transitions between phases was observed and some support was found. We were unable to support that either phase showed more conflict before a transition. Some transitions to mania were associated with a recurrent dream report at entrance into the manic phase. Recurrent dreams at transitions are an observation worth pursuing. The authors also observed that in the depressed phase the patient reported more dreams of being hurt while in the manic phase the fear is of destroying others. Utilizing the Beck Masochism scale (Beck, 1967), which scores injury to the dreamer, we found a higher masochism score in the manic (0.62/dream) than the depressed phase (0.39/dream). Dreams of being hurt were not more common in the depressed phase. The comment in the study that there was no reference to mother in the 21 dream reports is what might be expected as in 1000 dream reports of normals only one such dream report was found (Hall & Van de Castle, 1966). We believe that a systematic use of reliable quantitative measures delineates the reproducible aspects of the dream reports even of a single case report and focuses the areas that might be worth pursuing.

4. Redundancy in Scoring Systems

We have observed that there is considerable redundancy in the dream content scales that have been developed. Was it really necessary for each investigator to develop their own scaling system? Hauri (Hauri, 1975) showed that a series of dreams scored with different aggression content scales had an intercorrelation of .50. He showed that a significant and similar degree of the aggressive activity in dreams was captured by all of the scales. We tested the idea that a concept expressed in a dream content scale such as found in Beck's Masochism scale (Beck, 1967) could be captured by selecting items from a comprehensive scoring system such as the Hall-Van de Castle dream scoring system (Hall & Van de Castle, 1966) and not require developing a new scale. We scored a sample of dreams from depressed patients. Twenty-one were morning collected dreams of patients with manic depressive illness and 91 laboratory collected dreams of depressed patients. We scored them with both the Beck's Masochism scale and items selected from the Hall-Van de Castle system (Clark, Trinder, Kramer, Roth, & Day, 1972). The results were very similar from the two systems. The agreement for identifying masochistic content was 81% for the manic depressive patients' dreams and, for the dreams of the depressed, it was 91%.

E. Stability of Measurement Across Time

There is an interest in any measurement system about the stability of the measurement over time. We conducted a short-term study of the impact of time on dream content (Kramer & Roth, 1979). We collected dreams from subjects from the end of the first four REM periods of the night for 20 consecutive nights. Dream content showed a modest (.46) but significant correlation over two weeks. The mean first week correlation was a nonsignificant .22 but it was a significant .50 in the second week suggesting the content was beginning to stabilize. The stabilization effect was also shown in that night one correlated with night two a nonsignificant .05 and night 10 with night 11 a nonsignificant .30, while night 19 correlated with night 20 a significant .80. Hall and his colleagues (Hall, Domhoff, Blick, & Weesner, 1982) compared two nonlaboratory samples collected some 30 years apart from college students. The results are remarkably similar supporting an overall view of dream content stability across time. We have looked at gender differences in laboratory collected dreams and found similarities and some differences from the Hall-Van de Castle norms (Kramer, Kinney, & Scharf, 1983). Domhoff (Domhoff, 1996) discusses possible methodological problems with the results that do not support the replication of the Hall-Van de Castle norms and offers an alternative method of analysis. His effort is directed at refuting claims that the Hall-Van de Castle norms are out of date. The Hall-Van de Castle norms and method have held up remarkably well over time.

F. Critique of Measurement in Different Cultures

Barbara Tedlock and her anthropological colleagues claim that dream content analysis, the Hall-Van de Castle system being the case in point, is not sensitive to the cultural determinants of dream reporting nor does it take into account the interpersonal communication aspects of dream reporting (Tedlock, 1987). These assertions are of considerable interest but would be best refuted not by assertion but by the presentation of quantitative data demonstrating the limitations of content analysis and the superiority of another approach.

G. Conclusion

The quantification of the ineffable dream report is possible from a number of different aspects without the trivialization of the dream's essence. The measurement of dream report content can serve to solidify clinical observations by separating reproducible from nonreproducible results and need not lead to the endless multiplication of scoring systems. The dream report has been shown to be both stable and variable across short and long time periods, probably reflecting state and trait aspects of the dreamer. The examination of quantified manifest dream content can lead to meaningful insights about the so-called deeper meanings of the dream experience.

The demonstration of the orderliness of the dream is the goal toward which we are working. If the dream is orderly and not random, i.e., if its signal-to-noise ratio is greater than one, then it is the legitimate object of scientific interest. I will proceed by examining in the chapters that lay ahead the following questions: (1) Does the dream reflect meaningful psychological differences? (2) Does the dream respond to significant psychological influences? (3) Does the dream have a systematic relationship to waking thought? (4) Can meaning be extracted from a dream? (5) Can a function be attributed to dreaming? The answers to these questions should serve to expand our understanding of the dream experience.

CHAPTER 5

Dreams and Psychological Differences

A. Introduction

It is crucial in our exploration of the dream experience to raise questions about the orderliness or regularity of dreaming. If the dream is viewed as the unique personal experience of the individual, variability would be potentially so great that studying dreaming would really not be possible and, at best, we could only study the dreams of a particular individual. This has been the traditional scientific view of the dream that has rejected any scientific attempt at its study. In its extreme form the dream experience is described as a type of delirium or dementia in which the mind-brain is making the best of a bad job trying to organize the psychological output of a set of random stimuli coming from the subcortical pontine center (Hobson, 1988). The search for the structure and meaning of dreaming is a fruitless endeavor if psychological dreaming is a disorganized state, chaotic, and essentially random. The dream must be signal rather than noise, patterned rather than chaotic, stable rather than unstable, to support the possibility of scientific study.

The modern work directed at studying sleep has used the electrical output of the brain, the electroencephalogram (EEG) coupled with measuring the movement of the eyes and the tone of the chin muscles to describe the organization of sleep across the night. This approach has been codified by a scoring manual (Rechtschaffen & Kales, 1968) that describes the criterion to be used in classifying parts of sleep into either REM sleep or NREM and the latter into one of four so-called sleep stages reflecting the increasing depth of sleep. We wanted to determine if the stability of the physiology of sleep that was and is vigorously being scientifically measured in laboratories around the world was significantly different in its reliability from the measurement of dreaming with the Hall-Van de Castle scales. Would it turn out that measuring sleep was science and measuring dreams was not?

We did two studies (Roth, Kramer, & Roehrs, 1977; Kramer & Roth, 1979) to establish the reliability and stability of the measurement of sleep physiology and sleep psychology, dreams. First, we wanted to see if the reproducibility of the measurement of dreams approached that of sleep. This step, establishing inter-rater reliability, is essential to be sure that variability of measurement is not the result of randomness in scoring. Second, we wanted to explore whether the level of stability in dreaming approached that of sleep, which has been widely accepted as a legitimate subject for scientific study.

We examined the reliability of two judges "blindly" scoring two sleep records, polysomnograms, from each of 11 college age men who slept for 15 consecutive nights in the sleep laboratory (Roth, Kramer, & Roehrs, 1977). The average reliability, i.e., agreement, scoring every 30-second period of the 8-hour polysomnograms for seven sleep parameters for the 15 nights was 92.5%. We correlated actual time and percentage time of each sleep stage for successive night pairs and then averaged across them for the first and second week. The mean correlation for the time data overall was 0.28 and for the percentage data was 0.44, explaining 8%–19% of the night-to-night variability of these physiological parameters.

To establish the reliability and stability of dream content measurement, we had 14 college age men sleep for 20 consecutive nights in the sleep lab and collected dream reports from awakenings from the first 4 REM periods of each night (Kramer & Roth, 1979). The recorded reports were transcribed, coded, and scored "blindly" and independently by two scorers with the characters, activities, and descriptive elements scales of the Hall-Van de Castle dream scoring system. The overall exact percentage agreement dream by dream across the three content categories was 91%. A score for each scale for each night for each subject was established and successive nights were correlated and averaged for each scale and across the scales for the first and second week and then across the 2 weeks. The mean overall night-to-night dream content correlation is 0.46, which explains 21% of the night-to-night variability in dream content.

The reliability of measuring sleep or dream parameters is remarkably similar, 92.5% and 91%. The stability and therefore the predictability of sleep physiology and psychology across 2 to 3 weeks is also nearly identical with 19%–21% of the variability explained allowing the more liberal figure for sleep physiology to be used. It is apparent that the reliability of measurement and the stability of measurable parameters in sleep and dreams are so comparable that to suggest that the study of sleep is scientific and that dreaming is not is giving voice to bias and not to reasoned thought.

In the process of delineating the regularity of dreaming, a tentative description of the structure and process of dreaming will emerge. The question of the definition of dreaming remains so far unanswered (Hobson, 1999; Nielsen, 2003). I have explored it in another context (Kramer, Winget, & Roth, 1975). The contrasting and comparing of the mental content we obtain from sleep to other mental products across a number of conditions will begin to provide us with an empirically based definition of the dream. We start with the view that what the dreamer reports as a dream (Malcolm, 1959; Erickson, 1954) or his response on being awakened to the question of what was going through your mind (Goodenough, 1978) and not some idealized version of what a dream should be (Taub, Kramer, Arand, & Jacobs, 1978; Hobson, 1999) is our stating point.

To be the object of scientific study, the dream must be an orderly process. The dream can be approached scientifically from many points of view all of which presuppose its orderliness, its regularity. "The apparent randomness of dreaming at the physiological level is neutral with respect to the functional significance of dreaming at the psychological level" (Moffitt, Kramer, & Hoffmann, 1993, 3). My objective will be to demonstrate the orderliness of dreams by exploring whether, as we have reason to believe, there are psychological differences in the waking state, are there systematic differences in dream content as well? We will look at differences between groups of people, among individuals, within a night of an individual, and within a REM period.

B. Group Differences

1. Demographic Variables

The demographic variables, sex, age, and social class, to no one's surprise, show clear psychological differences during waking. This being the case, we asked if there are systematic dream content differences as well.

a. Sex It became apparent that the major organizer of dream content is the sex of the dreamer. We (Winget & Kramer, 1979) were able to find 34 nonlaboratory studies that found male/female differences in dream content. These varied from boys having more unpleasant dreams and dreams of mutilation to females having more intimacy themes in their dreams. The Hall-Van de Castle (Hall & Van de Castle, 1966) normative dream data, derived from 500 dreams of 100 college age men and 500 from 100 college women, compares the frequency and proportions of various categories of their scoring system. What is striking is the systematic and large number of male/female content differences. For example, women have more characters in their dreams than men, but men have twice as many male as female characters while women have essentially an equal percentage of each sex. Men have more physical aggressions than women. Women have more friendly interactions than men. Sexual interactions are not common in dreams but when they do occur they are three times more likely to appear in men's dreams than women's. Emotions are more common in women's dreams. Women's dreams are more likely to be set indoors and men's outdoors.

We compared the laboratory collected dream reports from the first four REM periods from 20 consecutive nights of 11 college age women and 11 college age men (Kramer, Kinney, & Scharf, 1983). We then content analyzed with 45 scales of the Hall-Van de Castle scoring system the 594 dreams of the men and the 596 dreams of the women. We found significant differences for 11 variables. Women had more cognitive activity (i.e., thinking) and more intensity references (i.e., probably an emotionality variable). Men had more male characters, strangers, auditory activity, achromatic colors, large sizes, and crooked or curved references.

In our study of a stratified random sample of adults in Cincinnati (Winget, Kramer, & Whitman, 1972), we found nine content differences related to the sex of the subject. Women had more dreams with characters, friendly social interactions, emotions, indoor settings, and home and family references. Men had more aggression, achievement striving with success, castration anxiety, and overt hostility. The aphorism that "anatomy is destiny" has some support from these results on gender differences in dream content.

In the present context, the issue is not the particular meaning of the sex differences in dream content but whether systematic differences exist. The four studies we briefly summarized clearly support that there are such differences and that among the results of the studies the frequency of many content categories are replicated. This, we believe, contradicts the contention that at the psychological level the dream is determined by random and meaningless pontine discharges. The extent and regularity of the differences do not suggest the result of the so-called mind/brain making the best of a bad job.

b. Age   Let's turn our attention to another demographic dimension, age. We found (Winget & Kramer, 1979) 20 studies that deal with dream content that suggest or show changes across the life span from 2 to 95. Unpleasant dreams decrease from ages 1–4 to ages 9–12. Children's dreams are lower in aggression than adults. Anxiety decreases with age while sex differences in aggression increase with age. Adolescents had more destructive themes, castration threats, and concern with self-safety than adults. Dream content changes between 3 and 15 mirror waking cognitive development. Older adults, over 65, had more dreams of lost resources, helplessness, or weakness. In our population survey (Winget, Kramer, & Whitman, 1972), we found that references to death and death anxiety were directly correlated with age. However, guilt anxiety was highest in young adults, age 21–34. Aggression had a complex relationship to age in this population sample. The young adult is concerned with right and wrong while the elderly are concerned with decline and dying. Dreams across the life cycle show systematic and understandable changes, which are difficult to encompass as the direct result of a random physiological process. The number of age related changes in dream content is less than what we see in our comparison of sex differences. More extensive examination of dreams in relationship to the age of the dreamer would be helpful. Age would appear, based on the data we have, to be less important in determining dream content than sex.

c. *Socioeconomic Class*   The relationship between dream content and the socioeconomic class of the dreamer has had very little limited study. In our population survey of the dreams of a representative sample of adults in Cincinnati (Winget, Kramer, & Whitman, 1972), we used the education, income, and occupation of each respondent to establish three social classes: lower, middle, and upper-middle and found six class related dream content differences. We found that the upper-middle class had fewer characters, less death anxiety, and fewer premonitions in their dreams. Misfortune was more common in the lower two social classes. For white respondents in the upper-middle class, there was less total anxiety and fewer dreams with home and family themes. The upper class has a relatively less troubled dream life than the lower classes.

d. *Race and Marital Status*   We found few differences related to the race or marital status of the dreamer. Blacks had more castration anxiety and penis envy and whites had more covert hostility directed outward. Widows had the most death anxiety. The formerly married (i.e., widowed, divorced, or separated) dreamed more of family members from their married family than their family of origin and had more premonition dreams. Cartwright points out the significance of who is dreamt about at the time of a divorce (Cartwright, 1991). To recap, the major determinant of dream content is the sex of the dreamer; age and social class were influential, but race and marital status had the least influence. It seems highly unlikely that chaotic or random processes determine the demographic differences that we reviewed.

2. Psychiatric Illness

We would expect to find differences in the dream life of patients suffering with the one of the major psychiatric illnesses. We collected and examined (Kramer, Baldridge, Whitman, Ornstein, & Smith, 1969) the most recent dream from 40 paranoid schizophrenic, 40 psychotically depressed, and 40 medical patients in a VA hospital. We examined the content for plausibility, hostility direction, and major character type. We found that the typical dream report of the paranoid schizophrenic patient finds him in an implausible situation in which he is the victim of a hostile attack by a stranger. The psychotically depressed patient typically is with a family member in his dreams, usually in a plausible situation, with hostility present about half the time, which is as likely to be directed at others as at the dreamer. The nonpsychotic medical patient, in his dreams, is with a friend in a plausible situation that is rarely hostile and, if it is, the dreamer is equally likely to be the expresser as the recipient of the hostility. The dreams of hospitalized women with paranoid schizophrenia and psychotic depression are similar to what was described for our male psychotics (Langs, 1966) with the dreams of the depressed having family members while family members are essentially absent from the dreams of schizophrenics whose dreams are most implausible and filled with conflict.

The dreams of depressed (Kramer, Whitman, Baldridge, & Lansky, 1966; Kramer, Whitman, Baldridge, & Ornstein, 1968) and schizophrenic patients (Kramer, Clark, & Day, 1973; Kramer & Roth, 1973; Kramer, Trinder, & Roth, 1972; Kramer, Whitman, Baldridge, & Ornstein, 1969) show systematic changes concomitant with improvement in their waking condition. The depressed patients with improvement show a decrease in hostility and anxiety and an increase in heterosexuality and motility. When improved, the schizophrenic patients showed more concise and better organized dreams with proportionately fewer aggressive interactions compared with friendly ones, fewer emotions, and more success and good fortune.

In our studies of REM dreams in the laboratory collected from hospitalized schizophrenic and depressed patients, we found as in our nonlaboratory study that the schizophrenics had strangers as their most frequent character and the depressed had family members. The schizophrenics had more groups of people than the depressed. And both patient groups showed changes in their dream life with improvement in their illness.

We examined with five Hall-Van de Castle scales (i.e., the character, social interactions, emotions, achievement outcome, and environmental press scales); the laboratory collected REM dream reports of a small number of middle aged brain damaged patients. We compared the dream content of those who were mildly damaged to those who were severely damaged (Kramer & Roth, 1975). The only statistically significant finding was that the more severely damaged had more characters than the mildly damaged. We also looked at recall rates in an elderly mildly brain damaged group. It was apparent that age and severity of brain damage contributed to decreasing dream recall, as dream recall was lowest in the older, severely brain damaged patient. Compared to the Hall-Van de Castle norms (Hall & Van de Castle, 1966), the combined middle-aged brain damaged groups had more family members, friendly social interactions, fewer aggressive ones, and had no scoreable emotions. Age and brain damage result in a significant change in dream content.

The orderly and systematic differences between psychotic patients, in and out of the laboratory, and the differences found in relationship to demographic variables, as well as their dream life changing when their condition improves, makes the notion of the brain making the best of a bad job increasingly implausible. Langs (Langs, 1966) offers an example of the dream of a paranoid schizophrenic woman, "Dreamed I was going over Niagra Falls in a barrel with a fat roly-poly man made of rubber. I think I had intercourse with the man." And for a psychotically depressed woman, "Dreamed I was with the whole family as it was in former times." The dreams may be implausible but hardly chaotic or resembling the confused verbalization of the delirious or demented patient. Heynick (Heynick, 1993) makes the point that speech in dream reports is well organized and generally grammatically correct.

C. Individual Differences

1. Between Individuals and Between and Across Nights of the Same Individual

All dream theories of a depth psychological nature assume three things about dreaming: (1) that dreams have meaning (i.e., that dreams are orderly and not random experiences), (2) that dreams are meaningful (i.e., that the content of the dream overtly or covertly is related to the waking subjective life of the dreamer), and (3) that dreams sub-serve some important psychological function and contribute to the adaptive capacity of the individual. We have already reviewed the evidence from our work that at the group level dreams are regular, orderly, and nonrandom and, therefore, have the characteristics necessary to have meaning and that the content of their dreams both at the trait and state level are meaningful as well.

The question emerges whether the orderliness found in the dreams of groups could be extended to individuals, both the normal and the psychiatrically ill (Kramer, Hlasny, Jacobs, & Roth, 1976). We gave three judges, of variable experience in working with dreams, 75 REM dreams from five different male college students, 15 dreams per subject; and 65 REM dreams from five male hospitalized schizophrenic patients, 13 dreams per subject. The judges' task was to sort the dreams into five groups of 15 dreams for the normal subjects and five groups of 13 dreams for the schizophrenic subjects. These tasks and the subsequent tasks were done throughout without the judges having any information about the dreamer to increase the likelihood that the judges were basing their decisions primarily on the dream report. All three judges were successful in sorting both groups, which supports the assumption that dreams of individuals are distinguishable one from the other at the trait level (i.e., reflect enduring aspects of personality).

Freud had suggested that the dreams of the night were related (Freud, 1955). A view clearly expressed as well in the Torah, "And Jacob had proclaimed that the dreams' of Pharaoh are one" (O.T., 1976, Genesis: 41:25). We next (Kramer, Hlasny, Jacobs, & Roth, 1976) gave our judges 15 dreams from each of 10 college students and from each of five schizophrenic patients and they were asked to sort each group of 15 into five sets of three dreams each. Each set of three dreams was from the same night. All three judges again were able to do this successfully. Not only were dreams distinguishable among people but they were distinguishable by nights for an individual. This systematic result supported the view that dreams were distinguishable one night from the other at the state level (i.e., day to day). For the individual, it underlines the reactive nature of the dream and opens the possibility that the dream is relatable to the previous day's activity, to the day residue. This is not to say that the dreams of an individual are not linked to one another across nights. We correlated the characters, activities, and descriptive elements in dreams of subjects from night to night for 20 consecutive nights (Kramer & Roth, 1979) and found that the overall mean night-to-night correlation was a significant 0.46.

We then asked our three judges (Kramer, Hlasny, Jacobs, & Roth, 1976) to place into their order of appearance in the night 50 sets of three dreams each from the college students and 34 sets of three dreams each from the patient groups. None of the judges were able to do this for the normal subjects, one judge was able to do it for the patient's dreams, and one judge showed a trend. It is fair to say that the judges, overall, were unable to sort the dreams by position in the night.

2. Dreams Across a Night

We were unable to demonstrate that the regularity of dreaming extended to the position of the dream within the night using judges and the dreams of individual subjects (Kramer, Hlasny, Jacobs, & Roth, 1976). We pursued the matter further by examining the dream content from REM periods across subjects (Kramer, Mcqarie, Bonnet, 1980). We collected dreams from the first four REM periods of 22 subjects for 20 consecutive nights. We found that the word count of REM I was shorter than REM II, that REM III was shorter than REM IV, but that REM II and REM III were not different from each other. These results could be the consequence of the REM periods being longer across the nights with more dream experience and therefore more to describe and more words per dream being reported. However, we found nine content differences across the night, with word length held constant; four were between REM I and REM II and five were between REM II and REM III but none between REM III and REM IV. The findings are suggestive of a positional difference for a dream within the night related to the content of the dream but at a group not an individual level and that tempers the position that the dream is independent in regard to where it appears in the night of an individual.

We had examined dream sequences across the night obtained both clinically and in the sleep laboratory, and described two basic patterns (Kramer, Whitman, Baldridge, & Lansky, 1964). One pattern is of a progressive-sequential nature in which a problem is stated thematically, worked on figuratively, and resolved subjectively. The other pattern is a traumatic-repetitive one in which a problem is experienced and reiterated figuratively in each dream of the night with little or no progress. Dreamers have both patterns probably depending on the immediate current concern they have before going to sleep and their emotional resources at the time.

A progressive-sequential pattern is illustrated by this dream series reported by a 27-year-old married woman to her analyst in her 497th hour:

Dream #1: "A man kept knocking at the back door. He said he wanted a knife. I said not to come in. I put the knife behind the washing machine. Finally he got in and got the knife. He was not threatening once he got inside."

Dream #2: "I was going to an old camp where there was a deep lake. Somebody drowned there and they were finding out the depth of the water by letting down a chain."

Dream #3: "There was some blood on my breast and I found out that it was partly cut but did not hurt at all."

The sequential progression thematically was from Dream #1: a threat by a male to enter with something penetrating but when he was inside it was not so threatening. Dream #2: someone died and was it caused by being in too deep? And Dream #3: you may be damaged, but it is not too serious, it doesn't hurt. Without adding the history of the dreamer and her associations to the dream and recognizing that much could made of possible meanings for the dream, thematically there is progression from a threat that decreased but that could be dangerous—even if there is a cut it is okay as it didn't hurt as anticipated.

A traumatic- repetitive pattern is illustrated by the dream series reported by a 24-year-old single woman to her analyst in the 54th hour:

> Dream #1: "I went to a beauty shop without an appointment. It was against the rules not to have an appointment. I was afraid that the beautician taking care of me would get fired and I therefore started sobbing dreadfully."

> Dream #2: "I was in the ladies room in the elevated station. I was looking for you at the usual time of our appointment and you were not there. I broke down and began to cry."

> Dream #3: "I was lost in a building like a maze. Couldn't find my way. A girl behind the bar in a tap room talked about going away. I was envious of the fun she was going to have and wished I could go."

> Dream #4: "I was at a bus stop. My friends, Helen and Mary, were there and were going somewhere. I was seeing them off."

The traumatic repetitive thematic pattern starts with Dream #1: seeking to be made better, but by not following the rules, running the risk of losing the person who can help and being upset. Dream #2: looking for a helping person but they are not there and upset again. Dream #3: a lost, person who provides is going away, envious. Dream #4: friends and potential helpers are going but she isn't. People who could help her (beautician, analyst, bar girl, friends) are or could be leaving in all four dreams—a highly repetitious theme. The affective tone appears to improve from tears to envy to neutral. Nevertheless, the theme remains essentially the same, loss of a helping person. Again much more could be made out of these dreams but the point we are making is to highlight the thematic similarity in all of the dreams.

3. Dream Content Across a REM Period

There has been some work which has suggested that the dream experience is different early as compared to later in the night (Foulkes, 1966; Verdone, 1965). Unfortunately, these studies compared only two points in time across the night and could describe only a linear relationship. We examined the content recovered from a series of six time points across the REM period (Kramer, Czaya, Arand, & Roth, 1974; Kramer, Roth, & Czaya, 1975). The content was rated for 12 factors on a Dream Inventory

Questionnaire (DIQ) on awakening by the dreamer and later by a judge and was content analyzed as well using the Hall-Van de Castle dream content scoring system. There was a significant effect across time for recall, emotionality, anxiety, and pleasantness. The change was linear for all four significant changes with emotionality also showing a quadratic curve. Each approach to the dream experience yielded the same result and was similarly significant. The rating, judgment, and content based curves for emotions rose steeply in intensity from 2.5 minutes into the REM period to 10 minutes then were flat for 20 minutes, then rose a little less steeply to 30 minutes, the last point sampled. This result supports the central role for emotions in guiding the dream experience.

There is a clear regularity to content development across the REM period. The curve, at least for emotions, seems to parallel the ebb and flow of eye movements across the REM period that Aserinsky (Aserinsky, 1971) described and we replicated (Johnson, Kramer, Bonnet, Roth, & Jansen, 1980). This may be an important point of psycho-physiological parallelism. More importantly, in the current context, is the fact that dream content is not randomly displayed across the REM period.

D. Conclusion

It is apparent that the study of dreaming can be a scientific undertaking. Dreams can be as reliably measured as their sibling, the physiology of sleep, and the two are equally stable (i.e., predictive night to night). The most conservative definition of dreaming is what the dreamer says, not the dramatic version we would all prefer dreaming to be. Plato offers a description of dreaming in the *Republic* (*Book IX*, 409f) that "In sleep... the beastly and savage part (of the soul) endeavors to sally forth and satisfy its own instincts.... It does not shrink from attempting to lie with a mother in fancy or with anyone else, man, god, or brute. It is ready for any foul deed of blood...which are revealed in our sleep." Fanciful, but empirically incorrect.

The biological randomness of aspects of REM sleep is not found at the psychological level of dreaming. Where we know there are psychological differences between or among groups awake we find meaningful differences in dreams. Dreams of individuals are different from each other and the dreams of one night are different from another. There is the suggestion that the content of a REM dream depends on its position in the series of dreams of the night. And, there is an orderly development of dream content within a REM period.

The disordered psychological production of an impaired brain, of a delirium or dementia, which can appear to be chaotic and disjointed, does not fit the ordered, structured, and nonrandom content of the dream experience.

CHAPTER 6

Normative Dreams, Typical Dreams, and Repetitive Dreams

A. Normative Dreams

The assumption of the infinite variability of the dream experience and therefore of the description of the experience, the dream report, poses a serious problem for those of us who wish to study the dream scientifically and to derive general statements about that experience particularly about the content of the experience. For those who take the dream seriously, the assumption of infinite variability reflects, I believe, both the sense of mystery that they contend surrounds the dream experience and a conviction that their inner experiences are unique. It is this uniqueness that makes the dreamer special, different, and the particular person they feel they are or aspire to be. The uniqueness of the dream experience confirms their individuality and the scientific study of dreaming, which is of common responses, is experienced as an assault on the very individuality they prize so highly. The response is in line with the reception given to other findings that diminished the centrality of man (e.g., Copernicus establishing that the earth was not the center of the universe, Darwin proposing that man was descended from preexisting biological forms, and Freud suggesting that behavior may be determined to a significant degree by processes outside of the person's awareness).

The study of normative dream content is directed at establishing the usual or common content of dreaming with no intent to destroy the individuality of the person. It answers the question, What do people usually dream about? This provides information for examining what people are experiencing across the night during sleep and what this might tell us about thinking or experiencing under conditions of reduced external involvement. It provides a point of reference to examine the effect of key demographic dimensions (e.g., gender, age, race, social class, marital status, and education, see Chapter 5) on the dreaming experience. Further, establishing normative dreaming allows comparisons of the dream reports of individuals or groups to such norms as this may serve to enhance our understanding of them as we evaluate their similarity to or deviation from such dream content norms.

We had the occasion to review the early English language literature on dream content studies (Winget & Kramer, 1979). The earliest studies were generally limited by the small number of subjects contributing dreams and often by the small number of dreams examined and the absence of systematic measuring devices. The earliest report of census data on the home dreams of normal subjects was reported by Nelson in 1888 on dream length and seasonal and male sexual cycles. Calkins (1893) found continuity between dream; life and waking life as did Andrews (1900) and Weed and Hallam (1896), the latter also noted the great variability in dream reports. W. S. Monroe (1898) exposed 20 subjects to crushed cloves while they were sleeping and collected 256 dream reports and found 17 (6.6%) references to taste and 8 (3.1%) to smell. Andrews (1900) found very little incorporation but noted the relatedness among the dreams of the night. Andress, (1911) in looking at the dream reports of 6 college students, observed that 25% had references to the school work of the previous day. Middleton (1933) studied 170 college students and there were references to the previous day in 51% of the dreams. Hartmann (1968) reported that in approximately 800 of his dreams he found 463 references (58%) to the previous day, most were unimportant and referred to the previous evening and not to just the time before going to bed. Food deprivation results in a decrease in sexual dreams and nocturnal emissions and an increase in dreams about food (Miles, 1919; Franklin, 1948). Bentley (1915), in training five students in introspection, observed in their 54 dream reports that unpleasant dreams were reported twice as often as pleasant dreams and that dreams tended to be more active than passive and more of them occurred late rather than early in sleep.

The topics addressed by these early investigators were (1) dream length and various cycles, (2) the continuity of dreaming and waking experience, (3) the variability of dream content, (4) the incorporation of stimuli during sleep, (5) the presence in dreams of events of the previous day, so-called day residues, (6) the response of dreaming to bodily deprivation; and (7) the affective tone of the dream experience and all continue to be explored by investigators of the dream experience. What is most disappointing is that although the later studies tend to confirm the results of these earlier studies it is done without appropriate acknowledgement.

It is when we get to the work of the great empiricist of dream research, Calvin Hall, that we get the first and the most successful attempt to provide a comprehensive system for describing and quantifying manifest dream content (Hall & Van de Castle, 1966). Richard Jones (Jones, 1962) described an approach to manifest dream content based on Erik Erickson's epigenetic description of psychological development. The focus for Jones is the intersection of the genetic, adaptive, and structural points of view in psychoanalytic theory. He gives examples of his approach but it is qualitative and subjective. The most comprehensive system that attempted to capture the personal meaning of dreams by utilizing both the manifest dream report and the associations to the report in a quantitative manner was described by David Foulkes in his Scoring System for Latent Structure (Foulkes, 1978). The scoring system is complex and has had only limited application.

Calvin Hall and Robert Van de Castle in their *Content Analysis of Dreams* (1966) provide a series of categories that encompass the characters, interactions, emotions, and items that appear in most dream reports. These dream content categories include the classification and scoring of (1) the physical surroundings in which the dream occurs, (2) the characters in the dream, (3) the social interactions that occur, (4) the activities, (5) the achievement outcomes of the characters actions in the dreams (i.e., their success or failure), (6) the results of environmental press (i.e., fortuitous consequences which are the result of external factors such as so-called good fortune or misfortune), (7) emotions expressed in the dream, and (8) descriptive elements that are essentially adjectival clarifiers of things in the dreams. They also provide several theoretical scales that have been less extensively used.

Hall and Van de Castle (Hall & Van de Castle, 1966) attempted to provide a set of numerical values and ratios for the various categories of their coding system that could be used as the normative description of what is found in dream reports. They used a convenience sample of dream reports that had been obtained in the late 1940s as part of a class assignment from college students, ages 18 to 25, in introductory psychology classes at Baldwin-Wallace College and Case Western Reserve University, both of which are in northern Ohio. The students kept diaries and the dream reports were written out by the student. From this pool of dream reports were selected five dream reports of 50 to 300 words in length from each of 100 male and 100 female students. This pool of 1,000 dream reports was scored for each of the categories in the scoring system. The reliability score for each scale for two judges was provided. Perfect agreement, a very high standard, varied from 63% for emotions to 85% for activities. The normative results were reported overall and then by the sex of the dreamer.

The composite picture of the normative dream that emerges from this remarkable undertaking is an interesting one that has stirred much comment and research (Domhoff, 1996). There are 1.30 settings for the 2.60 characters per dream including the dreamer who is engaging in 4.83 activities, qualifying aspects of the experience 2.57 times, and having 1.37 social interactions per dream. The normative dream has people in it who are doing things, evaluating things, and interacting with others in a setting that may change. The dream experience usually has an explicit emotion 70% of the time, but only 20% of them are positive. The dream report has negative modifiers 77% of the time, success 12%, failure 13%, misfortune 41%, and good fortune 6%. The reported dream has an explicit emotion in it frequently but not always and tends to be a negative experience emotionally with the cause of events attributed mostly to fortuitous occurrences. Responsibility, contrary to a poet's view, does not begin in dreams (Schwartz, 1939).

The question arises as to how representative the Hall-Van de Castle norms might be across a fuller age spectrum than 18 to 25. A number of studies have looked at the dream content in different age groups. In children, Kimmins (Kimmins, 1920) found that the content of their dreams was influenced by where they lived, at home or in an industrial school, and by the state of the child's health. Jersild and colleagues (Jersild, 1931; Jersild, Markey, & Jersild, 1933) found more similarity than differences between the dreams of older (11–12) and younger (5–6) children. Older children had more dreams of play and travel and more feelings of shame and guilt. Younger children had dreams of magical happenings and ghosts. Foster and Anderson (Foster & Anderson, 1936) observed that the frequency of unpleasant dreams drops from 40% in 1–4 year olds to 22% in 9–12 year olds. Polster (Polster, 1970) showed an increase in ego strength in dreams as the child gets older.

Foulkes (Foulkes, 1982) has given us the most informed developmental picture of dreaming. He studied a group of children that slept in the sleep laboratory and had their dreams collected. The subjects were studied for 5 years; one group starting at age 3–4 and continuing until age 8–9 and a second group was studied from 9–10 to 14–15. There were 8 boys and 8 girls in each of the age groups with replacements introduced to compensate for dropouts. Children were studied and dreams collected over 9 nonconsecutive nights in the first, third, and fifth year of the study in both groups. Foulkes concluded that REM dreaming follows a path parallel with waking cognitive development. Dream content is more related to what they are able to represent symbolically than what their emotional conflicts force on them to express. At ages 2–5, dreaming is of static imagery, without narrative, or affective content, an active self- character or social portrayal. Animals are common. At ages 5–7, we see dreams with sequential, narrative properties with physical and social activities but with little if any feelings. The dream has a setting, family members may be portrayed, but self-representation is limited and animals are still common. At ages 7–9, dream experiencing is richer with more of a dream like narrative with better sequencing and with a self-character that can view the dream, which has a wide range of activities and interactions. The dreamer can think and feel in the dream; most commonly has happy or pleasant feelings and can have characters beyond the family. At ages 9–13, there is increased self-participation in the narrative and concrete activities and social interactions are frequent with different types of feelings, positive or negative, but most dreams are without affect. Unfamiliar or fictional characters may appear. At ages 13–15, the dreamer can detach from the narrative and comment on a detail in the dream and entertain new self-representations. Content can be more abstract and less literal. Foulkes also comments on the relationship between dream development and personality noting that the emergence of dreaming is not associated with anxiety and impulsivity. Increased dream unpleasantness was associated with low anxiety. Dreaming does not seem to control drive states and the function of dreaming is probably more related to symbolic processing than to REM physiology. The continuity hypothesis of waking and dreaming is more likely than the compensation hypothesis, but it is the cognitive conceptualization of self-knowledge that is represented in dreams not simple waking behavior, therefore the correlations with behavior classified by others may not be very great. Social interaction in dreams fit a compensatory model, and activities fit a continuity model. He is very much in agreement with Hall's (Hall, 1953; Hall & Van de Castle, 1966) view of dreaming as a cognitive-symbolic process that shows how we think about ourselves in relationship to others and the world. Foulkes wonders about the change in the dream experience that accompanies later cognitive changes such as occur with aging: He says, "… there is (the) need to implement a full life-span developmental approach and to ask how dreams change with waking cognitive changes associated with the aging process. Other conditions associated with waking cognitive change should reflect change in the dream experience (e.g., schizophrenia and Parkinsonism)" (Foulkes, 1982, 288).

Changes in aspects of the dream experience were found to change across the life span. Hall (Hall, 1953) found that the ratio of unpleasant to pleasant dreams increases with age and that children have less aggressive dreams than adults. He found (Winget & Kramer, 1979) that anxiety in dreams decreases with age while coping with dangers was about the same in adults and children. Hall and Domhoff (Hall & Domhoff, 1963a, 1963b) observed that sex differences in aggression increased with age, with children and older adults being more likely to be observers of aggression than participants. They (Hall & Domhoff, 1964) noted that children and older females have fewer friendly acts in dreams and that males over 18 were more likely to initiate than be the recipient of a friendly act. Altshuler and coworkers (Altshuler, Barad, & Golfarb, 1963; Barad, Altshuler, & Goldfarb, 1961) noted that those over 65, whether living in an institution or independently, frequently had dream themes of lost resources, helplessness, and weakness. The increase with age of unpleasant dreams, of sex differences in aggression, of themes of vulnerability and loss, and the decrease with age of anxiety and of friendly acts in the dreams of older females all suggest that there may be meaningful changes in dream content that are age related.

We chose to examine the most recent dream report and earliest memory collected at home from a stratified random sample of 300 adults in the city of Cincinnati (Kramer, Winget, & Whitman, 1971; Winget, Kramer, & Whitman, 1972). We wanted to establish normative data on the content of dreams for adults and whether the early memory and dream reports were similar. We will report primarily the dream content findings at this point. We found that we had a fairly representative sample comparing the demographics of our sample to census data as our discrepancies only varied from 1%–14%. We obtained 182 dream reports (61%) and 256 early memories (86%) from the 300 subjects. The dream report frequency is similar to what we found in a study of dream report frequency (58%) in psychoanalysis. Our demographic differences (Kramer, Whitman, Baldridge, & Lansky, 1964) from Hall's sample may account for many of the differences we will report. Our group was 65% women, had 33% blacks, probably had fewer single people and our respondents were less educated and poorer than Hall's. The average dream report contained 21 words with a range of 2–68 words. The Hall-Van de Castle average was 125 words with a range of 50–300 words. The word length differences may also account for any differences between the two samples. The use of a 50-word minimum does not reflect the length of the usual dream report of a representative adult population sample.

The greatest number of differences was found comparing the dreams of men and women. More women reported dreams (65%) than men (53%). Women had more dreams with characters, friendly interactions, emotions, indoor settings, and home and family references. Men reported more dreams with aggression, overt hostility, castration anxiety, and success. Women in their dreams appear to be more interpersonally involved but more passive than men who appear more active and directly involved.

How predictive these sex differences are for waking behavior remains to be more carefully delineated, however, it is notable that the Cincinnati dream content frequencies are strikingly similar to Hall's norms.

Age was a less important factor than sex in dream reports. There was a variable relationship to dream reporting with age as those 21–34 and 50–64 reported dreams two thirds of the time while those 35–49 and over 65 reported them less often. Death anxiety and death themes had a direct correlation with age. Those over 65 had more death references than the three younger groups. Little guilt in dreams was found but most of it was in the 21–34 age group. Aggression and hostility were highest in the 35–49 year old group. The direct relationship of age with death is clear while the variable relationships are more difficult to understand. There is the suggestion that guilt, concern about right and wrong, is more a problem for the young and concern about death for the older person.

There have been no published systematic studies of dreaming related to social class (Bastide, 1966). Socioeconomic groups, i.e., lower, lower-middle and upper-middle, were developed in our population study based on the education, income, and occupation of the respondents. The upper-middle-class group had dreams with fewer characters, less death anxiety, and fewer premonitions. For upper-middle-class whites there was less total anxiety and fewer dreams with home and family themes than in the dreams of the lower two white classes. Misfortune occurred more frequently in the dreams of the lower two classes. The conceptualization of the world of the lower classes in their dream life is of a world in which negative events occur that are beyond their control in a world crowded with people, with poor whites focused on home and the family. The lower classes feel anxious, threatened by death, and experience negative events that are beyond their control, and believe that their dreams predict the future. It appears that this worldview might well mirror their waking worldview as well. No comparison to Hall's data can be made as his scoring system does not address social class and his college age sample is likely to be all in our upper-middle-class group. Buckley (Buckley, 1970) in an unpublished PhD thesis, used the Hall aggression scale and found that lower-class high school students had more aggression in their dreams than middle-class students.

Bastide (Bastide, 1966) and Ullman (Ullman, 1969) have both urged that the social aspects of the dream be more carefully examined and that a sociology of the dream be developed. Bastide believes that the sociology of the dream must contain (1) the study of the function of the dream in society, and (2) the social framework of dreaming thought. Ullman views the sociology of dreaming focusing on (1) the ways in which institutions are experienced in dreams, and (2) how dreaming experience relates to the social ambience and social structures. The examination of the dreams of our population study by social class is a beginning in the direction of a sociology of dreaming. We found (Kramer, Winget, & Whitman, 1971) that 51% of our dream reports had an institutional reference of which 79% were to the family, 59% to the family by marriage, and 41% to the family of origin. Work references made up 11% of the institutional references. Only 5.6% of our dream reports had a direct work reference. It is not the occupational world of the dreamer that is being manifestly conceptualized, but rather some aspect of the family as it is represented in 40% of the dreams.

There were very few racial differences in dream content as only 3 out of 30 variables studied showed a significant difference and those that were found were based on very small numbers. There was more castration anxiety and penis envy in blacks and more covert hostility directed outward in whites. Sex, age, and small numbers confounded the very few significant variations in dream content related to marital status. Widows had the most death anxiety. The postmarital group (separated, divorced, and widowed) dreamt more of their family by marriage than the currently married or single respondents (Cartwright, Lloyd, Knight, & Trenholme, 1984) and had more premonition dreams.

The differences between the Cincinnati sample (Kramer, Winget, & Whitman, 1971) and the Hall-Van de Castle norms (Hall & Van de Castle, 1966) may be due to the dream length and social class differences in the two samples. We found the mean number of characters including the dreamer to be very similar in the two samples (2.1/2.6). Assuming one per dream, the Cincinnati sample had a family reference in 40% of the dreams while the Hall sample had 39%. The Cincinnati sample had 5.6% of dreams with an occupational referent and Hall had 30.5%. The proportion in their sample of aggressive interactions to friendly ones was 1.32 for Hall and was 1.1 in the Cincinnati sample. Failures to success were 1.12 for Hall and 3.0 for the Cincinnati sample. The proportion of misfortune to good fortune was 6.0 for Hall and 6.8 for Cincinnati. The proportion for unpleasant to pleasant dream emotions in Hall's sample was 4.27 while it was 3.0 the Cincinnati sample. The proportion of indoor to outdoor was 1.22 for Hall and 0.90 for the Cincinnati sample. We were struck by the overall similarity of the proportions in the two samples despite the dream length, social class, and the differences in the number of male/female subjects in the two samples.

The only study that has attempted to establish normative data based on laboratory collected dream reports is that of Strauch and Meier in Zurich (Strauch & Meier, 1996). They studied 18 men and 26 women ages 19–35, for a total of 161 nights and generally report the results of having analyzed 500 REM dreams, 331 from women and 169 from men, who were selected because they were good dream recallers. There is no mention of the other demographic characteristics of the subjects or of the length of the dream reports. They conclude that dreams create novel situations from known circumstances. The dream experience is not just a series of images but is an integrated experience characterized by linear and event oriented stories. Dreamers are involved in their dream world and are dealing mainly with the events of the moment but with just part of what they know. Emotion in dreams may be wide ranging but many dreams have no specific emotion. The reported dream experience does not encompass all the feelings the dreamer will report about his experience on later inquiry. Negative feelings do not characterize most dreams. The dream setting is secondary to the narrative structure of the dream. A wide range of characters appear and strangers are prominent. The dreamer is active in the dream mainly in a social manner and the activities are largely those of everyday life but the familiar is inventively turned into the new but rarely becomes fantastic. The basis for the selection of the day residue is unclear but it commonly appears in dreams. The dream incorporates waking images and deals with them often in unique ways. Most surprisingly, Strauch and Meier conclude "...the dream world of both sexes does not differ basically" (Strauch & Meier, 1996, 239). They see dreams and waking fantasy as very much alike differing only in the lack of personal control in dreaming.

The fact that essentially twice as many dreams were contributed by women as men and that no attempt was made to deal with the question of dream length makes it difficult to compare this study by Strauch and Meier (Strauch & Meier, 1996) to other studies of so-called home dreams. The possibility exists that the differences are cultural as the earlier normative studies are of Americans but it is not a very compelling explanation, (Domhoff, 1996) especially as the frequency of emotions in their dreams is similar to what we found in the dream reports of patients in psychoanalysis (Kramer & Glucksman, 2006; Kramer & Glucksman, 2005).

B. Typical Dreams

The interest in so-called typical dreams relates to an interest in what they may tell us about the preoccupations of individuals and of various groups. Do typical dreams reflect the emotional concerns of people and does their frequency give us a sense of the relative importance of these themes? If a difference in frequency is found between two groups does it suggest a different psychological focus for the groups? These are questions of interest that have had some limited exploration (Antrobus, 1993; DeMartino, 1953a, 1953b; Domhoff, 1996; Gahagan, 1936; Griffith, 1958; Kramer, Winget, & Whitman, 1971; Langs, 1965, 1966; Rychlak, 1960; Rychlak & Brams, 1963; Schredl, Ciric, Gotz, & Wittmann, 2004; Ward, Beck, & Rascoe, 1961).

The typical dream has been described by Freud (Freud, 1955b) as a dream that has an essentially standard manifest content to which the dreamer usually provides no associations; but if the dreamer does provide associations they rapidly become obscure. These typical dreams are distinguished from dreams with identical content, as typical dreams have affect associated with them and their counterparts do not. Understanding the meaning of these dreams requires the use of symbolic interpretation, a secondary, auxiliary method of interpretation. Freud believed that as many people dream the same dream, they must have the same meaning and have the same source. He presents two major examples of typical dreams. One is the embarrassed dream of being naked, scantily or inappropriately dressed, and not being able to get away. This occurs in front of strangers who don't comment or notice the impropriety. The source is related to exhibitionistic wishes or behaviors from childhood. The second example is of the death of a loved one, usually a relative, associated with a feeling of grief. It has as its source the childhood feelings surrounding the Oedipus complex, the wish to possess the parent of the opposite sex to the dreamer and to remove the parent of the same sex.

The focus in Freud's discussion surrounding typical dreams is on the extreme egoism of the child and the centrality of infantile sexual feelings as the foundational basis for dreaming. He points out that the feelings revealed by analysis to the dreams' ultimate source may not represent the adult attitude of the dreamer. He attempts to show the great degree that the symbols that appear in all dreams are sexual in nature. The choice of symbols is influenced by the context of the dream. He rejects the criticism that all dreams have a sexual interpretation.

The other typical dreams Freud (Freud, 1955b) mentions are (1) flying through the air with agreeable feelings that may require an individual interpretation; (2) falling with feelings of anxiety that has an erotic implication; (3) losing teeth or having them pulled that may, for a man, have castration references or may be an expression of adolescent masturbatory impulses, while for a woman they may relate to birth fantasies; and (4) failing an examination with anxiety that one has already passed. It is seen as having a consolation meaning as it usually occurs the night before a test of some sort and serves to reassure i.e., "As I didn't fail the previous one, no matter how I worried at the time, I won't fail the one tomorrow"); (5) missing a train is a consolation dream, but related to fears of dying. Other dreams include swimming, which may be related to intrauterine fantasies, as are dreams of passing through narrow spaces or being in water. Dreams of floating in air and falling are associated with sensations that are often sexual but may need individual interpretation. Fire, going through narrow streets, or through a series of rooms may relate to sexual intercourse, while being pursued by wild animals and dreams of robbers occur in anxious people; dreams of burglars and ghosts may refer to parents.

Artemidorus of Daldis, the second century dream interpreter, does not deal explicitly with typical dreams. Nevertheless, I reviewed the frequency with which dream topics are mentioned in his *Oneirocritica* (White, 1990) as classified by his translator Professor Robert White of Hunter College. The top five topics based on frequency of appearance in the text are death—38 references, gods—35 references, clothing and eating—each 22 references, and the Head—21 references. The three most frequent typical dreams in recent studies are (1) of the object endangered (a person being hurt, in danger, or dead), (2) falling through space, and (3) being chased or pursued. It is suggestive, despite the differences in the manner the data was collected, that the theme of death was by far the most frequent dream theme in both the classical as well as the modern world. Mortality, to no one's surprise, has been a concern throughout the ages.

There have been a number of studies of typical dreams performed since Freud's description of them. These studies addressed the frequency of occurrence of various types of typical dreams, noting that there were gender differences in the types most commonly experienced and that the frequency of themes was related to psychopathology, as was the dream's theme. Gahagan (Gahagan, 1936) gave his questionnaire of 22 dream themes and asked if the subject ever had the dream type; if yes, he asked how often and give an example. Gahagan obtained responses from 228 male and 331 female college students. Overall, the highest percentage of positive responses was to falling (87%), being pursued by a person (64%), being pursued by an animal (62%), wish fulfillment (60%), and examination (60%). More women than men responded positively to being pursued by a person, examination, frustrated effort, being inappropriately dressed, a person now alive being dead, and being a child again. Men more often than women had dream themes of dying or being killed; being a historical, legendary, or literary character; being nude, and flying, soaring, or floating in air.

Griffith (Griffith, 1958) developed a list of 34 typical dreams that he administered. He found that college age men and women had a similar frequency of typical dream themes while hospitalized psychiatric patients had fewer themes than college age men. Subjects with more pathological MMPI scores were those with more typical dreams. Grade school boys with both typical dreams of falling and attack were more likely to have unpleasant early memories and were found to be more insecure and nonsociable. The number of typical dreams was related to self-awareness and insight.

DeMartino (DeMartino, 1953a) developed a questionnaire asking whether the subject had any of 21 dream themes (some of which can be considered as typical dreams). He administered the questionnaire to 150 male and 150 female southern college students and found that women reported more dreams with color, falling, frustration, inability to move, and premonition themes while men had more dreams with sexual feelings. DeMartino (DeMartino, 1953b) applied a nine-category dream categorization scheme to the dreams of 50 male and 50 female institutionalized mentally retarded subjects and gave them a simplified 15-item theme questionnaire and found that home was the most frequent dream theme for both sexes and that males dreamed more often of aggression, boys, and sports. On the questionnaire, males reported more dreams of eating food, finding money, and hitting others; females reported dreams of color, falling, and being chased. The dreams were predominantly pleasant for both sexes.

Rychlak (Rychlak, 1960) found that in grade school subjects, 26% of boys and 56% of girls reported at least one affiliative dream theme over a 12-week period of study. Rychlak and Brams (Rychlak & Brams, 1963) found no sex related differences in dream themes of 41 college students.

Ward and his colleagues (Ward, Beck, & Rascoe, 1961) have delineated most carefully, from a psychoanalytic point of view, a small number of dreams, 17, that have been designated as "typical" or "universal." They include dreams of a person endangered, falling, being chased, being naked, missing a train (conveyance), or taking an examination. These dreams have the characteristics of being repetitive, easily recalled, resisting interpretation using free associations, and require symbolic interpretation in the context of their appearance. They provide both early Freudian "id" oriented interpretations as well as later ego psychology oriented interpretations. Ward and his colleagues inquired of 748 psychiatric patients if the patient ever had each of the dream types. They found that the object endangered dream had occurred to 57.4% of the patients, falling to 52.3%, and being chased/pursued to 45.2%. The lowest frequency of 6% was of caves. No dream type was truly universal, i.e., reported by all respondents. There was no typical dream that showed a differential distribution between the sexes. There was a tendency for teeth dreams to occur more often in women and finding money, flying, and rescue dreams in men (Colby, 1958; Harris, 1957; Hall, 1955). However, Gahagan (Gahagan, 1936) and Schredl's group (Schredl, Ciric, Gotz, & Wittmann, 2004) have found for some typical dreams a sex related differential frequency.

The 748 subjects of Ward and his colleagues' study (Ward, Beck, & Rascoe, 1961) had their data collected in three groups of 229 patients, 254, and 265. The rank order of the typical dreams was essentially the same in the three groups. Harris (Harris, 1948) found among military selectees that the three most unpleasant dreams were of the object endangered 38.7%, falling 65.0%, and being chased or pursued (attacked) 72%. Griffith

(Griffith, 1958) in 473 college students (half of the group was American and half Japanese) found falling in 78.9% and attack/pursued in 83.5% with the overall rank order being quite comparable statistically to Ward's. Schredl and colleagues (Schredl, Ciric, Gotz, & Wittmann, 2004) found, in studying a German sample, a very high rank order correlation of their results using a 55-item typical dream questionnaire with that reported by a Canadian group. We found in our stratified random sample of the population of the city of Cincinnati (Kramer, Winget, & Whitman, 1971) that a typical dream was reported by our subjects about half the time but only 9 of the 17 typical dream types were reported. The most frequent typical dream was of the object endangered and was reported by 51.9% of the population. Notably the rank order of occurrence of typical dreams in the Cincinnati subjects and Ward's sample were very similar. The Cincinnati results extend Ward's findings to a normative sample.

The Ward group (Ward, Beck, & Rascoe, 1961), in attempting to establish the possible meaning of the ordering of typical dreams, offers a grouping of the 17 dream themes into 4 clusters. The 3 most frequent dreams (the object endangered, falling, and chased/pursued) from an ego psychology viewpoint are related to unresolved interpersonal conflicts with people from the dreamer's past. The second group (dreams of water, food, money, fire, nakedness, and flying), from an "id" viewpoint, has libidinal motivations. The third group that refers to teeth, being lost, or losing things, examinations, and missing trains seems to reflect superego activity. Lastly and least frequently, the group of dreams that include dreams of being rescued, of narrow spaces, and of caves may reflect regressive impulses or birth fantasies.

In a series of studies, Harris attempted to explore the meaning of two of the most frequent typical dreams. He noted that that dreams of falling (Harris, 1951) are related to a fundamental fear of losing mother. Dreams of the object endangered (Harris, 1957) are associated with anger toward an overly intrusive parent.

Typical dreams and dream themes, although they are not universal (i.e., are not reported by everyone), do seem to have a fairly stable frequency of occurrence across many diverse populations. The frequency of occurrence may be influenced by sex differences. The thematic focus of typical dreams provides clues about the areas of personal concern we all share. The meaning of our behavior and of our dreams remains a topic of considerable interest, one we touched on in our introductory chapter and to which we will return more specifically in chapter 9.

C. Repetitive Dreams

A type of dream experience has been described that has as its central feature that the same or a very similar dream reoccurs from time to time. The notion of the infinite variety of dream experience is challenged by such experiences. The reoccurring dream causes some consternation among dreamers as to why is that "old thing" back again; often, but not always, the feeling tone of such recurring dreams is a negative one.

The contribution of Artemidorus of Daldis (White, 1990) to the understanding of repetitive dreams is worthy of note. He, in his search for the meaning of a given dream, recommends that the state, status, and life circumstance of the dreamer must be taken into account. Such things as the age, gender, civil status (free man or slave), occupation, marital status, mood, and geographic location must be known to render a correct interpretation. He observes that dream reoccurrences that are close in time may well have the same meaning, and that we should pay attention to them as when we have something important to say we usually say it frequently.

Artemidorus illustrates the contextual basis for dream interpretation by describing how a reoccurring dream separated by a long period of time may have a different meaning as the life circumstance and therefore current concern of the dreamer may be different. Artemidorus reports the dreams of a man who was a perfume dealer who dreamed he "lost his nose" and subsequently he lost his store and stopped selling perfume, as he no longer had the means to test his product. The next time the man dreamed he "lost his nose," he had been caught in a crime. The dream interpretation was that the lack of a nose disfigures and degrades the face and, as the face is the image of respectability and reputation, the man felt disgraced. The man had the same "lost nose" dream during an illness. He died shortly thereafter. The skull of a dead man has no nose, therefore the dream was a death dream. Speculative, certainly, but interesting nevertheless. Artemidorus offers an alternative to the view that recurrent dreams always reflect the same personal concern of the dreamer.

Freud (Freud, 1955b) in the *Interpretation of Dreams* discusses repetitive dreams as they illustrate that the historical source experience for dreaming lies in childhood experiences. He accepts the view, as did Artemidorus, that dreams that occur close together in time have a similar meaning. For example, a dream expressing an intention was repeated every night until it was carried out, and, of course, behind this manifest intention a sexual wish is found (Freud, 1953). Freud does not deal with the possibility of change based on new circumstance but rather that when a similar situation to the childhood one arose, an analogous intention reappeared in the dreamer's dreams. In reporting a recurrent dream of his own (Freud,

1955b) in which his inadequacies as a chemical analyst are experienced, Freud sees the connection to his having become a psychoanalyst but the desire or wish is to be young again.

Cartwright (Cartwright & Romanek, 1978; Cartwright, 1979) sees the repetitive dream as reflecting difficulties not being coped with adequately during waking and that they may reveal the stable memory concepts to which new emotional experiences are related. Their reappearance reflects the concern currently in focus. The dream recurrence may disappear with adequate resolution of the concern.

Domhoff (Domhoff, 1996) offers an expanded view of what he terms the "repetition dimension" in dreaming that exists across the gamut of dream types from traumatic dreams to recurrent dreams to typical dreams to repeated dream themes to frequent dream elements. He vigorously reviews this neglected aspect of this manifest element in dreaming. He attributes this repetitiousness to the unfinished business in every person's life. He offers this as evidence that we dream about our ongoing personal concerns much like our waking concerns. I am certainly in agreement that our dreams reflect our personal concerns and that dream meaning can be established through viewing the dream as metaphor. However, the notion that the reappearance of an item or an entire dream always addresses the same personal concern remains to be demonstrated. Jung (Jung, 1964a) pointed out that the appearance of a dream character with whom you are currently involved represents that person while the appearance of someone with whom you are no longer involved suggests that the character is symbolic. That in dreams the frequency of an item reflects its intensity is a reasonable starting assumption that Domhoff makes, but many one-time events in waking can have intense consequences (e.g., birth, marriage, divorce, and the death of a loved one). He offers the view that the similarities between waking and dreaming thought lead to a view that they are on a continuum rather than distinctive forms of thinking. Content similarities do not address whether the form of thinking is different in waking and dreaming. We found that even content similarities were different between the two states as there were greater content similarities between pre-sleep and post-sleep waking thought than among the REM dreams of the night (Kramer, Moshiri, & Scharf, 1982). The form of laboratory collected dreams is more fragmented and poorly organized than the same dream reported the next morning, but this may be due to the different level of arousal at the time of reporting.

Psychopathologic Dreams (Nightmares) and Dreams in Psychopathologic States

A. Introduction

There is potential confusion between a psychopathology of dreams and dreams in a psychopathologic state. The former refers to alternations in the dreaming process that may be seen as abnormal, whereas the latter refers to the dreams that are the concomitants of a mental disorder. A dream that awakens the dreamer in a terrified state generally with accompanying frightening dream content, a nightmare, would be a psychopathologic dream. A dream report from a patient suffering from schizophrenia would be a dream from a person in a psychopathologic state. The dream may or may not be unique, either pathonomonically or statistically, to that state. Strangers occurring more frequently in the dreams of schizophrenics than in normal or depressed individuals are a statistical change in dream content in a psychopathologic condition (Kramer, Baldridge, Whitman, Ornstein, & Smith, 1969)

B. Nightmares

The recognition that a category of frightening dreams existed has been documented for two millennia. The work of Artemidorus (White, 1990) from the second century distinguishes dreams that refer to future events (*oneiros*) from those that reflect the present state of affairs (*enhypnion*). Enhypnion relate to what is on the sleeper's mind before going to sleep.

The frightened person will see in his dreams what he fears. Gruppe (1906), cited by Freud (Freud, 1955b), describes a classification of dreams given by Artemidorus in which dreams can have a future significance or reflect the current state of the dreamer. This latter group, which sounds like enhypnion, was divided into the insomnia which gave a direct representation in the dream to an idea or its opposite and a group, the ephilaltes or nightmare, that gave a fantastic extension to the idea.

The nightmare is a topic that captures the imagination but how common is it? The frequency of nightmares in a college age population (Feldman & Hersen, 1967) was that 5% had them once a week, 24% once a month, 47% once a year, and 24% less than once a year. The Belickis (Belicki & Belicki, 1982) surveyed 314 college students about nightmares and found that 10% reported more than one a month and 64% between one a month and one a year. Herzen (Herzen, 1972) did a study of nightmares in psychiatric inpatients and noted 7% had them once a week, while 43% had them less than once a year. No gender differences were noted in either of the Feldman/Herzen studies. Wood and Bootzin (Wood & Bootzin, 1990) report that about 50% of college students report one nightmare per two weeks. The variability is high among studies of college students but the differences between college students and psychiatric patients is low. The frequency of nightmares does not differentiate a normal from a psychopathologic population.

Bixler (Bixler, Kales, Soldatos, Kales, & Healey, 1979) found that 5% of 1,000 people in a metropolitan area had nightmares as a current problem. Bixler further noted in a national survey of 4,000 physicians that 4% of patients had nightmares as one but not their major complaint. Hartmann (Hartmann, 1984) estimates the incidence of nightmares in adults to be one to two per year and that they decrease with age but may increase with depression and psychiatric medicines. He is of the opinion that nightmares may start as early as eight months at the time when the infant experiences stranger anxiety. Hartmann concludes that occasionally having nightmares is common for adults and children, especially children under the age of six and that the sex of the dreamer is not a determinant of nightmare frequency but in adults it may be a determinant of nightmare reporting as women report a higher frequency than men (Garfield, 1984).

Freud's formulation of the nature of the dream in the *Interpretation of Dreams* (Freud, 1955b) was that a dream is a (disguised) fulfillment of a (suppressed or repressed) wish, and he felt that anxiety dreams and punishment dreams, often considered nightmares, were not exceptions. In 1920 in *Beyond the Pleasure Principle* (Freud, 1955a), Freud acknowledged that there was an exception to his wish fulfillment thesis namely the dreams experienced in traumatic neuroses, the modern day equivalent of

Post Traumatic Stress Disorder (PTSD). Freud had previously explained that anxiety dreams and punishment dreams could be seen as wish-fulfillments. However, dreams of childhood and adult traumas, such as those of war, arise as part of a compulsion to repeat. The traumatized dreamer is trying to go from passive to active in the dream, in order to master the stimulus and the attendant anxiety associated with the trauma for which the individual was not prepared psychologically. He observes that the original function of dreaming, to protect sleep, may not be the case as he goes beyond the pleasure principle to something more primitive, the mastery of the anxiety of an associated trauma. He added to his formulation that the dream was the "attempted" fulfillment of a wish.

Ernest Jones, a disciple and biographer of Freud's, in his *On the Nightmare* (E. Jones, 1959) gives three cardinal features of nightmares: (1) agonizing dread, (2) a sense of oppression or weight at the chest which alarmingly interferes with respiration, and (3) a conviction of helpless paralysis. He views the nightmare as an anxiety or dread attack that is essentially due to an intense mental conflict centering on a repressed component of the psycho-sexual instinct, essentially concerned with incest. Jones then establishes the possible causal connection between the nightmare experience and certain medieval superstitions namely incubus, vampires, werewolves, the devil, and witchcraft. Jones relates the suppression of devil worship and these other myths by the church to their recognition, even if unconsciously, of the incestuous longings intrinsic to such phenomenon. Jones' book is of interest because of its exploration of medieval myths that may have a relationship to nightmares, but is of limited value in enhancing our knowledge of the nightmare experience. A major problem is whether what is being described is a nightmare, a dream experience, or a night terror, a frightening arousal out of deep sleep with little if any content associated, or a combination of the two.

John Mack published *Nightmares and Human Conflict* (Mack, 1989) in 1970 and updated it in 1987 by including some of the sleep laboratory findings and later work of Hartmann (Hartmann, 1984) and Fisher (Fisher, 1965a, 1965b). This is a major work on the nightmare that captures the personal element in the experience. It provides a thoughtful presentation of the history of nightmares and a sensitive presentation of case material from nightmare sufferers he has treated. Dr. Mack's intention is to understand the nightmare, in his view a REM state experience, from a depth psychological viewpoint. He sees no need to separate the night terror from the nightmare. He rejects Jones' (E. Jones, 1959) libidinal emphasis on incest as too narrow. Mack tries to relate the nightmare to the life situation, psychological development, personality, and adaptation strategies of the dreamer. He sees the nightmare as an adaptational attempt to deal with external threats connected with internal fears that create an experience that seems to threaten survival itself. He sees in the nightmare the consequence of the breakdown in the social contract between the individual and the society that by its rules is supposed to protect the individual. The nightmare therefore has a political dimension. The treatment of a nightmare sufferer needs to have a spiritual dimension. He speculates that the anxiety of nightmares may reflect the birth experience as Freud (Freud, 1955b) and Otto Rank (Rank, 1952) had suggested. The fear of the nightmare sufferer is of actual death and has for Mack a transcendental dimension. He tries to argue that the nightmare is not a failure in dream function but that the nightmare response is related to vigilance and survival theories of dream or REM function. His arguments are unpersuasive and inconsistent as he himself describes the nightmare response as exaggerated and inappropriate to a threat which is not real.

The most comprehensive work on nightmares is by Ernest Hartmann (Hartmann, 1984). He points out the necessity, as had Broughton (Broughton, 1968), to distinguish the night terror from the nightmare, both are awakenings from sleep, the former from deep sleep, feeling frightened with extreme autonomic activation (i.e., accelerated heart rate, blood pressure, and respiration and with no or little memory for a dream) and the latter is from REM sleep usually with memory for a long, vivid, frightening dream, and autonomic variability rather than acceleration. He suggests that the nightmare of the patient with PTSD may be of a different order than the more usual nightmare of his subjects with life-long, once a week nightmares that he studied. Hartmann feels his subjects have what he calls "thin boundaries," some features of schizophrenia, an artistic temperament, and an openness and sensitivity. He notes that nightmares are very rare occurrences in the sleep lab. Hartmann enumerates the factors that may stimulate nightmares as (1) physical illness, especially if febrile; (2) neurological diseases such as epilepsy or Parkinsonism; (3) mental illnesses especially at the onset of a psychosis; (4) stress which involves feelings of helplessness; and (5) medications like beta blockers. He explores the biology of nightmares, which he views as a long and intense REM dream. He offers the hypothesis that an alteration in the forebrain in the balance between four neurotransmitters (i.e., a relative increase in acetylcholine and dopamine and a relative decrease in norepinephrine and serotonin) increases the tendency toward nightmares.

Hartmann (Hartmann, 1984) had selected for intensive study 50 subjects that responded to an ad for people with frequent nightmares and who gave a history of weekly nightmares. They, for the most part, turned out to have had nightmares since childhood but reported no obvious childhood traumas. He did a detailed history and a series of psychological tests but had only 11 of the subjects each sleep four nights in the sleep laboratory. He is aware that his subjects may not be representative of the general nightmare population. His subjects do not appear to be what has been called nightmare sufferers as it is possible to have nightmares but not be troubled by them (Belicki & Cuddy, 1991). Further, the absence of a history of abuse in his subjects may also suggest they are atypical nightmare sufferers (Cuddy & Belicki, 1992). His concept of "boundaries" is central to his explanation of the psychological structure of his nightmare subjects. Boundaries, thin or thick, are measured by his boundaries questionnaire, which has limited explanatory power (Hartmann, 1989). The boundary questionnaire did not predict decreased dream recall in people with thick boundaries which one would expect if boundary thickness is a significant determinant of dream recall (Moffitt, Hoffmann, & Galloway, 1990).

We compared the content of a dream experience to a nightmare to a made up (i.e., a confabulated nightmare) (Taub, Kramer, Arand, & Jacobs, 1978) using Hall-Van de Castle scales (Hall & Van de Castle, 1966). We found the difference between the dream and actual nightmares to be what one might expect. Nightmares had more aggressive interactions, physical activities, color and institutional-residential-vocational settings, and more castration anxiety. Dreams had more friendly interactions, less apprehensive feelings, more happy emotions and fewer misfortunes. Confabulated nightmares compared to real nightmares were higher in aggression, movement, intensity, color, misfortune, and indoor settings. The confabulated nightmare was half the length of the real nightmare and the normal dream. The confabulated nightmare reflects an idealized version of the nightmare which may influence our expectation of what we should find in studying nightmares while the differences between the real dream and nightmare supports that they are different experiences.

We extended our exploration of the possible differences between nightmares and dreams to nightmare sufferers. We compared the reports of sleep and dreams of a group of nightmare sufferers to a group of vivid dreamers, both groups were civilians (Kramer, Schoen, & Kinney, 1984). We found that the nightmare group in their dream diaries reported four times as many bad dreams per week as the vivid dreamers, while the latter had dream recall 89% of the days compared to 54% for the nightmare subjects. The rank order of the 17 descriptors used to describe the disturbed dream experience was essentially the same (i.e., very highly correlated r = .87) for the two groups. However, the responsivity to the dream experience (e.g., screaming, crying, and sleep walking) was greater among nightmare sufferers and the responsivity was confirmed by the reports of others. This increased motor behavior in nightmare sufferers raises question as to whether the nightmare comes only out of REM sleep where behavioral inhibition would be more typical or whether it arises out of non-REM (e.g., stage 2 or 4) (Fisher, Byrne, & Edwards, 1968) or perhaps there is an impairment of the motor inhibition in REM sleep as occurs in a REM behavior disorder (Mahowald & Schenck, 2000). The frightening dream was reported by the nightmare group to be more common following a day of high stress with feelings of anxiety, anger, or fatigue. The personality measures showed clear differences between the groups. The mean of the eight MMPI clinical scales were all higher for the nightmare group with five of the eight being two standard deviations or more above the mean. The three highest were the Sc, Pa, and Pd scales for the nightmare group and Pd, Ma, and Pt scales for the vivid dreamers. The very elevated Sc score mean of 82.5 supports the observations of Hartmann (Hartmann, 1984). The Cornell Medical Index (CMI) showed elevated nervousness and tension scores for the nightmare group and they had significant correlations between their CMI scores on anger, sensitivity and general emotion, and dream frequency. The descriptions suggested that the nightmare experience was not content dependent but was rather a reaction to the dream experience, perhaps in the awakening process, similar to the "Goblot" phenomenon (Freud, 1955b) in individuals predisposed by daytime stress and who were already hyper-aroused.

In the sleep laboratory, we studied two comparable groups of Vietnam combat veterans, one of whom reported disturbed dreaming at least once a week and the other who was free of bad dreams (Kramer, Schoen, & Kinney, 1984). The disturbed dreaming group had PTSD, while the control group had symptoms, of it but did not have PTSD. Over the four nights of observation, each time the subject awakened, a dream report was obtained. The disturbed dreaming group had to have more bad dreams out of non-REM sleep and did, 84%. For 50% of the subjects, the bad dreams were only from stage 2 sleep; for the other half, they were out of both REM and non-REM. Both groups awakened frequently (7–8 times per night] and overall recalled dreams at the same rate (45%–55%). The control group had a lower rate of recall from REM awakenings, 50% compared to 77%, suggesting they may be avoiding the disturbing dream experience. The disturbed dreaming group had military themes in half their dreams while the control group essentially had none. The military content dreams were as likely to come out of REM as non-REM. In PTSD patients, their dreams were half the time manifestly related to nonmilitary aspects of their lives. The dream reports as gathered in the laboratory do not reflect that the reports are stereotyped replications of the traumatic event. The avoidance of disturbing dreams either through repression or suppression may contribute to a less troubled life adaptation as seen in our control subjects and as reported in better adjusted holocaust survivors who also had decreased

REM dream recall (Kaminer & Lavie, 1991). The psychological structure of our nightmare subjects shows them to have had more combat and stress experiences and increased scores on tests of anxiety and depression as well as two standard deviation elevations on their Sc, Pd, and Sc MMPI scale scores and higher Rotter Locus of Control scores than the control group (Kramer & Kinney, 1985; Kramer, Kinney, & Schoen, 1983). The results of the psychological aspects of our study of Vietnam combat veterans are similar to our report on civilian nightmare sufferers (Kramer, Schoen, & Kinney, 1984) and to aspects of Hartmann's 50 lifelong nightmare sufferers (Hartmann, 1984).

The sleep stage results in our PTSD study showed (Kramer & Kinney, 1988) that for the nightmare subjects and the control group, the sleep was lighter and more disrupted with very low deep sleep (stages 3/4) as Neylan and colleagues have also reported (Neylan, Lenocchi, Maglione, Rosenlicht, Metzler, Otte, et al., 2003) and with the nightmare group having a longer REM sleep latency, and more spontaneous awakenings in the first half of the night (Schoen, Kramer, & Kinney, 1985). These findings have not been confirmed by some other sleep studies of Vietnam veterans (Hurwitz, Mahwold, Kuskowski, & Engdahl, 1988). The Hurwitz study did not select subjects with weekly nightmares from non-REM sleep. Neylan (Neylan, Malman, Metzler, Weiss, Zatzick, Delucci, et al., 1998) found that frequent nightmares appear to be virtually specific for PTSD. The abnormality in our subjects of increased early night awakenings, decreased stage 3/4 sleep, and a prolonged REM latency suggests an underlying circadian irregularity. The less intense but similar sleep abnormalities in the control group, all of whom had some PTSD symptoms, may reflect their biological susceptibility to later breakdown.

It was apparent that nightmare sufferers may well be in a hyper-aroused state that predisposes them to having nightmares. Yet Vietnam veterans told us they had been since Vietnam light sleepers, vigilant, and easily aroused. We studied our subjects from the dream phase of the experiment for an additional five nights and established their arousal thresholds and responses using both an ascending limits and super-threshold startle approach to white noise (Kramer & Kinney, 2003; Schoen, Kramer, & Kinney, 1985). The nightmare group had a higher, not a lower, awakening threshold than the control group across the night in both REM and non-REM sleep. The autonomic response frequency (heart and respiratory rate and motor movement) is higher in the nightmare group across the night. The disturbed dreaming group is more responsive to the startle tones across the night than the control group (93% of trials compared to 84%) but more so in NREM in the first half of the night. The subjects' awareness that they were awakened by white noise was lower, occurring in only 8% of trials in the nightmare group in NREM compared to the control group's 21% (Kinney & Kramer, 1985). The results appear counter intuitive as the nightmare subjects had higher awakening thresholds. However they were hyper-responsive to above threshold stimuli but hypo-cognitive in identifying the source of the disturbance. The elevated thresholds were also found by Dagan (Dagan & Lavie, 1991) and Lavie (Lavie, Katz, Pillar, & Zinger, 1998) but they did not ask the subject if they knew what awakened them.

With the elevated awakening thresholds and decreased dream recall in nightmare patients, avoidance may well be an adaptive strategy. Those veterans who had previously had PTSD but do not have it now show psychological and biological alterations that take an intermediate position on many variables between those who have never had PTSD and those who currently have it (Kramer & Kinney, 1985; Kinney & Kramer, 1985; Kramer, Kinney, & Schoen, 1983). This raises the possibility that they may be more vulnerable to a recurrence of PTSD given the correct precipitant e.g., the loss of a significant relationship (Kramer, 1991; Kramer, Schoen, & Kinney, 1987).

The nightmare sufferer clearly shows psychological and biological changes. Whether the nightmares that come on after traumas and those that occur in lifelong sufferers are the same or not phenomenologically, and in the stage of sleep from which they emerge, remains to be resolved. The centrality of altered REM mechanisms (Ross, Ball, Sullivan, & Caroff, 1989) in PTSD remains an open question. It has been concluded from the work I have just described and a review of the literature on dreams in PTSD that the hallmark of PTSD may be an alteration in the psychological aspects of dreaming (Kramer, 1979; Neylan, Malman, Metzler, Weiss, Zatzick, Delucci, et al. 1998) and possibly of NREM sleep in the first half of the night but not of REM sleep (Kramer, 1999).

The nightmare experience whether part of PTSD or some other psychopathologic condition or as an isolated recurring event can be very troublesome and many different treatment approaches have been tried. Halliday (Halliday, 1987) has divided treatment approaches into (1) behavioral procedures such as desensitization, 2) psychotherapy and ventilating approaches, (3) alteration of the dream scenario, and (4) confrontation. There have been efforts to treat nightmares with sedative medication of which Fisher's is an early one (Fisher, Kahn, Edwards, & Davis, 1973b) but pharmacological approaches have had variable success. Kellner and colleagues (Kellner, Neidhardt, Krakow, & Pathak, 1992) have demonstrated the value of the rescripting approach which Krakow has systematically shown in additional studies to be reasonably effective (Krakow, 1992).

C. Dreams in Psychopathologic States

1. *Introduction*

There long has been the assumption that there was an intimate relationship between dreams and mental disorders. Epigrammatic statements cited in Freud (Freud, 1955b, 90) and elsewhere that "the madman is a waking dreamer" "that dreams (are) a brief madness and madness a long dream" that if we "let the dreamer walk about and act like a person awake..., we (would) have the clinical picture of dementia praecox (schizophrenia)" (Jung, 1960, 86) and that if "we could find out about dreams, we would find out about insanity" (Jackson, J., 1958, 45) reflect the conviction about the close relationship between dreams and profound emotional disturbance. This view enlivened efforts to study dreaming to gain insights into the problems of the mentally ill.

In the literature review that introduces *The Interpretation of Dreams*, Freud (1955b, 88) has a section on "The Relations between Dreams and Mental Diseases." He points out that when he "speaks of the relationship of dreams to mental disorders [he] has three things in mind: (1) etiological and clinical connections, as when a dream represents a psychotic state, or introduces it, or is left over from it; (2) modifications to which dream-life is subject in cases of mental disease; and (3) intrinsic connections between dreams and psychosis, analogies pointing to their being essentially akin."

The published work on dreams and psychopathologic state touches on all three areas of Freud's concern (Frosch, 1976). There are reports of psychotic states appearing to begin with a dream or a series of dreams, and there is certainly a literature, which continues to pursue analogies between dreams and psychosis. However, the vast majority of the work that has been done on dreams and psychopathologic states devotes itself to "...modifications to which dream life is subject in cases of mental disease" (Frosch, 1976, 39) and will be the focus of these comments. Freud was of the opinion that as we better understand dreams, it will enhance our understanding of psychosis. Hartmann (Hartmann, 1984) is of a similar opinion.

Ramsey (Ramsey, 1953) published a review of studies of dreaming. These were all from the pre-REM literature. Overall, he cites some 121 articles and books of which 20 at most were studies of the dreams of six patient groups. The amount of information available from 20 publications would be woefully inadequate to characterize the dreams of psychopathologic groups. Ramsey concludes that the research was scientifically inadequate. Very few of the studies were so designed and reported that they could be replicated to validate their findings.

The literature dealing with the nature of the relationship between dreaming and mental illness has been reviewed on several occasions

(Kramer, 1969, 1970, 1981; Kramer & Roth, 1978; Kramer & Roth, 1979), the last of which was a detailed review published in 1979. The scientific adequacy of the publications covered in that review (Kramer & Roth, 1979) was quite problematic, but a picture of dream content in some psycho-pathologic states began to emerge. I have reviewed the literature since 1979 for this section and combined it with previous reviews.

2. Schizophrenia

Schizophrenics (Kramer & Roth, 1979) were less interested in their dreams and their dreams were more primitive (i.e., less complex, more direct, more sexual, anxious, and hostile; and showed evidence of their thought disorder in being more bizarre and implausible). Strangers were their most frequent dream characters. Hallucinations and dream content were relat-able and the degree of paranoia, awake and in dreaming, was similar, con-trary to Freud's compensatory view of waking and dreaming in paranoia. An updated literature review yielded only six additional articles on dream content in schizophrenic states (Deutsch, 1985; Meloy, 1984; Ohira, Kato, Namura, & Ishikawa, 1979; Ushijima, 1988; Van de Castle, 1974; Wilmer, 1982), a surprisingly small number which added little to our understand-ing. Lobotomized schizophrenics (Jus et al., 1973) had a lower dream recall rate in the laboratory (10.4%) than nonschizophrenics (46.7%) but both were higher than in another study (Solms, 1997).

3. Depression

The depressed (Kramer & Roth, 1979) patient was found to dream as frequently as the nondepressed, but the dreams were shorter and had a paucity of traumatic or depressive content even after the depression had lifted. Family members were more frequent in their dreams. When hostil-ity was present, it could be directed at or away from the dreamer, while in schizophrenia it was directed at the dreamer. The depressed had in their dreams more friendly and fewer aggressive interactions than schizophren-ics but more failure and misfortune. With clinical improvement, hostility decreased while intimacy, motility, and heterosexuality increased.

The view that begins to emerge more clearly from the updated review is that in depression there is a decrease in the frequency (Barrett & Loeffler, 1992; Beauchemin & Hays, 1996; Firth, Blouin, Natarajan, & Blouin, 1986; Greenberg, Pearlman, Blacher, Katz, Sashin, & Gottlieb, 1990; Mathew, Largen, & Claghorn, 1979; Riemann, Low, Schredl, Wiegand, Dippel, & Berger, 1990; 1990) and length (Barrett & Loeffler, 1992; Cartwright, Lloyd, Knight, & Trenholme, 1984; Firth, Blouin, Natarajan, & Blouin, 1986; Rie-mann et al., 1990) of the dream reports. Their dreams are often common-place but at times have content characteristics (Beauchemin & Hays, 1995,

1996; Firth, Blouin, Natarajan, & Blouin, 1986; Trenholme, Cartwright, & Greenberg, 1984) of high interest. There is an increase in dreams with death themes in depressed suicidal patients and in bipolars before becoming manic (Beauchemin & Hays, 1995; Firth, Blouin, Natarajan, & Blouin, 1986). An increase in family roles in the dreams of the depressed may also be the case (Barrett & Loeffler, 1992; Brenman, 1982; Riemann Low, Schredl, Wiegand, Dippel, & Berger, 1990).

Masochism in the dreams of the depressed (Beck, 1967; Cartwright & Wood, 1993; Clark, Trinder, Kramer, Roth, & Day, 1972; Dow, Kelsoe, & Gillin, 1996; Hauri, 1976; Trenholme, Cartwright, & Greenberg, 1984) appears more clearly in women than in men and is more likely a trait than state characteristic. It was evident that a past focus (Barrett & Loeffler, 1992; Beauchemin & Hays, 1996; Cartwright, Lloyd, Knight, & Trenholme, 1984; Dow, Kelsoe, & Gillin, 1996; Firth, Blouin, Natarajan, & Blouin, 1986; Greenberg, Pearlman, Blacher, Katz, Sashin, & Gottlieb, 1990; Hauri, 1976) was not universal in the dreams of the depressed nor was it unique to the depressed state. Affects such as anxiety and hostility were not prominent in the dreams of the depressed (Beauchemin & Hays, 1995; Dow, Kelsoe, & Gillin, 1996; Strauch & Meier, 1996; Trenholme, Cartwright, & Greenberg, 1984). The content of their dreams may have prognostic significance for the response of the depressed patient to treatment or the spontaneous outcome of the depression (Cartwright & Wood, 1993; Greenberg, Pearlman, Blacher, Katz, Sashin, & Gottlieb, 1990).

A most striking implication of these findings about dreaming in the depressed is that the affective state of the dreamer co-varies with the content of the dream (Beauchemin & Hays, 1995, 1996; Cartwright, Lloyd, Knight, & Trenholme, 1984; Levitan, 1977; Riemann et al., 1990; Trenholme, Cartwright, & Greenberg, 1984). And, that changes in dreams across the night may contribute to the dreamer's coping capacity (Cartwright, Lloyd, Knight, & Trenholme, 1984; Cartwright, 1991; Trenholme, Cartwright, & Greenberg, 1984), as was suggested by Kramer in "The Mood Regulatory Function of Dreaming" (Kramer, 1993b). Changes in dream content across the night alter the affective condition of the dreamer and contribute to the adaptive state of the dreamer the next day.

4. Post Traumatic Stress Disorder (PTSD)

A widespread interest in PTSD, and the dreams that sometimes accompany the disorder, has developed since the Vietnam War. PTSD was only included in the official nomenclature of the American Psychiatric Association in 1980, although it had been described in the psychiatric literature for over 100 years (Erichson, 1882).

In a review article, Ross and his colleagues (Ross, Ball, Sullivan, & Caroff, 1989) attempt to demonstrate that a sleep disturbance is the hallmark of PTSD. They base their hypothesis on the mentation difference between REM and non-REM sleep. They characterize the dreams of PTSD patients as vivid, affect laden, disturbing, outside the realm of current waking experience (although representative of an earlier life experience), repetitive, stereotyped, and easy to recall. They are of the opinion that the dream disturbance is relatively specific for the disorder (Reynolds, 1989) and that PTSD may fundamentally be a disorder of the REM sleep mechanism. However, as the nightmare in REM sleep occurs early in the night when there is less REM and is associated with gross body movements, they (Ross, Ball, Sullivan, & Caroff, 1989) acknowledge that abnormal non-REM sleep mechanisms may be involved as well and speculate that the neural circuitry involved in PTSD may be similar to that in accentuated startle behavior. Ross and colleagues (Ross, Ball, Sullivan, & Caroff, 1990) take exception to the suggestion (Reynolds, 1989) that the dream in PTSD is the same that occurs in traumatized depressives and point out that the dreams of traumatized depressives are not dreamlike and do not incorporate the trauma. They (Ross, Ball, Sullivan, & Caroff, 1989) see the dream in PTSD as repetitive and more importantly stereotyped.

Kramer (Kramer, 1979) in contrast views the disturbing dream as the hallmark of PTSD rather than the sleep disturbance. Green and collaborators (Green, Lindy, & Grace, 1985) suggest that the unique aspect of PTSD is indeed the intrusive symptoms including intrusive images and recurrent dreams and nightmares. They point out that not all dreams are directly recapitulations of the trauma. For them, these intrusive images may be the hallmark of PTSD. The view of Green's group was based on the suggestion by Brett and Ostroff (Brett & Ostroff, 1985) that there has been a neglect of post traumatic imagery, which they postulate is the core of PTSD. They lament the lack of research into the range, content, and patterning of the imagery. Interestingly, Fisher and coworkers (Fisher, Kahn, Edwards, & Davis, 1973a) point out that trauma sufferers may have disturbing arousals that can come out of both REM and non-REM (stage 4 and stage 2) sleep. This is a view Schlosburg and Benjamin (Schlosberg & Benjamin, 1978), Kramer and Kinney (Kramer & Kinney, 1988), and Dagan and Lavie (Dagan & Lavie, 1991) confirm. Questions arise whether the sleep disturbance in PTSD involves more than REM sleep mechanisms and whether the imagery, dreams, reported by PTSD patients are stereotyped and REM-bound, as Ross and colleagues (Ross, Ball, Sullivan, & Caroff, 1989) postulate.

Although there has been a relative lack of attention to the range, content, and patterning of the nightmares in PTSD, it is clear that there can be different types of nightmares (Dowling, 1982; Schreuder, 1996; Siegel, 1980) with themes unrelated to the trauma (Mellman, Kulick-Bell, Ashlock, & Nolan, 1995; Watson, 1993) and that the traumatic dream can change across time (Titchener & Kapp, 1976). The traumatic nightmare is seen to reflect classical Freudian dream work mechanisms (deSaussure, 1982; Dowling, 1982; Lansky, 1991; 1995; Siegel, 1980; Silvan-Adams & Adams, 1990) and not to be a meaningless re-enactment of the trauma.

An adequate characterization of the phenomenology of the disturbing dream in PTSD remains to be done. The dream experience is disturbing, but this may be more a reaction to the dream than the dream itself (Kramer, Schoen, & Kinney, 1984). The affect laden nature of the disturbing dream cannot be confirmed and expectations may influence the perception of what the dream should be like in PTSD (Taub, Kramer, Arand, & Jacobs, 1978). The content of the disturbing dream may be outside the realm of current waking experience but it is linked to earlier childhood experiences (deSaussure, 1982; Dowling, 1982; Lansky, 1991, 1995; Puk, 1991; Silvan-Adams & Adams, 1990) and can be reactivated later in life (Goldstein, van Kammen, Shelly, Miller, & van Kammen, 1987; Kuch & Cox, 1992; Mollica, Wyshak, & Lavelle, 1987; Siegel, 1980; Van Dyke, Zilberg, & McKinnon, 1985; C. Wells, Chu, Johnson, Nasdahl, Ayubi, Sewell, et al., 1991). The vividness of the dream has not been adequately addressed. The dream in PTSD is not easily recalled. Patients with active PTSD have a lower dream recall (Dagan & Lavie, 1991; Hefez, Metz, & Lavie, 1987; Mellman, Kulick-Bell, Ashlock, & Nolan, 1995) rate than normals, but higher than well adjusted former PTSD patients (Lavie & Kaminer, 1991).

A consensus has begun to emerge from the PTSD dream literature suggesting that the hallmark of PTSD is a disturbance in psychological dreaming and possibly of non-REM sleep early in the night. Disturbed dreaming co-varies with combat exposure (Neylan, Marmer, Metzler, Weiss, Zatzick, Delucchi et al., 1998) and being tortured (Shrestha, Sharma, Van Ommeren, Regmi, Makaju, Komproe, et al., 1998) not with the complaint of a sleep disturbance. The disturbing dream tends to occur early during sleep (van der Kolk, Blitz, Burr, Sherry, & Hartmann, 1984) as do increases in movement (Hertz, 1976; Lavie & Hertz, 1979; Mellman, Kulick-Bell, Ashlock, & Nolan, 1995), spontaneous awakenings (Kramer, Schoen, & Kinney, 1984; Schoen, Kramer, & Kinney, 1985; Wilmer, 1996), autonomic discharge (Wilmer, 1996), an elevated arousal threshold (Dagan & Lavie, 1991; Kramer & Kinney, 2003; Schoen, Kramer, & Kinney, 1984), and a heightened startle response (Kinney, Schoen, & Kramer, 1983; Kramer & Kinney, 2003). The disturbing dream is not sleep stage-bound and may emerge out of REM or non-REM sleep (Fisher, Kahn, Edwards, & Davis, 1973a; Kramer & Kinney, 1988; Schlosberg & Benjamin, 1978).

Stereotypical dream content is not the sine qua non of the dream in PTSD. The failure or avoidance of dream recall may be an adaptational strategy in PTSD (Kramer, Schoen, Kinney, 1984; Lavie & Kaminer, 1991).

5. Eating Disorders

Anorexics and bulimics both report dreams and their dreams are seen as useful in therapy (Brink & Allan, 1992; Dippel, Lauer, Riemann, Majer-Trendel, Krieg, Berger, 1987; Frayn, 1991; Hudson, DeTrinis, Ware, & Karacan, 1978; Jackson, Beumont, Thornton, & Lennerts, 1993; Jackson, Tabin, Russell, & Touyz, 1993; Levitan, 1981; Sprince, 1984; L. Wells, 1980; Wilson, 1983). For eating disorder patients, the rate of dream recall is low on self-report questionnaires but normal in the sleep laboratory. Dreaming of food is high in eating disorder patients, and higher in bulimics than anorexics. Aggressive dreams are less common in eating disorder patients than in normals.

6. Brain Damage

The previous review (Kramer & Roth, 1979) found five articles on brain damaged patients. These studies reported that there was a decrease in dream reporting with age and dementia. The more recent studies (Askenasy, Gruskiewicz, Braun, & Hackett, 1986; Benyakar, Tadir, Groswasser, & Stern, 1988; Nathan, Rose-Itkoff, & Lord, 1981; Stern & Stern, 1985; Stern & Stern, 1990) of brain injured patients report the value of dream exploration in psychotherapy with them. A questionnaire study of aged individuals found no relationship between dream report frequency and the degree of brain atrophy on CT scan. Repetitive visual imagery in brain damaged patients was not REM-bound. Focal brain damage studies suggest the anatomical substrate for dream formation (Solms, 1997).

7. Alcoholism

In the previous review (Kramer & Roth, 1979), the dreams of alcoholics could be distinguished from those of nonalcoholics. The alcoholic had more oral references in his dreams, was more often the object of aggression and had fewer sexual interactions. Those detoxifying alcoholics that dreamed about drinking maintained sobriety longer. The implication of dreaming about drinking as a predictor of abstinence remains unclear (Cernovsky, 1985; Cernovsky, 1986; Christo & Franey, 1996; Denizen, 1988; Fiss, 1980). However, it raises the possibility that what one dreams about may have adaptive significance.

8. Conclusion

It is apparent that the mysteries of psychosis have not been revealed through the study of dreams. The paucity of studies in some conditions and the relative lack of scientific rigor throughout continue to plague the study of dreams in psychiatric conditions. However, in some areas, such as depression and PTSD, we do know more about dreaming than was previously known.

The most intriguing insight that emerges from this review is that what one does or does not dream about may contribute to the waking adaptational process (Denizen, 1988; Koulack, 1991; Kramer, 1993; Kramer, Schoen, & Kinney, 1984; Lavie & Kaminer, 1991; Trenholme, Cartwright, & Greenberg, 1984). Manipulating the dream by the controlled incorporation of characters or events into the dream (Kramer, Kinney, & Scharf, 1983) and assessing the daytime consequences would treat the dream as an independent variable and contribute to our understanding of the functional significance of dreaming.

CHAPTER 8

The Reactive Nature of Dreaming

A. Introduction

The dream experience is an organized event as reflected in the fact that psychologically different groups have different dream experiences. The nature of those differences implies but does not demonstrate that the dream is responding to psychologically meaningful experiences rather than just being a concomitant of them. We want to explore more specifically whether the dream experience is responsive to external events or is essentially so stable, at least in the adult, as to be endlessly repetitive. By postulating a strict biological determinism, Hobson and colleagues (Hobson, Pace-Schott, & Stickgold, 2000) maintain that it is the random neural signals from the pontine centers that is determining of the content of the dream experience. Domhoff (Domhoff, 1996), in emphasizing the constancy of dream themes across the adult life span and in advocating the use of content norms derived from college age subjects in studies of adult dreaming and describing what he believes to be a neglected aspect of dreaming, the repetition dimension, implies that the reactive nature of dreaming, if it exists, is of less importance than the stability or impenetrability of dreaming.

B. Techniques to Search for Dream Reactivity

There are a number of techniques that have been used to study the reactive nature of dreaming. These include externally determined, personally meaningless, usually nonemotional stimuli presented during sleep such as water, touch, light, and sound (Dement & Wolpert, 1958); or arousing films shown before sleep (Witkin & Lewis, 1967); or hypnosis with instruction to dream during hypnosis or with post hypnotic suggestion (Moss, 1967); or simple suggestion (Tart, 1979). All are intended to study the incorporation of the stimuli into the dream. Generally, the rate of incorporation of impersonal stimuli into the dream has been disappointing. Techniques such as lucidity (LaBerge & Rheingold, 1990) are not examples of dream reactivity and incorporation but rather of altered dream awareness. The re-scripting techniques of Kellner and colleagues (Kellner, Neidhardt, Krakow, & Pathak, 1992) are self-determined suggestions to alter troubling emotional dream experiences. The techniques are often successful and are an example of the reactive capacity of dreaming.

C. Studies of Dream Reactivity

We had been able to distinguish one night of dreaming from another in the same subject (Kramer, Hlasny, Jacobs, & Roth, 1976). The emotionally impersonal stimuli in the disappointing incorporation experiments suggest that a stimulus might have to be emotionally intense and personally meaningful to find its way into the dream experience. The re-scripting techniques that were successful in altering upsetting dreams were both. We considered that the differences among nights of dreaming that permitted us to sort one night of dreaming from another might be related to some personal and prominent activity having occurred to the dreamer during the day which had stirred some significant degree of emotional arousal.

1. Responsive to Activities of the Preceding Day

We undertook to explore the influence of the day's activities and emotional state of subjects by having them keep a daily activities record (DAR) each hour as well as an hourly emotional tone report (ETR) on each of the 10 nonconsecutive days before they slept in the laboratory for REM dream collection (Piccione, Jacobs, Kramer, & Roth, 1977). Three judges were separately given for each subject the 10-day packet of DARs, the 10 nights of transcribed REM dream reports, and the 10-day packet of ETRs and REM dream reports. The three judges were unable to match past chance either the DAR or ETR to the corresponding nights dreaming for the subjects. The result is disappointing as it underlines the fact that the relationship between waking activity and dreaming is not an obvious one. Freud had observed that the day residue to which the dream appeared to be connected was often a seemingly indifferent event.

The judges were then presented with the set of REM dreams properly matched to the DAR of the day before sleeping in the laboratory. The judge's task was to select an activity from the DAR of that day that appeared in the matching night's REM dreams. We then compared the emotional intensity scores from the ETR for that activity/time to the other emotional intensity scores. Overall there was a significant difference between the emotional intensity scores of the daily activity chosen by the judges as being represented in the dream and the emotional intensity of the activities not represented in the dream. The activity chosen by the judges as most prevalent in the dream was the same activity the subject had rated as more emotionally intense. This result demonstrates that dream content is most concerned with the activity of the day which is accompanied by the more intense emotion. This is the opposite of what one would predict from Freud's description of the day residue being an inconsequential daytime event. It should be kept in mind that the so-called meaningless or inconsequential day residue described by Freud is linked to other usually unconscious material of great importance to the dreamer.

We had some confirmation that an event during waking that was personally meaningful and emotionally charged for a person was more likely to be represented in his dreams that night. To establish that dreams are meaningful, i.e., "...they can be inserted into the chain of intelligible waking mental acts" (Freud, 1955, 12), to the dreamer requires that dreams are nonrandom events (as we demonstrated in chapter 6) and that dreams can be systematically related to the waking preoccupations of the dreamer. Much of the early work on the relationship of waking and dreaming thought has related trait aspects of the person, particularly their fantasy life, to their dreams (Cartwright, 1969; Cartwright, Kasniak, 1991; Winget & Kramer, 1979). We chose to test the hypothesis that dreams are responsive to the immediate concerns of the dreamer.

2. Responsive to Emotionally Significant Daytime Events

We wanted to select an event of emotional significance to the dreamer thinking that such an event ought to be discernable in the subject's dreams. We reasoned that the beginning and ending of an experience are events of high emotional charge. We were of the opinion that coming into the sleep laboratory as a subject for 20 consecutive nights for dream collection was such an event (Kramer, Roth, & Cisco, 1977; Whitman, 1963). Judges were asked to choose which of a pair of night's dreams belonged to beginning to sleep in the laboratory and which to ending the experience. In the first task, the judges were given all the dreams from all of a subject's nights and asked to put them into their night of occurrence. In the second task, the judges were given all the dreams of each subject for a pair of nights (i.e.,1–20, 3–18, 5–16, 7–14, 9–12, and 10–11) and asked to place them correctly as to which of the two nights the dreams were from. The three judges were unable to accomplish either task at greater than a chance level of accuracy. On the third task, the judges were given all the dreams of a night (not individual dreams) and were asked to place each member of the pair as either beginning or ending. Overall, the judges were able to place the nights in the pairs well past a chance level. Placement was significant for night pairs 1–20 (69% correctly placed), and 3–18 (67%) but not for 5–16 (62%), 7–14 (50%), 9–12 (60%), and 10–11 (62%). The meaningfulness of dreams cannot be discerned at an individual level but can at the level of an entire night of dreaming. It seems reasonable to conclude that the dreams of a night, if not individual dreams, are meaningful and could be "inserted into the chain of intelligible waking mental acts."

3. *Responsive to Emotionally Significant Interpersonal Circumstances*

We have examined the interpersonal relationships in the sleep laboratory to explore their effect on dreaming, speculating that the interpersonal situation with its emotional charge might be a significant influence on dream content. The selective communication process to the technician at night and to the psychiatrist in the morning that we described in chapter 3 may be a case in point (Whitman, Kramer, & Baldridge, 1963b). The male patient that we described earlier reported dreams to the psychiatrist that highlighted his masculine capabilities and did not report dreams with homosexual implications. The woman volunteer reported veiled criticism of the technician to the psychiatrist and dreams with sexual implications that reflected her sexual concerns and fears of psychiatrists and psychiatric treatment only to the technician.

We recognized that in our study of the differential reporting of dreams in the therapeutic dyadic relationship (Whitman, Kramer, & Baldridge, 1963b) that we had examined the impact of the relationship on only one half of the pair and had not looked at the impact of the relationship on the dreams of the psychiatrist. To examine the dreams of both participants in the therapeutic relationship, we had 10 therapist-patient pairs sleep in two different sleep laboratories on the same night to examine the possibility that the dreams are relatable to each other (Whitman, Kramer, & Baldridge, 1963a). To enhance the importance of the patient to the psychiatrist, we chose to have the pair sleep the night before the psychiatrist was going to present his work with the patient at a group supervisory conference. The patient knew nothing about the psychiatrist's participation in the lab or at the conference, which was composed of a senior psychiatrist supervisor and a group of the presenting psychiatrist's peers. Our hypothesis was that the patient would dream about the psychiatrist and the psychiatrist about the patient and that the dreams might serve to illuminate the relationship between them. The patients dreamt about the therapist in

41.4% of their dreams. The therapists dreamt about their patients in only 12.5% of their dreams, 37.5% of their dreams had references to the supervisory conference, and in 53.6% there were references to the experiment or experimental situation. A dream could have references to more than one category. The supervisors reported that 33% of the dreams they recalled from the night before the conference were about the experiment and none were about the conference.

The dreams of the patients were unusual in their lack of concern about the experiment in contrast to volunteer nonpatients (Whitman, Pierce, Maas, & Baldridge, 1962) who revealed in their dreams being concerned about being sexually assaulted or exploited. The major concern of the psychiatrists in relation to the supervisory conference was the fear of being exposed as inadequate and ganged up on by a group with subsequent feelings of shame. Avoidance of and competitiveness with the supervisor were present as well. The conference supervisors' morning recalled dreams revealed concerns about how adequate the research team would view their supervision and competitiveness with the research group. Discomfort over being looked at was present in both the psychiatrists' and supervisors' dreams. The patient dreamed about his psychiatrist, but contrary to our expectations, the psychiatrist dreamed about supervision, and the supervisor about the research team. Everyone was dreaming "up" concerned about how they appeared to those watching them. When the researchers were asked who they dreamed about, it was The National Institute of Mental Health, the provider of funding for the research. Participants in the research were described (*New Yorker,* 1964) "[as] a bunch of sleepy social climbers."

We were interested in examining further the impact on the dream experience of the interpersonal situation in the sleep laboratory. We undertook a study in which we varied the sex of the dream collector and dreamer so we could observe whether in a heterosexual interpersonal laboratory situation the dream reports were systematically different from those in a same sex, a homosexual, laboratory pair (Fox, Kramer, Baldridge, Whitman, & Ornstein, 1968). The study is described in chapter 3. The differences between experimenters were age, status, and sex. We found clear dream recall and content differences. Subjects' dream recall percentage was higher with the male than female experimenter. Crowds and groups and characters of unstated sex were much more frequent when there was a heterosexual pairing. The central theme for the female subject was dependency. When paired with the male psychiatrist, she viewed doctors fulfilling her patient's needs; with the female experimenter, her patients were waiting to have their needs met. With the male experimenter, there were dreams of intravenous fluids running smoothly. With the female experimenter, the fluids ran dry. The male subject with the male experimenter had satisfying dreams of performing well. With the female experimenter, the themes were of being hurt. References to the experimental situation, almost all indirect, occurred 66% of the time and the frequency was the same in the first three and the last three nights.

The concluding impression is that experimental dream subjects respond in their dreams to the person of the dream collector in an idiosyncratic and ongoing manner. There was a consistent theme in each of the four sets of dreams related to how the subject viewed the experimenter which was elaborated over the dream collection period. The presence of crowds and characters of unstated sex in dreams appeared only at times when the pair was heterosexual and may be related to avoiding sexual temptation by having others present or denying the sexual designations of characters in the dream (e.g., identifying a character as a person rather than as a man or a woman). There was no evidence of adaptation to the experimental situation as the frequency of references to the experiment is the same in the first and last half.

In these three interpersonal relationship studies we have demonstrated that the dreamer is responsive to the immediate current concerns in their lives at the time of dreaming. The interpersonal situation in the laboratory, which has a preemptive quality, becomes for some the immediate concern which is then elaborated across the nights of dreaming. Cartwright (Cartwright & Kasniak, 1991) has come to an identical view of the focus of dreaming on current concerns which is elaborated across the nights of dreaming. She points out that when the external concern is intense enough, like in a divorce, the laboratory situation is less pre-empting but does not disappear (i.e., 12% in her divorced subjects compared to 28% in her controls). As we saw in our study of patients and resident psychiatrists, the patients represented their personal problems in 58.6% of their dreams, the experimental situation in 6.9%, the resident psychiatrists focused on the upcoming supervision in 42.8% of their dreams, but the experimental situation was still very much represented in 53.6% of their dreams. The experimental situation was much more of a current concern for the psychiatrists as some members of the research team were their teachers.

The pre-empting influence of the interpersonal situation makes the point that the dream is responsive to an immediate circumstance or current concern of the dreamer. However, if other concerns are excluded in favor of the laboratory, then trying to study other nonexperimental concerns becomes problematic. Clearly this is not the case in Cartwright's study of divorcing women (Cartwright & Kasniak, 1991) or in our study of patients and their psychiatrists (Whitman, Kramer, & Baldridge, 1963a). We examined the frequency of direct and indirect references to the laboratory situation and reviewed some of the literature. Whitman and colleagues (Whitman,

Pierce, Maas, & Baldridge, 1962) reported that out of 110 dreams of experimental subjects one third made direct and another third made indirect references to the experimental situation, which included concerns about the equipment and the room, the subject's behavior in the experiment, and the subject's attitude toward the experimenter. The female volunteer subjects had rape fantasies about being in the experiment and the men had exploitation fantasies in their dreams. The laboratory experience clearly was a powerful force affecting their dreams. Domhoff and Kamiya (Domhoff & Kamiya, 1964) noted that 30% of the dreams in their study made a direct reference to the experimental situation. Dement (Dement, Kahn, & Roffwarg, 1965) reported that 21.9% of a pool of laboratory dreams made a direct reference to the experimental setting and that 15.4% had an inferential reference. He saw a drop in laboratory references on the second night but then a gradual increase occurred reflecting the subject's involvement generally with the experimenter. The Whitman (Whitman, Pierce, Maas, & Baldridge, 1962) and Domhoff (Domhoff & Kamiya, 1964) studies showed no evidence of adaptation.

We undertook a more extensive study (Piccione, Thomas, Roth, & Kramer, 1976) of the frequency of representation of the laboratory in the dreams of experimental subjects to see if adaptation to the laboratory took place over a more extended period than previously had been reported. We collected REM dreams from the first four REM periods of the night for 20 consecutive nights from 14 college age male subjects. We obtained a recall rate of 82%, which gave us 754 dream reports. The reports were scored blindly by two judges for the presence or absence of laboratory references in the dreams with a reliability of 90%. There was no significant decrease across the 20 nights of the percentage of dreams with laboratory incorporation either when comparing the first night (39%) to all the other nights (34%) or when comparing the first five nights (33%) to successive five night blocks (28%, 33%, and 33%, respectively). The laboratory remains a potent stimulus for these relatively untroubled subjects across the 20 nights.

The night to night percentage incorporation varied greatly from a low on night five of 2.05% to a high on night 10 of 44.3%. We computed the variability of laboratory representation in the first 10 nights (standard deviation of 24.6%) and of nights 11–20 (standard deviation of 13.5%). There was a decrease in the standard deviation in the second half of the nights but it wasn't significant. We then compared the night-to-night variability of dreams incorporating the laboratory to the variability of dreams with characters other than the dreamer. The variability of the percentage of laboratory incorporation dreams was significantly greater in the first 10 nights than the variability of character incorporated dreams. This variability difference disappeared when the last 10 nights were compared. This suggests that the laboratory situation had lost some of its emotional intensity as the variability difference from character variability decreased. Variability was assumed to be a major component of an emotional response.

A more complete set of 820 dreams from the 14 subjects (Kramer & Roth, 1979) was scored with the Hall-Van de Castle dream content scales (Hall & Van de Castle, 1966) for three content categories: characters, activities, and descriptive elements. The scale scores were correlated night to night and the mean correlation across the three content categories was 0.22 for week one and 0.50 for week two, which was significant. Further, the mean correlations for each night pair across the three content categories was for nights 1–2, 0.05; for nights 10–11, 0.30; and for nights 19–20, 0.80. The night 19–20 correlation is significantly different than the night 1–2 correlation. The laboratory incorporations show minimal evidence of adaptation but the content categories clearly show evidence of adaptation without becoming stereotyped. The variability in dream content supports the concept that the dream is responsive but not without some limits to the responsivity.

4. Responsiveness to Pharmacological Alteration of the Emotional State

It is apparent that the dream is responsive to the waking affective state of the dreamer. We wanted to pursue this possibility outside of the realm of the immediate waking current concern of the dreamer.

Would a pharmacological intervention with the potential to alter affective state result in altering dream content? We had reviewed the impact of centrally active drugs on dreaming (Kramer, Whitman, Baldridge, & Ornstein, 1966) and saw systematic changes across drugs that included a rise in anxiety and dependency scores and a decrease in intimacy. We were of the opinion these were related more to the interpersonal situation of being given a medication than to the medication itself. We did observe that imipramine, an anti-depressant, tended in normal subjects to increase hostility in dreams. Given the central role attributed to hostility in depression (Freud, 1957), we studied the REM dreams of a group of depressed patients. Our initial effort to relate dream content changes to clinical improvement in depressed patients given imipramine was unsuccessful (Kramer, Whitman, Baldridge, & Lansky, 1966). Our approach led to demonstrating that depressed patients had more depressive themes such as low self-regard, self-blame and criticism, and feelings of helplessness and hopelessness than normal subjects, but we were unable to show changes in the frequency of these categories with clinical change in the patients. We considered that as we had dealt with the dream content thematically using a categorical system (e.g., was a theme of helplessness present in a dream or not), we may have missed changes in significant state aspects of the dreams that were dimensional rather than categorical. We rescored the dreams of the depressed with a series of intensity or interval scales that included measures of hostility, anxiety, intimacy, heterosexuality, motility, dependency, and homosexuality (Kramer, Whitman, Baldridge, & Ornstein, 1968). We had the hospitalized depressed patients sleep in the first week for two baseline nights for REM dream collection and then one night a week for three additional weeks, a total of five nights. By the fifth night, the patients had essentially recovered from their depression. Comparing the first to the fifth night, we observed that there was a decrease in hostility, anxiety, and intimacy but no significant change in the other four scales. These results lend some support to the proposition that the dream is responsive to the changing affective condition of the dreamer. They are of particular interest as we established and altered the waking emotional condition of the patient and measured the consequent change in aspects of the dream experience.

5. Directly and Selectively Altering Dream Content

We attempted to alter the ongoing dream experience itself by introducing significant material during dreaming. This would be the most direct experimental demonstration of the dreams responsiveness. Previous attempts to show differential dream incorporation based on the meaning of the stimulus had been unsuccessful. Berger (Berger, 1963) had demonstrated that incorporations of verbal material could occur during dreaming but he concluded that the incorporations were based on the phonetic not the semantic properties of the stimulus. Castaldo and Holtzman did two studies (Castaldo & Holzman, 1967, 1969) in which the voice of the dreamer was played during sleep and the result was that the main character in the dream was more active, assertive, and independent compared with when the dreamer heard someone else's voice which led the main dream character to be more passive. There studies suggest the effect of dreaming is related to meaning not the phonetic properties of the stimulus. Utilizing the technique Castaldo and Holtzman described, we did two studies (Kramer, Kinney, & Scharf, 1983). One study was with nine subjects and the other with seven subjects. Each subject slept for three nights in the laboratory. However before sleeping each subject generated and recorded in their own voice 20 high meaning, (H) names, and 20 low meaning, (L) names. The H names were of family, friends, and living companions; L names were not of people the subject knew or had known. Across the night during a REM period and through an earpiece, one stimulus name was presented one time. Each subject heard randomly selected three H and three L names. At 2, 8, and 10 minutes after the stimulus presentation, the subjects were awakened and asked to report their dreams and if they had heard anything through the earpiece. Incorporation was scored: (1) as *representational* (if the person appeared in the dream), or (2) as *direct* (if the person's name appeared in the dream), or (3) as *assonant* (if a phonetically similar phrase appeared in the dream), or (4) as *associational* (if the subject made a voluntary comment about the person while reporting the dream). Overall dream recall was essentially the same 85%–94% in both experiments for both H and L exposure dreams. Hearing the actual stimulus word in the first experiment was 29% H and 15% L, while in the second it was 9% H and 19% L. In both studies incorporation was greater for the H than the L exposure (59% vs. 11% and 39% vs. 5%). The most frequent type of incorporation was representational 56% in Experiment 1 and 87% in Experiment 2.

Meaning does matter; high-meaning stimuli are more likely and reliably to be incorporated into dreaming. Dreamers while dreaming are responsive as they are capable of making distinctions between stimuli based on the meaning of the stimuli and incorporate them into their dreams. These results open the possibility of experimentally studying the function of dreaming by being able to manipulate the characters in dreams and examining the consequences, if any, of the manipulation in waking. The success or failure of such experiments could address directly a possible adaptational role for dreaming.

D. Summary

We have explored the influence of the emotional preoccupation (immediate current concern) of the dreamer as the significant influence on the individual's subsequent dreaming. It is the more intense emotional experiences of the day that appear in dreams; emotionally laden experiences such as beginning and ending a relationship are identifiable in dreams; and the emotional nature of the interpersonal experience helps determine which of the multiple dreams of the night is chosen to be reported, which of several situations is chosen as the focus in a night's dreams and how an emotionally charged relationship is elaborated across several night's of dreaming. The dreamer's immediate current concern is structuring and influencing of the dream content of the night. A medication that alters the emotional condition of the dreamer results in systematic changes in dream content. Evidence that the content of dreams adapts across nights has been difficult to establish but dream content appears to be both stable and variable. The meaning of a presleep experience determines its impact on dreaming.

CHAPTER 9

Dreams and Waking Thought

A. Introduction

We have shown that where we know there are psychological differences in the waking state, there are corresponding and related differences in the content of dreams. These observations we have offered as support for the structured orderly nature of dreaming and the importance of meaning in understanding dream content. We also have shown that the dream is responsive to experiences of emotional significance to the dreamer. All of the studies on which these conclusions are based relate waking and dreaming thought. We want to review a series of studies which we believe explore even more directly the relationship between waking and dreaming thought.

B. Clinical Utility and Uniqueness of Dream Reports

In a number of reports we have illustrated the clinical value of obtaining dream material from the patient (Kramer, 1966; Kramer, Ornstein, Whitman, & Baldridge, 1967; Whitman, Kramer, & Baldridge, 1969; Whitman, Kramer, Ornstein, & Baldridge, 1967; Whitman, Kramer, Ornstein, & Baldridge, 1970). The dream can contribute to the diagnostic process, to our understanding of the patient's psychodynamics, to an understanding of the transference that may develop, to possible counter-transference issues, and to treatment planning. We were persuaded of the clinical utility of dreams but wanted to see if the dream made a unique contribution to the process of clinical assessment.

We explored whether examining REM dream reports systematically contributed to the psychological understanding of the dreamer and, if it did, was its contribution unique or essentially the same as other types of information about the patient. To pursue this question we compared inferences drawn from different sources about the dreamer. We had three volunteer patients who were in psychotherapy sleep in the sleep lab and collected five REM dreams from each (Kramer, Roth, Clark, & Trinder, 1972). The clinical history of the patient was provided by the intake psychiatrist, the therapists' notes from his interviews were made available, and a clinical psychologist prepared a report about each patient based on a Thematic Apperception Test (TAT) and a Rorschach test he had administered.

Using a 100-item Q sort which describes attributes a patient might have, four judges independently sorted the items basing their judgments on the information source provided: (1) dream reports, (2) projective test report, (3) clinical history, and (4) psychiatric interview notes. Each judge blindly and randomly sorted each information source for each patient. A correlation for each information source was done among the four judges' results and then averaged across the four sources. The correlation of the judges' sorts for each data source was significant as was the average correlation for the four data sources. Psychological tests correlated with the clinical history and with psychiatric interview notes in all three subjects. The dream report based item sorts correlated with other data sources in only one of the three cases.

The inference drawn from this pilot study was that dreams may provide in some cases a similar picture as other data sources about the dreamer. However, dreams may potentially add a different dimension than projective tests, therapist interviews, and clinical history which tend to lead to similar inferences. Cartwright (Cartwright, 1969) has pointed out that no relationship between dreams and projective tests has been effectively demonstrated. She is of the opinion that this is due to the lack of the necessary state conditions of high cerebral arousal and low sensory arousal present during dreaming but absent during psychological testing. Cartwright's view would be consonant with our finding that dreams do not mirror other information sources about patients. Beck, in his discussion of Cartwright's paper (Beck, 1969), makes the point that in patients his studies have shown that the cognitive schema operative awake and in dreaming are similar if not identical. Subsequently, we reviewed some 28 studies that compared non-laboratory studies of dreaming with other psychological measures (Winget & Kramer, 1979) and that of the 20 that addressed the issue of the relationship of psychological test data to dream content, three quarters showed a positive relationship. Methodological differences among the studies may account for the differences and the different conclusions drawn about the relationship between fantasy as measured in psychological tests and morning reported dreaming and REM collected dreaming. The uniqueness of dreaming remains an intriguing but open question.

C. Trait and State Relationships Between Waking Thought and Dreaming

1. TAT and Dreams (a Trait Relationship)

We were interested in continuing our exploration of the relationship between waking and sleeping mentation. We saw dreams as a fantasy production, and, since we wanted to compare it to a waking fantasy, we chose the TAT as the source of our waking fantasy material for comparison to the content of REM dreams. We tried to take the methodological problems that had been identified into account in our study design. We had 24 subjects of college age, 12 men and 12 women, sleep for three nonconsecutive nights and collected their REM dreams (Kramer, Roth, & Palmer, 1976). The subjects were given a 10-card TAT test, half of them took the test before sleeping in the lab and half afterward. The dream reports and TAT stories were scored on 10 need press variables described by Murray (i.e., abasement, achievement, affiliation, autonomy, aggression, counteraction, deference, dominance, order, and sex). The average TAT story is twice the length of the average dream report and contains more scoreable items. The average intensity score correlation for the 10 variables across the entire group of 24 subjects was a significant 0.72. When the correlations are done separately for men and women, the range of correlations for both the frequency and the intensity of the 10 need press variables were significant and ranged between 0.86 and 0.98. We may safely conclude that waking and sleeping fantasy, at least as indexed by the TAT, are highly related and does not support a view of the dream, at least from a content point of view, as a unique type of fantasy. This would suggest, if fantasy is all of a whole, that studying the function of waking fantasy could contribute to an understanding of dream function. If the TAT is seen as tapping a long range aspect of the personality, then this study of waking and dreaming indicates that they have a trait relationship in addition to the more short term changes of a state relationship that we have already described (e.g., in our showing that dreams of an individual are different night to night).

2. Verbal Samples and Dreams (a State Relationship)

The limitations on our showing a state relationship between waking thought and dreaming would be improved if we could more directly link the content of the two forms of consciousness. Looking at the evening experience as the waking source most likely to be connected to dreaming is suggested by the work of Breger (Breger, Hunter, & Lane, 1971). In a small number of subjects he had shown that the content of thought in subjects who had been placed under intense personal scrutiny in a focus group before going to sleep was thematically represented in their REM dreams that night. Hartmann (Hartmann, 1984), commenting on an extensive set of his own morning recalled dreams, observed that the day residue came most often from some evening experience than one earlier in the day.

We taped 5-minute spontaneous verbal samples from 20 college age women and 20 men immediately before and after they slept in the sleep lab and had REM dreams collected (Kramer, Roth, Arand, & Bonnet, 1981). The content of the 356 dreams and 240 verbal samples were scored with 18 scales of the Hall-Van de Castle (Hall & Van de Castle, 1966) dream content scoring system. The 18 scales included eight characters, five activities, three descriptive elements, one environmental press, and one emotions scale. Across all 40 subjects, we found for all 18 contents a significant total average correlation of 0.31. Nine of the 18 correlations individually were significant and these included total number of characters, individual characters, male characters, female characters, relatives, negatives, location changes, emotions, and verbal activities. The mean of the nine significant correlations was 0.38. The distribution of the 18 correlations was significant. For men, five of the 18 content correlations were significant including total characters, single characters, male characters, negatives, and location change with an average correlation of 0.49. Women had three of 18 content correlations significant including single characters, location change, and total emotions with an average correlation of 0.45. Men had 14 positive and four negative correlations and women had 15 positive and three negative. This distribution of positive correlations is significant. There were no significant differences in the dream/verbal sample content correlations between men and women. It is reasonable to conclude that dream content and aspects of waking thought are significantly related.

We believe the dream-verbal sample study (Kramer, Roth, Arand, & Bonnet, 1981) is a clearer demonstration of a connection between dreaming and waking mentation at the state or short term level as it provides specific content from both waking and sleeping consciousness. It also supports a continuous rather than compensatory view of the relationship as all of the significant relationships are positive (i.e., continuous, and overall 14 of the 18 correlations are positive). We continue to find connections and organization in studies of dreaming and it serves to bolster our understanding of the dreaming experience as an orderly process, not a random one. The content areas of connection between waking and dreaming in men and women certainly are interesting as they point to characters as central to our preoccupations awake or asleep with men being more critical and women more concerned about feelings while the setting of the dream experience is unstable for both. Awake or asleep, life is with people in a changing evaluative context.

3. Thematic Connections Between Waking Thought and Dream Content

We had shown a clear specific content connection between waking thought and dreaming. We wondered if there were thematic similarities between waking thought and dreams (Kramer, Moshiri, & Scharf, 1982). To test for that possibility, we collected 5-minute verbal samples from 10 women and 10 men before and after sleeping in the sleep lab for three nonconsecutive nights where they had their REM dreams collected from each of the first four REM periods of the night. The contents of the verbal samples and the dream report of each subject were searched for thematic similarities. The percentage similarities by individual were determined. We found thematic similarities between night and morning verbal samples in 95% of the subjects and dream-to-dream similarity in 75% suggesting that thematically waking thought, although further apart in time, is more connected than dreaming thought which is more diverse or diffused. The thematic connection between night verbal samples and dreams was found in 85% of subjects while dreams have a thematic connection to morning verbal samples in 70% of subjects. Thematically the dream appears more reactive to waking thought at night than proactive to morning waking thought.

4. Inability to Predict Hypnotically Induced Psychological Conflict in Dreams

My colleagues did a study (Whitman, Ornstein, & Baldridge, 1964) in which subjects were hypnotized and had a psychological conflict, of a type similar to what has been described by French (French, 1952), implanted from one of 25 conflicts such as independent strivings versus the need to be dependent. They were told they would immediately have a dream about the intense conflict. They did and reported the dream while still hypnotized. They were then made amnesic for the entire hypnotic session. They then had a free associative anamnesis type interview and slept that night for REM dream collection. They were tested for amnesia by questioning after the hypnotic session and at the start of the interview. The hypnotic session dream, the interview, and the REM dream reports were recorded, transcribed, and coded. The task for the two psychoanalyst judges was to select the implanted conflict from the predetermined list of 25, first from each part of the data separately (i.e., only the interview, or only the hypnotic dream, or only the REM dreams, and then from all the material). All the material rated by the judges was consistently less than chance. They were given feedback about their results and, again, did less well than chance in their judgments. The failure to achieve even a modicum of accuracy in selection of the conflict was so discouraging that it was never reported. I was familiar with the study as I had prepared and analyzed the data. In a personal communication to Tart (Tart, 1979), the senior author indicated that the "complex and contradictory" results lead to a discontinuation of the project.

D. The Relationship Between Affect Awake and Sleep-Physiology and Psychology

I had wanted to explore French's concept of the focal conflict (French, 1952) in dreams to establish how the conflict is processed across the night (i.e., solved or not) and leads to psychologically successful or unsuccessful outcomes. Once I had such a clear demonstration that consensus on what the conflict might be was not attainable, even when only a fixed number of conflicts were possible, I knew I had to find another option. I reasoned that a conflict had to have an accompanying feeling state (e.g., fear, anger, anxiety, unhappiness, or others). There were affective adjective checklists that were quantifiable reliable and valid (Nowlis, 1970). I selected the Clyde Mood Scale (Clyde, 1963; Roehrs, Kramer, Lefton, Lutz, & Roth, 1973) to index the affective state of the person, as I couldn't count on establishing the focal conflict, to then relate the affective state to dream content. The Clyde Mood Scale is made up of 48 adjectives describing how a person feels each of which is rated as not at all, a little, quite a lot, or extremely. The results of standardizing studies have been factor analyzed to produce six major factors: friendly, aggressive, clear thinking or alert, sleepy, unhappy, and dizzy or anxious.

1. The Relationship of Pre-Sleep Mood to Post-Sleep Mood

The initial issue was to see what, if any, relationship pre-sleep mood had to post-sleep mood. This would lend support to our looking at intervening events, sleep, and dreams, as possibly accounting for or being related to any affective change that may occur from night to morning. Our subjects were eight men: four aged 20, two aged 50, and two aged 70. They slept 15 nights in the sleep lab and filled out the Clyde Mood Scale immediately before and on awakening in the morning (Roth & Kramer, 1976). We found the six mood subscales to be different from each other in intensity and variability and that the night scores were different from the morning scores along the same dimensions of intensity and variability. Mood scores were largely higher and more variable at night than in the morning. The sleepy subscale was higher in the morning than at night, while the other five were higher at night and decreased in the morning. The significant mean scale changes were in the sleepy, unhappy, and friendly subscales. The variability in all the subscales decreased across the night. The sleepy subscale was higher in the morning because of how close to awakening the rating was made. A replication with 11 college age male subjects who slept 15 nights and did Clyde Mood scales before and after sleep gave essentially identical results. The mood change across the night shows a decrease in level and variability suggesting a funneling effect as if sleep was acting like a regulator, sort of an "emotional thermostat" that resets how a person feels each morning. Mood changes in intensity and variability across the night were consistent and supported the possibility that a relationship existed between an affective aspect of wakefulness, in addition to thought, and the sleep that intervened.

We wanted to look at the relationship of pre-sleep mood to post-sleep mood in female subjects as well (Kramer, Sepate, & Leavengood, 1990). We collected Clyde Mood Scales before and after sleep from 15 women between the ages of 19 and 52 sleeping at home for 21 consecutive days. We averaged each subject's score on each of the six mood subscales: friendly, aggressive, unhappy, sleepy, clear-thinking, and dizzy for their 21 night and morning scores and did a between subject rank order correlation for each subscale. All the between subject correlations were significant, but sleepy (0.15). The significant correlations ranged from a low of 0.53 for dizzy to a high of 0.93 for friendly. The average within subject correlation night to morning for each of the 15 subjects for each of the six mood scales found the only significant subscale was unhappy (0.46). The average mood is stable between individuals but highly variable within an individual, except for the unhappy aspect of mood. All subjects have at least two significant night morning correlations but the significant aspect of mood varies from person to person. Mood relationships across a night reflect both trait and state aspects of the individual. How a person feels before and after sleep is different from person to person but varies within a person day to day. This combination of stability and variability in feeling state is similar to what we found for dreams (Kramer & Roth, 1979) and for sleep (Roth, Kramer, & Roehrs, 1977). The relationship between waking thought and feeling and aspects of sleep appear to show similarities in form, stability, and variability but whether they are interrelated remains our question.

2. The Effect of Sleep Deprivation on Mood Change

If sleep was involved with the change in mood from night to morning, we should be able to show an effect on mood from sleep deprivation. We had 11 college age male volunteers complete a Clyde Mood Scale at home before going to sleep and on awakening in the morning (Roth, Kramer, & Lutz, 1976). They came to the lab and were kept awake as a group all of the next night. They filled out the mood scale at the time they would have gone to bed and again in the morning when they would have awakened. They then slept at home on the next, or recovery, night filling out mood forms before sleep and on awakening. The study was repeated one week later. There was an effect on mood at night, namely that the sleepy score on the deprivation night was lower probably an alerting effect in anticipation of being awake all night. The morning mood scores indicated that the sleepy score was higher on the morning following deprivation than on the baseline or recovery mornings, showing that mood was sensitive to one night of sleep deprivation. The friendly score was higher following the deprivation night than on the baseline morning but not after the recovery night, probably reflecting the fact that the deprivation was done in a group. The aggressive scores were higher after deprivation than at baseline or after recovery. One night of sleep deprivation leaves the subject feeling sleepy and angry. Whether it is the loss of the physiological or psychological aspects of sleep that are related to the change in feeling remains to be demonstrated. In addition to a content relationship between waking thought and dreams, the probability is again demonstrated of an affective relationship between waking and sleep.

3. Pilot Studies of Mood Change and Sleep Psychology and Physiology

a. Mood Change and Dreams   We had linked the change of feelings from night to morning, to what all people know intuitively, to the intervening period of sleep. Our next task was to make explicit whether the relationship was to the psychology of sleep (i.e., dreaming) and/or to the physiology of sleep as it is currently quantified (i.e., various sleep stages). As a beginning, we collected the REM dreams of two men who slept in the lab for 20 consecutive nights and filled out Clyde Mood Scales before and after sleeping (Kramer & Roth, 1973). They were awakened from each of the first four REM periods for dream collection. The dream reports had been recorded and were transcribed and coded and scored blindly with the scales of the Hall-Van de Castle dream scoring system. We correlated for each subject the rank order of the average frequency of 31 Hall-Van de Castle dream content scores (Hall & Van de Castle, 1966), 12 character subscales, 9 activities subscales, and 10 descriptive elements subscales for each of the 20 nights to the rank order of the average night to morning mood difference scores for each subject on each of the six mood subscales (unhappy, friendly, aggressive, clear-thinking, sleepy, and dizzy). Overall, the total number of significant correlations was 54, with 92% involving the character dream content scales or the unhappy mood subscale, and 26% of the significant correlations were directly between the two, characters and unhappy. Our pilot study showed the connection between change in feeling state in waking to the intervening dream content particularly to who was in the dream and how much happier the dreamer was in the morning. A promising beginning, but we only had studied two subjects and we had no idea whether the physiology of sleep participated in the change in feelings as well.

b. Mood Change and Sleep Physiology (Sleep Stages) In another pilot study, we explored the relationship between the physiology of sleep (i.e., total sleep time, the stages of sleep, and the number of awakenings) and the difference in the six mood subscale scores across the night (Kramer & Roth, 1973). We recorded the sleep of six men who slept for 15 nights and filled out Clyde Mood Scales before and after sleeping. We correlated for each subject the rank order of the average of each of the five sleep measures to the rank order of the average mood difference score on each of the six subscales. Overall, we obtained 26 significant correlations, with 69% involving either the sleepy mood subscale or total sleep time, with 22% of the significant correlations being between total sleep time and the sleepy subscale of mood. In these two pilot studies, the mood subscale most involved with dreaming is unhappy and with sleep physiology it is sleepy. This opens the possibility that there is a differential effect of mood on the two aspects of sleep, dreaming and sleep physiology. For us, these results provided an intriguing possibility. Might this account for the "I slept long enough but I am still feeling down" sensation that many people experience?

c. Differential Relationship of Mood Change to Dreams and Sleep Stages It appeared at this point that the change in various aspects of feelings across the night was differentially related to dreams and sleep. We found that the distribution of the actual frequencies of the significant correlations was different in the two pilot studies of dreaming and sleep physiology (see Table 9.1) (Kramer & Roth, 1973). It suggested that the change across the

Table 9.1 Percentage of Significant Correlations with Each Mood Subscale Change from the Dream and Sleep Pilot Studies

Mood Subscales	Dream	Sleep
Unhappy	43	15
Friendly	15	7
Aggressive	16	7
Clear-thinking	6	19
Sleepy	9	27
Dizzy	11	25

Note: Chi square performed on actual frequencies shows the frequencies to be significantly different, $p < .05$.

night in the mood subscales unhappy, friendly, and aggressive was more likely related to the dreams of the night and the change in the sleepy dizzy and clear-thinking mood subscales to the physiology of sleep. We had only studied 8 subjects, 2 in the dream pilot study and 6 in the sleep pilot, and a larger number of subjects needed to be studied to ensure the validity of our observations.

4. Mood Change and Sleep Physiology Study

We undertook to expand our two pilot studies. We looked at the mood change physiology of sleep relationship first as a matter of personal convenience; it is an easier study to do as it requires no nighttime awakenings. We had 15 men sleep for 15 consecutive nights in the lab and recorded their sleep, and they filled out Clyde Mood Scales before and after sleeping (Kramer, Roehrs, & Roth, 1976). The sleep records were scored reliably for seven sleep parameters: (1) total sleep time, (2) stage one time, (3) stage two time, (4) stage three/four time, (5) stage REM time, (6) sleep latency, and (7) REM latency. We found significant correlations between the sleep parameters overall and the mood subscale differences on four of the six subscales: sleepy (0.42), friendly (0.42), aggressive (0.26), and clear-thinking (0.26). The correlations ranged from 0.42 to 0.22 for unhappy and 0.20 for dizzy (see Table 9.2). The two highest correlations, sleepy and friendly, were significantly different than the two lowest ones, unhappy and dizzy, supporting a differential relationship between mood change and sleep and leaving open the possibility that the other aspects of mood such as unhappy may be related to dreams.

We were curious as to whether a differential relation among the sleep parameters to the mood changes across the night would be found. The sleep parameters stage two, stage three/four, and sleep latency significantly predict mood changes but total sleep time, stage one time, stage REM time, or REM latency do not. It is worth noting that it is only non-REM sleep that is related to the mood changes and that REM sleep and unhappy mood are not involved. The correlations between mood change and sleep variables

Table 9.2 Multiple Correlation Coefficients Between Sleep Parameters and Mood Subscale Differences

	Sleepy	Friendly	Aggressive	Clear-thinking	Unhappy	Dizzy
r =	0.42**	0.42**	0.26*	0.26*	0.22	0.20

* $p < .05$
**$p < .01$

in individual subjects is considerably higher, 0.70–0.80, than the 0.42 we found for the group. Intersubject variability is what probably accounts for the difference in correlative levels and it needs to be explored and clarified. There are a number of conditions in which waking mood is altered and the relationship between mood change and sleep should be explored (e.g., in insomnia, drug addiction, and depression) to see if the possible mood regulatory function of sleep has been changed, disrupted, or exceeded.

5. *Mood Change and Dream Content Study*

We next turned our attention to expanding our dream-mood change pilot study. We had 12 male college students sleep for 20 consecutive nights in the sleep lab and they had their dreams collected from the first four REM periods of the night (Kramer & Roth, 1980). They also completed the Clyde Mood Scale before and after sleeping. The dreams were scored with 32 subscales of the Hall-Van de Castle dream content scoring system (Hall & Van de Castle, 1966) and included 8 character subscales, 9 activity subscales, and 15 descriptive elements subscales. We correlated for each subject (12) the mood change score on each of the mood subscales (6) with the subjects' scores on each of the dream scales (32) averaged across the 20 nights. We found that overall mood change and dream content are significantly related. It was the change in the mood subscales (unhappy, sleepy, aggressive, dizzy, and clear-thinking) that were significantly related to dream content. The distribution of the number of correlations across the six mood subscales was significantly different. In particular, the number of correlations with dream content was significantly different and higher for the unhappy mood subscale. The dream content scales that were significantly related to mood change were characters and activity. The significant content scale correlations are proportionately distributed across the three scales (characters, activities and descriptive elements) and are not significantly different from each other. However, the correlations with mood change were significantly different across the character subscales. And it was the relationship between the character's subscales and the change in the unhappy mood subscale that was significantly different. We found a striking confirmation of our results from the pilot study (Kramer & Roth, 1973) in our replication study. The change in mood across the night is correlated with the dreams of the night and, in particular, the change in unhappiness from night to morning relates to the characters that appear in the dreams of that night.

Conclusion

It appeared to us that we have shown there is a clear, regular, and significant relationship between waking thought (i.e., cognition, waking feelings, and dreaming). Scores on the unhappiness mood subscale are reduced across the night and related most particularly to the characters that appear in the intervening dreams. Sleepiness changes across the night appear related to the amount of non-REM sleep one obtains. Sleep may act as a selective affective regulator with its psychological dimension directed at feelings of unhappiness and its physiological dimension directed at feelings of sleepiness. The question of sleep function will be addressed more specifically in chapter 10.

It is of some interest to observe that in two clinical situations in which there was an intensified mood, a relationship between dreaming and mood was found. In our analysis of the work of Miller and Buckley (Kramer, Brunner, & Trinder, 1971), some of the clinical changes in dreaming they described as the patient moved from his depressed to his manic phase were confirmed with content analysis. More specifically, we showed changes in dream content in hospitalized depressed patients treated with imipramine (Kramer, Whitman, Baldridge, & Ornstein, 1968). Changes in dream content track changes in mood in the patient with an affective disorder and may be involved in the process directly or serve as a window on the process of change.

CHAPTER **10**

Dream Meaning

A. Do Dreams Have the Necessary Order to Support Meaning?

The question that inevitably arises when the dreamer reflects on or shares his dream with another person is what is the meaning of that dream. This view is reflected in the observation in the Talmud that "A dream that is not interpreted is like a letter that is not read."

However, there are two concepts that need to be recognized as a basis for an exploration of the meaning of dreams. First, for dreams to have meaning requires that dreams be orderly and organized and nonrandom. Second, meaning does not exist in dreams but is brought to the dream by the interpreter who applies some external system of meaning. This latter point is captured as well in the Talmud when it is observed that the dream follows its interpretation.

1. Evidence to Support that Dreams Are Orderly

Dreams have been shown to reflect psychological differences and to be structured events in our studies of (1) the organization of dreams across the REM period (Kramer, Czaya, Arand, & Roth, 1974); (2) the differences in dream content in each REM period across the night (Kramer, McQuarrie, & Bonnet, 1981); (3) the differences in dream content night to night within an individual (Kramer, Hlasny, Jacobs, & Roth, 1976); (4) the correlation of dream content night to night within an individual (Kramer & Roth, 1979); (5) the differences in dream content among individuals, whether normal or mentally ill (Kramer, Hlasny, Jacobs, & Roth, 1976); and (6) the differences in dream content among groups based on demographic variables (sex, age, social class) (Winget, Kramer, & Whitman, 1972) and mental illness variables (schizophrenia and depression) (Kramer, Baldridge, Whitman, Ornstein, & Smith, 1969; Kramer & Roth, 1973). The observations that dreams are structured and show differences and connections lends credence to the possibility that dreams may have meaning.

2. Evidence to Support Dreams Are Responsive

There are a number of studies that have demonstrated that dreams are responsive to significant (i.e., emotional) concerns of the dreamer. The meaning of dreams may lie in viewing them as an emotionally determined response to a significant event. We have shown that (1) it is the more emotionally rated experience of the day that is found in the dreams of the night (Piccione, Jacobs, Kramer, & Roth, 1977); (2) judges can distinguish the reflections of significant, immediate (Kramer, Roth, & Cisco, 1977), and ongoing (Piccione, Thomas, Roth, & Kramer, 1976) emotional events in dreams (e.g., the beginning and ending of the laboratory experience and the impact of the laboratory as an ongoing experience); (3) charged interpersonal experiences influence the content and reporting of the dream (e.g., the choice of the dream to be reported in therapy) (Whitman, Kramer, & Baldridge, 1963b), the impact of the supervisory experience in psychotherapy (Whitman, Kramer, & Baldridge, 1963a), and the relationship in the laboratory of the dreamer to the experimenter (Fox, Kramer, Baldridge, Whitman, & Ornstein, 1968); (4) mood altering drugs change dream content (Kramer, Whitman, Baldridge, & Ornstein, 1968); and (5) the dream experience, as it is occurring, can be influenced by meaningful input (Kinney, Kramer, & Bonnet, 1981; Kramer, Kinney, & Scharf, 1983; Kinney, Kramer) (e.g., the differential incorporation of names based on meaning).

3. Evidence to Support Dreams Are Linked to Waking Life

It is in connection to our waking lives that we seek the meaning of dreams. We have done a number of studies that have looked at the relationship of dreaming to our waking experience. We have found that (1) both similar and different inferences can be drawn about a patient from dreams as from psychological testing and clinical history (Kramer, Roth, Clark, & Trinder, 1972); (2) dreams reveal both trait and state connections between waking and dreaming, the TAT study showed a significant correlation between dream content and TAT stories (Kramer, Roth, & Palmer, 1976), and the verbal sample study showed a significant correlation between dream content and the content of verbal samples (Kramer, Roth, Arand, & Bonnet, 1981); (3) waking mood and dreams are related (Kramer & Roth, 1980), dreams reflect state changes in a patient with a manic depressive disorder

(Kramer, Brunner, & Trinder, 1971), and dream content changes when the patient's depression changes in response to anti-depressant medication (Kramer, Whitman, Baldridge, & Ornstein, 1968); and (4) most people (70%–85%) show a thematic connection between waking and dreaming mentation (Kramer, Moshiri, & Scharf, 1982).

The dream has the necessary relationships to contain psychological meaning. It is an orderly event that is structured and reflects important psychological differences, responds to immediate emotional concerns, and is significantly related to the waking preoccupations of the dreamer.

4. Source of Dream Meaning

In searching for the meaning of dreams, it is necessary to recognize that meaning does not exist in dreams but is brought to dreams from some external system of meaning. The various interpretive systems (e.g., the in-depth psychological ones) are meaning systems employed to explain and to give meaning to behavior outside of dreams. It is the understanding of these meaning systems (e.g., Adlerian, Freudian, Jungian, or personal) that is brought to the dream by the interpreter, whether trained or naïve.

The ancient dream interpreters had a code book (Van de Castle, 1994) which was of greater or lesser sophistication to extract meaning from dreams (White, 1990). The modern depth psychologist applies his system, associationist or amplifying, to dreams with a more or less well defined notion of what meaning is and when one has found it. I have described a system to establish the meaning of dreams (Kramer, 1991, 1993; Kramer & Roth, 1977) based on treating the dream as a figure of speech, utilizing neo-Freudian interpersonal parameters of psychological significance as the endpoints, and assuming a relatively strict determinism in approaching the actual dream text. The approach can result in establishing a meaning which can often fit well into the ongoing life of the dreamer. It is this system of "dream translation" that is illustrated in the example in the next section.

B. "A Dream Translation"—Establishing the Meaning of a Dream

The question that a dreamer is most likely to ask about a dream he has had is not why he can't remember it, or how can he measure it, or the other questions we have discussed so far, but rather what his dream means. The following dream was reported by a 26-year-old Vietnam War veteran to his psychiatrist at a VA hospital where he had just been admitted (Kramer & Roth, 1977).

> I dreamed I was back in Vietnam and I had thrown a grenade into one of the Vietnamese huts. I went inside and there was one of the babies blown up all over the inside of the hut. I woke up and was terrified, nauseated, and crying.

The dream was presented by the psychiatrist who was treating the dreamer to a group teaching conference on how to approach a dream report to establish a possible meaning without the participation of the patient. The psychiatrist read the dream to the group a phrase at a time in the order he had recorded it. He provided no additional information about the dreamer until the discussion about the dream and dreamer was concluded. The group responded by providing their associations to the report to develop a substitute text of meaning for the actual dream text. I have called this substitute text a "dream translation" to distinguish it from an interpretation. The underlying assumption is that the "meaning is in the metaphor" that is the dream.

1. Translation of the Veteran's Dream

The patient begins his dream report by placing himself in a foreign environment of danger, a war zone, and indicates he has been there before. The focus for him may be the fact that this is away from his current setting and it may, therefore, have an escape or desirable implication. However, the initial impression of being in a familiar, dangerous, destructive situation is the most striking possibility. The patient then throws a grenade into one of the Vietnamese huts. The patient, without apparent duress, engages in this aggressive, potentially destructive act. If one makes the inference that the patient is in the military, then the act of aggression and potential destructiveness is a sanctioned act in keeping with his work as a soldier. It is not an unbridled outburst of hostility, but a controlled and legitimate undertaking. The controlled or channeled nature of the destructive act may be of importance. It could avoid feelings of loss of control and it could serve to deal with issues of guilt or fears of retaliation. The plea or rationale might be, "it was my duty to engage in such potentially unacceptable acts for which I cannot be held personally culpable. It is the honorable thing for me to do." It is the difference between a madman with a butcher knife and a surgeon with a scalpel. The vehicle used for the expression of feeling is likely to reveal something about the person and the feeling itself because they are considered to be determined and not random choices.

A comment should be made about the attack being at a distance. It is not from direct contact but from something thrown that the damage will come. It is safer than hand-to-hand combat. Must he, for some reason, be distant from his destructiveness?

One of the Vietnamese huts is the object of the aggressive or destructive impulse. It is not his own, but that of the other. If we assume that our patient is an American soldier, a not unreasonable one as he is in a VA hospital, then the assault is on the non-American object, the foreign, the different, the strange. It is not an American but a foreign object that is attacked. It remains unclear what the foreign refers to at this point.

Further, in speculating about the object which is attacked, it is of interest that it is not a person being thrown at, but an inanimate object. Grenades are not usually thrown at empty huts, although that is possible to prevent the later use of the hut by the enemy. It is a reasonable inference that the patient is overtly concerned with a possible occupant of the hut. Nevertheless, the object of the assault is a relatively impersonal inanimate thing. Is this impersonal assault reflective of some discomfort about or disguise of aggressive impulses directed at some person? Given our explanatory system, it is people not things that matter, so that speculation must be given some credence, but at this time it can be given little further specification.

One further specification could be in relation to the relatively fragile implication of the idea of a "hut," a hut is hardly a house. Is delicacy implied? In addition, it is just one of the huts, not a specific hut, not personal in nature. Does the impersonal nature of the hut indicate that it makes no difference, or does it perhaps make too much of a difference?

If the hut is given a symbolic interpretation, some further specification can be made. The notion of the hut as a building being a person is well explicated by Freud in his dream book (Freud, 1955). This speculation would allow us to recast the dream into a sanctioned assault on a foreign, strange, distant, exotic, perhaps, fragile person.

Our attacker from a distance enters the scene of his destructive or potentially destructive act. Is this simply appropriate behavior? Is it curiosity, or whatever else one can think of? Nevertheless he enters the place of his aggressive action.

The scene is one of infanticide. "One of the babies (is) blown up all over the inside of the hut." To everyone this is a horrible sight. It is not the noble work of a warrior hero. No affect is expressed at this point. Not unusual for a dream. Affects, according to Freud (Freud, 1955), are generally muted in the manifest content compared to the latent dream text.

The baby in the hut is confirmation of the symbolic speculation that the hut may be representative of a person particularly a woman. Our assumption that we may be dealing with a woman and perhaps a uterus is simply that the only place, from a biological point of view, that contains a baby is a uterus, and that the only possessors of uteri are women. One should note that it is "one of the babies," perhaps implying others were present.

The child is "splattered" over the inside of the hut. If the hut is a woman, then a splattered child inside is a dead child in a mother, and the next idea is of an abortion, or a macerated fetus.

Perhaps we can take our translation a bit further at this point. Our patient has committed a sanctioned, aggressive (destructive) act, at a distance, against a fragile possibly pregnant woman and caused her (perhaps unborn) child to die or abort. Implied again, is the fact that he doesn't want to be held responsible for the act.

The last line of the dream report indicates that the dream ended in the dreamer awakening, feeling terrified, nauseated, and crying. From a psychoanalytic perspective, these awakening feelings are part of the dream and are not to be seen as reactions to the dream. Either way, the affect did appear and would be seen as appropriate to the content of the dream. The least altered aspect of the dream, Freud says, is the affect (Freud, 1955). To be terrified, nauseated, and tearful if one has "splattered" a baby with a grenade would be considered the appropriate affective response.

What of the awakening? It is a failure, well-recognized by Freud (Freud, 1955), in the function of the dream. The dream is a protector of sleep and not a disturber, provided it can meet the demands of the censorship and discharge the desire for gratification in the unconscious without arousing too much affect. If not, the dream fails its sleep protective function and an awakening from an anxiety dream occurs.

2. Formulation

What kind of man is our patient based on the "dream translation"? He is one concerned about his hostile impulses in relationship to mothers and particularly their children. From a psychogenetic perspective, he is, most likely, not the youngest child in his family. He might well have experienced displacement by younger siblings with relative hostility, at least at the fantasy level, directed at his mother and/or siblings. We noted the possibility of more than one baby earlier. The anxiety dream and the impersonal, sanctioned, distant mode of hostility, both suggest he finds the hostility intolerable. This was considered an appropriate stopping point. One could pursue a number of other dynamic speculations. One could extrapolate from the dream translation implications for transference, counter-transference, clinical diagnosis (a traumatic neurosis?), and treatment planning.

3. Therapist's History, Formulation, and Comment

This was the first VA hospital admission for this 26-year-old white male. He was brought to the admitting area late at night on September 6, 1974 in an ambulance by his girlfriend. At that time, he stated that he was afraid that he was going to hurt himself or others. On the evening of the admission, he was with his girlfriend at a war veterans club and was talking about the war. He found himself getting increasingly anxious and he finally went home. The patient said he began drinking, became more and more fearful, tried to go to bed and sleep, but he had vivid dreams about the war and killing. His girlfriend became frightened and called an ambulance. The patient was taken to the hospital and admitted.

a. Brief History of the Present Illness   The patient was in the Army as a rifleman in Vietnam in the later part of 1970. The last 12 months of his stay in Vietnam were in a heavy combat zone. While there, he was injured several times and a number of his friends were killed. He was awarded several medals for his service, which he keeps on his Army shirt at home. Now, when he looks at the medals, he gets very anxious. He married his second and present wife 4 months after returning from the service. In late 1972 while bowling with his wife, the people at the bowling alley began talking about the war. He started to get anxious and wanted to leave. His wife did not. He became more anxious, and the evening culminated in his hitting her in the back of the head with his fist, causing a large cut. He stated he went out of his mind with anxiety and fear while he was on the way to the hospital with his wife.

b. Past History   The patient is of a rural background. He is the oldest of nine children. His childhood was characterized by disagreements with his father, an alcoholic. His father was out of the home much of the time, but would come back for brief periods, often getting his mother pregnant. During those times, the patient would often find himself in the position of protecting his mother and would actually hit his father and run, fearful that if his father caught him he would kill him.   When he was 10 years old, he had to help his mother give birth because the doctor could not come and they were unable to get her to the hospital in time. He knew a great deal about the delivery of babies already because of animals on their farm. He reported that his mother had lost several children in the past through miscarriage, but none of the ones he had helped deliver.

c. Hospital Course   The patient talked at length about his military service, of the many friends that he saw killed and mutilated, and of the people he was told to torture. He stated that he would be terrified and confused at times. In addition, he shamefully noted that many times he actually got pleasure out of the killings and mutilations that he was ordered to do. He had a great deal of grief over these feelings of pleasure because they were in contrast to his pre-war ideals. He thought these ideals were now destroyed and he would never be at peace with himself again.   Just prior to enlistment, he and his first wife were not getting along very well. About 6 months before enlistment, he accidentally caused his wife to lose their baby. He was told that the miscarriage was the result of his breaking her membranes during intercourse.

d. Concluding Remarks   The patient's psychiatrist stated that he was in almost total agreement with our thoughts on the dream, though there was little content about the father. However, that in a sense seemed to the psychiatrist to be a separate problem. The psychiatrist noted that in session six, the patient reported a dream similar to the one presented here which was from session two, only the child in his dream was his daughter and he was terrified and revolted by the dream.

The descriptive historical material provided by the psychiatrist is provocative and superficially congruent with the "dream translation." Unfortunately, no explicit formulation was provided to specify more particularly the correctness of the translation. The psychiatrist was in his first 6 months of training and the lack of a definitive and more sophisticated formulation is understandable.

The word length of the effort to understand a dream is significantly longer than the description of the dream experience. The dream report of our veteran patient has 47 words and the dream translation included 1,353 words for a multiple of 28.8. The ratio of the words in Freud's associations to the word length of the Irma dream was 18.2 (Freud, 1955).

C. The Assumptions and Guidelines for Applying a Dream Translation

1. The Differences Between an Interpretation and a Translation

The traditional position taken in regard to the dream is that without the dreamer's associations little light can be shed on the meaning of the dream (Fliess, 1953; Freud, 1955). The associational methodology is of great value in direct therapeutic work with patients, as it involves the patient collaboratively in the search for meaning and enhances the patient's conviction as to the validity of what is found.

We have tried to show with the illustration in the previous section; that a meaning for the dream relatable to the dreamer's waking life can be established even without the patient's associations. We have called the methodology a "dream translation" in order to (1) distinguish it from a dream interpretation which requires the dreamer's associations, (2) call attention to its similarities to symbol interpretation that Freud called a "translation," and (3) to capitalize on a nuance in the philological difference between interpretation and translation, which is also captured in the difference between the two methods. Namely, that interpretation is a collaborative process, i.e., a negotiation between patient and therapist, requiring the patient's cooperation, while a translation is a transfer from one text to another and is done independently of the patient.

2. Assumptions Made to Establish Dream Meaning

All attempts to understand and find meaning in the dream assume certain things about the nature of the dream experience. First, that there *is* a dream experience. Second, that the dream report is an adequate reflection of that experience. And third, that an examination of that experience will lead to a meaning for the report. The first assumption is supported by experimental work that confirms that the dream experience occurs (Jones, 1970), is extended in time (Foulkes, 1966), and has a developmental course (Kramer, Roth, & Czaya, 1975). The second assumption finds support in the work that confirms a relationship between the experience and report of the dream (Kramer, Kinney, & Scharf, 1983; Kinney, Kramer, Bonnet, 1981). And the third by the work that points out that the dream is a non-random event (Kramer, Hlasny, Jacobs, & Roth, 1976) and relatable to the waking subjective life of the dreamer (Kramer & Roth, 1980).

3. Specific Dream Translation Methodology

a. Assumptions: Deterministic and Causal   The "dream translation" methodology has a particular series of assumptions, orientations, and rules that serve to guide the translation. There are three deterministic and causal assumptions: (1) that the dream report is determined, (2) that the order of elements in the dream report is determined, and (3) that the order of elements in the dream report is causal. These assumptions are not in accord with the psychoanalytic position about the manifest dream report. Psychoanalytic theory rejects the notion that all elements are similarly determined and that the order is determined and that the sequence is causally related. The assumptions in a dream translation require that all the material be systematically examined and the actual relationships in the dream report be taken into account. This avoids wild speculation and forces a dynamic view of the dream elements

b. Viewpoints and Responsive Roles   Establishing dream meaning can be approached from one of three psychological points of view and from any of three responsive roles that dreams may play in the mental economy of the dreamer. The three psychological orientations with which the translator can approach the dream are (1) the interpersonal, i.e., the dreamer in relationship to other things or people, the Jungian objective interpretation (Jung, 1956); (2) the intra-psychic, i.e., the dream is read as if the parts of the dream are to be seen as aspects of the dreamer and highlights the internal conflicts of the dreamer, the Jungian subjective interpretation (Jung, 1956); and (3) the narcissistic or self-psychological, i.e., the dream is seen as a statement about the dreamer related to vicissitudes of his self-esteem (Kohut, 1971).

The dream may be seen in one of three responsive roles (Breger, Hunter, & Lane, 1971): (1) reflective, i.e., the dream simply displays the preoccupations of the dreamer and the translator's task is to recast the metaphorical language of the dream to capture the meaning; (2) reactive, then the task in addition to undoing the metaphor is to speculate to what in the dreamer's life the dream is a reaction; a view of the dream that is adopted in the problem solving theories of dreaming (French, 1952; Schulman, 1969); (3) If the anticipatory role is adopted by the dream translator, then his additional task is to restate the figurative language of the dream and to speculate on what is being anticipated, i.e., the future goals of the dreamer. This anticipatory role is more often adopted by Adlerian and Jungian therapists than Freudian ones.

None of the responsive roles of dreaming are enough in themselves to demonstrate a functional role for dreaming. Dreaming to be functional must contribute to the adaptive capacity of the dreamer. In Piagetian terms (Piaget, 1962), for dreams to be functional, they must be assimilative, accommodative, or both.

The dream's meaning can be approached from any of the three points of view or roles that the translator chooses. The context or goal may guide the translator's choices.

c. Rules for Doing a Dream Translation   The dream interpreter and translator both assume that the meaning of the dream is other than what is apparent from a literal reading of the dream text. The dream translator makes no assumption as to the reason or purpose of the metaphorical nature of the dream report and does not preclude the possibility that the dream is a dynamically disguised product of a latent text. The approach to the dream text by the dream translator is to consider the text as a figurative statement (Fromm, 1951; Sharpe, 1951). The translator substitutes his own controlled associations to the elements of the dream text for those of the dreamer's. He tries to elaborate the maximum number of associations to each element of the text that he can.

The dream translator recognizes the danger if he does not use the associations of the dreamer to establish meaning is that his own personal biases may lead to his reading into the text his own predilections. He also must guard against the application of a too rigidified symbolic approach. And he must be particularly careful to avoid the excessive use of sexual symbols and basic psychogenetic paradigms in the final translation as the resultant translation is then too reductive and removed from the immediate subjective experience of the dreamer to be useful.

It is crucial in examining the dream text to work systematically from the beginning to the end, rather than reading for major themes or headlines (Saul, Snyder, & Sheppard, 1956) or working back and forth from some point of initial understanding (French & Fromm, 1964) in order to capitalize on the hypothesized causal sequence in the text which helps in ordering the translator's thinking. To begin at the beginning spurs as many textual translations, associations, to each element as possible and enables the translator to use later material as confirmatory of prior speculation, thereby assisting him in making choices from among several possibilities. The association of the translator to successive dream elements serves to constrain the possibilities and focus the translation. Moving across the text invites a narrative description of the dream report rather than treating each portion as separately determined as Freud did (Freud, 1955). Freud connected the interpretations to each part of the manifest text using the model of the rebus to create the latent dream text. The connections at the level of the manifest dream report were to be ignored. The secondary revision that Freud finally decided was not part of the dream work is treated in a translation as intrinsic to the process of dreaming and of the search for meaning and expresses the narrative structure of the dream.

The approach of dream translation is based on our common human experience as described by Dilthey (Palmer, 1969) incorporating a cognitive and empathic point of view. The constraining effect of associations to successive parts of the dream directs the search for meaning and is analogous to the corrective value of dialogue to establish meaning described by Schliermacher (Palmer, 1969). Dream translation is a hermeneutic as it is a search for meaning in which the relationship between part and whole determine meaning. We are searching for an understanding that fits the situation of the dreamer and to see how it may be useful. The search for meaning in addition to being denotative is connotative, figurative, and associative. It incorporates the metaphoric structuring of our subjective world (Lakoff & Johnson, 2003) as the meaning of the dream is in the metaphor. The translator needs to be spontaneous in his associations but secondary control is essential. The translator needs to be aware of how his own tendencies toward a positive, negative or sexual bias and the influence of his own recent experience may color his associations. The dream has to be seen as its own context, the translator has to get into the dream experience and have that determine his associations (Jung, 1964). The observation in the Talmud (Talmud) that "The interpretation doesn't create meaning rather interpretation highlights latent elements of meaning already there" captures the essence of the approach. The questions that need to be pursued are related to the dreams responsiveness (i.e., reflective, reactive, or anticipatory). Meaning has to be understood as highly contextual (e.g., is a snake a medical, sexual, or personality reference). The value of starting at the beginning has been noted as it has the constraining effect of successive associations. The choice between possibilities is guided by likelihood. Dreams as texts can have multiple meanings, overinterpretations. The Bible, *Hamlet*, and other texts have been approached from many points of view with different meaning systems (e.g., Marxian, psychological, social, feminine, or Freudian). Overinterpretation was Freud's term for multiple meanings which should be relatable. It often appears in doing a dream translation that the conclusion is implicit in the beginning. Parsimony should operate across the text in establishing a meaning.

The understanding of the structure of dreams by the dream translator provides an additional basis for his controlled associations to the elements of the text. The translator may use one of the theories of depth psychology as he searches for exemplars of the theories basic explanatory paradigms. The basic paradigm in the psychoanalytic theory is the oedipal triangle. Any three-person situation in the dream is potentially oedipal and permits an analysis of the dreamer's oedipal interactions which could contribute to an understanding of the dreamer's attitude toward men, women, authority, dependency, and sexuality, among other aspects of his inner life. Other explicit psychoanalytic paradigms are (1) same and opposite sex pairs, the former being at core homosexual and the latter heterosexual, modified as are all structures by the social context in which they are represented; (2) peers that are potentially sibling in nature; (3) movement that has an attraction-repulsion dimension and implications for desire, longing, and anticipation and rejection, leaving, and separation (Horney, 1945); and (4) activity and passivity that have assertive and receptive implications.

Other psychoanalytic paradigms have an implicit structure. The identification of hostility in the dream invites the assumption of a prior expectation and disappointment associated with the object of the hostility even if the expectation and disappointment are not expressed in the dream. The constellation of which the hostility is the final expression is based on the supposition that behavior is motivated. Dependency is another paradigm with an implicit structure in which a constellation approach is useful. If someone in a dream is dependent, it is reasonable to assume that they are dependent on someone for something, even if the someone and something is not expressed in the dream. The formula "on someone for something" is applicable to any impulse, desire, or action and is derived from the concept that an impulse has an aim and an object.

It may be useful to illustrate paradigms from other theories of depth psychology. The spatial orientation in dreams along an above or below perspective in individual psychology (Adler, 1956; Schulman, 1969) reflects the striving to overcome. From the position of analytic psychology (Jung, 1964) same sex unknown figures in the dream suggest the shadow aspect of the personality.

The dream translator must stay close to the text and only translate what is in the text with the exception of the constellation forms discussed earlier. If an inference is drawn from the text, each step in the process must be spelled out and should remain consistent with the referent and its textual relationships. Cleaving to the rule of translating only what is in the text diminishes wild speculation. The translator cannot deal with the possibility of reversals in the text and "reads" the text as given. However, our knowledge of dream structure does permit us to recognize, in general, that dichotomies are closely if not inevitably linked; when love appears hate is implied. Freud (Freud, 1955) suggested this linkage based on the antithetical meaning of primal words. The translator first responds to the explicit reference of a possible dichotomy and secondarily takes into account the antithetical pole of the dichotomy which is not explicitly present in the text. In attempting to provide a substitute text, the translator applies Occam's law (sometimes the simplest solution is the best) and chooses those inferences that tie together the largest amount of the dream with the fewest assumptions.

d. Role of Psychoanalytic Dream Formation Mechanisms in Dream Translation   In some cases, dream translation views the psychoanalytic dream formation mechanism's condensation, consideration for representability, displacement, symbolic interpretation, and secondary revision as similar to and in others as different from how they are viewed in the psychoanalytic methodology. Condensation, for example, is seen similarly in both systems. The generation of multiple associations by both to a single textual element reflects the conviction that the element may be a multifaceted representation. Although Freud distinguished composite images from intermediate common entities, little effort is made to distinguish between them in clinical work. For the sake of simplicity, we will treat them both as condensations.

The central idea in the mechanism of regard for representability is that one of the determinants which accounts for what is chosen to appear in the manifest dream, as expressive of the latent content, is the capability of the element to be represented visually. The dream translator relies heavily on this concept as he presumes that the major basis for the choice of a dream element is that it represents the figurative concept in a literal form. This embodies the concept that "the meaning of the dream is in the metaphor."

The use of symbol interpretation which Freud saw as an auxiliary interpretive method is done without the dreamer's associations. The judicious use of symbolic interpretation is done in dream translation with careful attention to the context of the dream experience.

Displacement of emphasis in which what is central in the latent content is peripheral in the manifest content is very common in the psychoanalytic approach but is not a useable presumption in the translation methodology. The manifest dream text is responded to at face value by the translator and points of emphasis are accepted as such because there are no rules to indicate when a shift in emphasis should be assumed.

Freud rejected secondary revision as one of the core dream work mechanisms. He recognized secondary revision as the mechanism that gives the dream its superficial organization and connectiveness but in order to conceal rather than reveal. The hypotheses of dream translation, that all of the dream text is strictly determined and sequentially and causally related, rejects the psychoanalytic concepts that part of the dream text is just filler and the dream text is ordered to give apparent coherence but primarily to mislead. The ordering of the dream elements in dream translations is seen as part of the narrative structure of the dream and intimately related to the meaning of the dream. Freud fragmented the dream narrative associating to each part and establishing meaning and continuity in the latent dream thoughts and denying it existed meaningfully in the manifest content. The value of *post hoc ergo propter hoc* (after the fact therefore because of it), is assumed by many subjective psychologies and provides a dynamic to the dreaming process.

There are two other processes, the mode of dealing with feelings and the complexity of regression, that are central in the psychoanalytic system to the transformation of the latent dream thoughts into the manifest dream. Feelings are potentially subject to the same changes: intensification, diminishment, displacement, reversal, and omission, as are any other portion of the latent thoughts. As there are no rules for choosing which mechanism is active, the translator deals with affects as they appear in the reported dream. Affects are evaluated against what the situation in the dream would elicit in the real world and deviations from the expected are then clues to be taken into account when making the translation.

Regression, in all of its aspects, can be accepted by the dream translator as it would be by the dream interpreter. Regression, although not used explicitly in the process of dream translation, could be invoked to explain the manner in which ideas are linked together in the dream, the visual nature of the dream experience and the historical sources of the dream content.

D. What Does Meaning Mean?

The title for this section poses in an awkward manner the core question that this chapter is attempting to address. Let us start to understand meaning with a dictionary definition. What is offered is that to mean something is to convey or denote, to signify or represent like a symbol, to indicate or to have an intention or being about something as in a consequence. All dream interpreters have taken the position that dreams do not "speak for themselves" even those who profess the view that dreams reveal rather than conceal. Meaning in the literal sense can be used to state what a dream means. The Vietnam vet's dream we explored previously is literally about killing a baby in a hut in Vietnam. We expanded and offered an additional meaning through a dream translation. This does not deny the validity of the literal meaning.

Connotation describes the relationship between the word and the images and associations it evokes or implies while denotation refers to the relationship between the expression and the thing represented. In all types of dream interpretation, we are interested in the connotation as the source of additional meanings. Freud took an extreme position that the literal or manifest dream is of no interest as it is meant to hide the real meaning that is found in the latent dream thoughts and which the interpretive process is to recapture. He lamented later on that his colleagues had not given more attention to the manifest dream content. Freud acknowledged that the content of the manifest dream was condensed compared to the latent dream content. The manifest dream content was overdetermined as an item from the latent content could be represented in more than one manifest dream item. In addition, affect could be displaced from several parts of the latent content onto one item in the manifest content which would have greater intensity and account for the difference in focus between the manifest and latent dreams. Freud did acknowledge that a dream could have more than one interpretation, more than one meaning, but, generally, these meanings were layered. He referred to this as overinterpretation. The Talmud tells the story of the Rabbi who took his dream to 24 different interpreters in Jerusalem and got 24 different interpretations and they were all right. This is in keeping with the Talmudic view that the meaning of a dream follows its interpretation. These may capture an aspect of what Freud meant in his idea of overinterpretation.

The dream is treated as a figurative statement and not a literal one even when it describes a thing or event in the real world. It is this metaphoric view of the dream which is addressed by the dream translation methodology. Ullman (Ullman, 1969) has referred to the dream as "a metaphor in motion" and we have said that "the meaning is in the metaphor." It is the work of Lakoff and Johnson (Lakoff & Johnson, 2003) that has so convincingly called attention to how we experience the world and describe those experiences through metaphor. The deep and surface concepts in Chomsky's work (Chomsky, 1968, 1980) and the manifest and latent concepts in Freud's work (Freud, 1955) are addressing different issues and Edelson's (Edelson, 1972) effort to unite them is unconvincing. The use of surface and deep has to be understood metaphorically in both cases and recognized as not being identical.

In the introduction to their work, *The Measurement of Meaning*, Osgood and colleagues (Osgood, Succi, & Tannenbaum, 1978) pointed out that the various disciplines have developed different definitions of meaning. The mentalist view held by many psychologists and others continues the mind/body dichotomy. They point out that Ogden and Richards (Ogden & Richards, 1989) present the most sophisticated presentation of this view, which is of interest as Richards had a major influence in literary textual analysis. The effort of Osgood and colleagues to measure meaning has lead to a system that describes a concept along three dimensions: activity, intensity, and value. They use a spatial model to place a concept along these three dimensions and relate other concepts as to how close in the hypothetical spatial model they are along these dimensions to the comparison concept. Their view is in keeping with the connotative, figurative meaning of a concept not a literal one.

Our world is not made for us in some objective manner. We create our own world and that is the world in which we live: a subjective, affective, figurative one. As the Buddha said: "With our thoughts we make the world."

E. The Dream of Irma's Injection: The Specimen Dream of Psychoanalysis Revisited

As so much of our discussion has focused on the psychoanalytic view of dream interpretation, it is worthwhile to look at "The Dream of Irma's Injection," the dream specimen of psychoanalysis, as it was the dream that Freud used to illustrate his interpretive method in *The Interpretation of Dreams*. We will attempt a dream translation and make some comparison to what Freud achieved. The caveat is that we know Freud's associations and conclusions and the extensive literature about the dream so we cannot be sure to what extent this has colored our translational effort. A reprise of the dream as Freud reported it is in order.

1. The Dream of Irma's Injection

A large hall—numerous guests, whom we were receiving. Among them was Irma. I at once took her on one side, as though to answer her letter and to reproach her for not having accepted my "solution" yet. I said to her: "If you still get pains, it's really only your fault." She replied: "If you only knew what pains I've got now in my throat and stomach and abdomen—it's choking me"—I was alarmed and looked at her. She looked pale and puffy. I thought to myself that after all I must be missing some organic trouble. I took her to the window and looked down her throat, and she showed signs of recalcitrance, like women with artificial dentures. I thought to myself that there was really no need for her to do that. She then opened her mouth properly and on the right I found a big white patch; at another place I saw extensive whitish grey scabs upon some remarkable curly structures which were evidently modeled on the turbinal bones of the nose. I at once called in Dr. M., and he repeated the examination and confirmed it...Dr. M. looked quite different from usual; he was very pale, he walked with a limp and his chin was clean-shaven. My friend Otto was now standing beside her as well and my friend Leopold was percussing her through her bodice and saying: "She has a dull area low down on the left." He also indicated that a portion of skin on the left shoulder was infiltrated. (I noticed this, just as he did, in spite of her dress.)...M. said: "There's no doubt it's an infection, but no matter; dysentery will supervene and the toxin will be eliminated."...We were directly aware, too, of the origin of the infection. Not long before, when she was feeling unwell, my friend Otto had given her an injection of a preparation of propyl, propyls...proprionic acid...trimethylamin (and I saw before me the formula for this printed in heavy type)... Injections of that sort ought not to be made thoughtlessly....And probably the syringe had not been clean (Freud, 1955b, 107).

Let us offer the dream translation of the Irma dream before turning to the additional information provided by Freud such as the day residue or stimulus for the dream, his associations, and the meanings he derives for the dream. In working with a dream independent of the dreamer's associations in a translation, we are trying to illustrate what one might do in trying to gain clues about the dreamer in an initial assessment or at a point of impasse in therapy or supervision or in working on one's own dream.

2. Translation of the Dream of Irma's Injection

We begin with a statement about the setting of the dream, *"A large hall."* This places us in a big open public space, impersonal, and vulnerable. The next statement, *"numerous guests,"* makes the situation more personal and friendly as we are dealing with guests which implies an invitation and a party. Play rather than work. The hosts for the party are described in the next remark *"whom we were receiving."* The "we" indicates more than just the dreamer but he is included, knowing the dreamer is married the most likely other is his wife, if we hadn't known that then a significant other who is likely to be specified rather than described as part of a "we" (The relationship to his wife has been invoked as a contributing stimulus for the dream). *"Among them was Irma"* singles out a particular person, close enough to the dreamer, in fact or in his desire, to be a guest at the party and be called by her first name. Irma is a woman; we experience a focusing from the guests to a particular female guest.

"I at once took her on one side," which serves to reinforce the focus on her and the relationship, the one to one or intimate relationship to her and excluding the other guests and the other part of the hosting pair, the we, probably his wife. *"As though to answer her letter,"* they appear to have had a prior relationship or at least prior communication, and there was an urgency on the dreamer's part to respond. *"And reproach her for not having accepted my 'solution' yet."* It sounds like in their relationship the dreamer has offered her some advice about something and he is troubled perhaps disappointed and/or annoyed she has not taken it. The "solution," which is set off in the text suggests perhaps a play on words and may refer to a liquid he recommended. When this sort of liquid association arises in the context of a relationship of intimacy and the dependency of advice seeking and giving one may be forgiven for having a sexual thought. *"I said to her: 'If you still get pains, it's really only your fault.'"* The focus at this point is on deciding whose fault or who is responsible for the continuation of the problem. The dreamer clearly makes it Irma's responsibility, but who else could be responsible? Is someone else in Irma's life at fault? Why is the dreamer so exercised about the pain continuing? If the dreamer offers advice, must others take it or he feels hurt, rejected, disappointed, or inadequate? (If we knew Irma is a patient, this line of association would be less likely and the questions answered more easily and quickly.) *"She replied: 'If you only knew what pains I've got now in my throat and stomach and abdomen—its choking me'*—Irma indicates that she has pains and is choking right now so that the answer, *"It's your own fault for not taking the solution I offered"* is countered with a pathetic description of her suffering. The dreamer might well feel, even if inappropriately, that he has failed her. The specific nature of the complaints might well suggest a number of diagnostic possibilities or metaphorical associations such as a multi-system disease to account for the array of symptoms or ambivalence about oral pregnancy fantasies. The physical diagnostic exercise will take us away from the relationship and the impregnation fantasies will have to emerge as the dream progresses if they emerge at all. *"I was alarmed and looked at her."* Irma's complaints

had upset the dreamer and he looked specifically at her, and having gotten his attention, he was past blaming her. *"She looked pale and puffy,"* which apparently was different than usual and it worried him. The intimate tone and involvement continues without leading us in a particular direction toward a medical diagnosis or a fantasized impregnation. *"I thought to myself that after all I must be missing some organic trouble."* The dreamer becomes concerned about a missed medical problem, momentarily moving in a medical direction. If he missed it and he is a physician (as we know from outside the dream), as he appears to be, then he made a mistake and the fault is his and not Irma's and, by implication, his "solution" would now not be appropriate.

"I took her to the window and looked down her throat,"—the dreamer and Irma move further away from the guests to a place where she can be more carefully inspected. The social situation has been abandoned and turned into a clinical one perhaps to cover the intimacy. *"and she showed signs of recalcitrance, like women with artificial dentures."* The response to being examined, looked into, with the exposure and intrusiveness that it entailed, leads Irma to be resistant like other women who are exposing something embarrassing. *"I thought to myself there was really no need for her to do that."* The dreamer's response is to deny any impropriety in the situation. *"She then opened her mouth properly and on the right I found a big white patch; at another place I saw extensive whitish gray scabs upon some remarkable curly structures which were evidently modelled on the turbinal bones of the nose."* The shock at what is seen must be enormous and confirms that something was indeed missed by the dreamer. A guilty feeling could be experienced but is not explicitly mentioned. The roof of the mouth is gone and the patch and scabs are spread, infection, tumor, or other conditions come to mind but something serious is suggested and discoverable by simply looking, nothing subtle. The reference to "right" should at least be noted. The dreamer is at fault, has made a mistake, and is open to censure. Why the particular anatomic location of the problem has been a source of speculation in the literature about the dream.

In response to the discovery of the extensive lesion, the dreamer says *"I at once called in Dr. M. and he repeated the examination and confirmed it."* The dreamer's concern was great enough that a consultant was called in and confirmed the physical problem. Now he was open to being held responsible for his error, an unpleasant prospect. *"...Dr. M. looked quite different from usual; he was very pale, he walked with a limp and was clean shaven."* The comments are directed not at the implications of the results of the consultation but to the appearance of the consultant. Dr. M. is pale so is he sick, as Irma is sick and pale and, like her, he is feminine and not manly. He walks with a limp, which also calls attention to his being less than whole, a cripple and therefore limited. He is beardless, and so he is missing another aspect of manhood or of maturity. A most negative and depreciating picture is painted of the consultant, Dr. M. who had confirmed the dreamer's error. If you don't like the message, you can at least depreciate the messenger and question his adequacy and masculinity.

"*My friend Otto was now standing beside her as well. And my friend Leopold was percussing her through her bodice and saying 'She has a dull area down on the left.'*" The dreamer sees the two men in the dream as peers or juniors as he refers to them by their first names, as he did with Irma, in contrast to how he addressed Dr. M. One, Otto, stands beside her and may in some sense be siding with Irma while the other continues the examination, but in a modest manner, and finds more evidence of disease lower down. Below and left may be negative references and perhaps a genital reference. "*He also indicated that a portion of the skin on the left shoulder was infiltrated. (I noticed this, just as he did, in spite of her dress.)*" Another reference to left and the competitive response to Leopold that is present in the dreamer noting it at the same time. It would be easier with women if they could be explored, examined, undressed. "*... M. said: 'There's no doubt it's an infection, but no matter; dysentery will supervene and the toxin will be eliminated.'*" The consultant who was belittled has lost his professional designation and provides a folk tale explanation for cure. He need not be taken too seriously.

"*... We were directly aware, too, of the origin of the infection.*" We, he now knows whence the problem came, how convenient. "*Not long before, when she was feeling unwell, my friend Otto had given her an injection of a preparation of propyl, propypls...propionic acid...trimethlamin (and I saw before me the formula for this printed in heavy type).*" It is apparent that somehow Otto, a male friend who was by Irma's side, had done something wrong and was the cause of the problem. What she was injected with is a bit uncertain but it was a liquid "solution," (of some importance as it is in bold type) that was given through something being stuck into Irma. Our earlier sexual speculations may have some basis. "*...Injections of that sort ought not to be made so thoughtlessly...And probably the syringe had not been clean.*" Injections of what sort? Is more being alluded to that may be sexual and then the syringe, in addition to the solution, is not "clean," pure or correct has caused the problem. Otto's sexual behavior is to blame for the illness and the dreamer, who may be envious and competitive with men, is not at fault.

3. Freud's Preamble and Interpretation

The night before the dream a family friend, Otto, had come to visit Freud and reported that Irma, Freud's patient, was "better but not quite well."

Freud spent the evening writing a summary of Irma's illness and his treatment of her for Dr. M., a high status physician in Freud's professional and social circle. The dream is seen by Freud as a response to the issues stirred up by what Freud feels is the criticism implicit in Otto's comment about Irma's health, namely, "better but not quite well." The dream is interpreted as an effort to justify himself as not responsible for Irma's illness, to avenge himself against Otto, and to plead that more accepting individuals be provided for him than some in his life. Freud protests that he is a conscientious physician, concerned about the health of others—patients, friends and family—as well as his own. He latter adds a sexual theme in a letter to Karl Abraham (Abraham & Freud, 1965).

4. Commentary and Questions

The dream is 369 words long, his associative interpretive effort is 16 and one half pages long and is about 6,715 words. The dream translation consists of 1,223 words. The effort to understand the dream takes considerably more words than the dream report itself and led to Freud's view that the latent content contained so much more than the manifest. The points of overlap between the translation and the interpretation are fairly clear. The fear of error, the self justification, and the blaming of others is striking even in reading the dream at the literal level. It is hard to understand why Freud was so convinced that the dream could not be understood as a wish fulfillment without using his interpretive method.

The dream, from a Freudian point of view, is to be seen as the attempted, disguised, hallucinatory, fulfillment of an infantile, often sexual wish (libidinous) in the service of maintaining the continuity of sleep. It is striking that in Freud's interpretation of the dream there is no infantile source provided nor does he provide a libidinous basis although the letter to Abraham (Abraham & Freud, 1965) indicates he was aware of one and he recognizes that displacement, a key dream work mechanism, does not take place in this dream.

There are a number of unanswered questions about the Irma dream that I have tried to answer in another context (Kramer, 1999). They include:

i. Who is Irma?
ii. What is the nature of her illness in the dream?
iii. What is the "solution" Freud offers?
iv. What is the infantile source of the dream and why wasn't it established?
v. Why was there no recognition of the competitive relationship with men?

    vi. How well does Freud follow his own techniques for exploring the dream?

   vii. Is the construction of the dream experience explained or explored?

I have concluded, based on an extensive literature review, that Irma was Anna Lichtheim Hammrerschlag, the daughter of a close family friend. Irma's illness in the dream was tuberculosis. And, that the solution Freud offered was sexual intercourse. The infantile source of the dream was not identified nor any awareness of his difficulty with men. The latter according to Freud is based on his relationship to his nephew John, despite his shabby treatment of his friends Otto, Dr. Oscar Rie, the family pediatrician, and Leopold, Dr. Ludwig Rosenberg, a former assistant to Freud, and Dr. M., Dr. Josef Breuer, a friend, colleague, and scientific collaborator. The last two questions need more extended comment.

It is curious that Freud, who contrasted his detailed approach to the block method of previous interpreters, does not follow his own methodological suggestions. The dream Freud argued is a strictly determined product requiring an examination of all its elements. He does not adhere to these principles in his analysis of the Irma dream. He ends up dividing the dream into 24 parts as a basis for his associating to the dream. In only six of these does he use the identical phrasing given in the dream report to start his associative process. In 13 parts, a change occurs from how the dream is reported in the dream text and how Freud labels it before giving his associations to the part. The change in most cases appears to be trivial. They may be attributable to translation problems as illustrated by the dream in German being reported in the present tense but in Strachey's translation it is done in the past tense, but a few of the changes, perhaps, were more significant. For example, leaving out that the big white patch in Irma's mouth was on the right. There are two parts of the dream to which Freud terminates his associations either because it would take him too far afield or because he doesn't want to penetrate more deeply. There are three parts to which he doesn't associate at all.

A reading of the two sections in which Freud chooses to limit his associations suggests that a sexual theme may be beginning to emerge for him. In one, he is dealing with women who won't yield who are recalcitrant and he associates to women he may prefer because they will yield, and he finally limits his associations because "they are taking him too far afield." In the second case, the starting point is seeing through Irma ("in spite of her dress"). He terminates his associations with the comment, "he doesn't want to penetrate any further."

The three sections Freud does not identify for association seem to establish with Irma the intimacy of a one-to-one relationship, "among them was Irma"—the initial singling out of Irma and "I at once took her to one side, as though to answer her letter." The third part underscores his concern about and his focusing on Irma's appearance—"I was alarmed and looked at her."

Freud did not always provide the close reading one might have expected given his commitment to an en detail approach. Those sections in which he chose to stop his associations or which he left out are very suggestive of sexual issues in regard to Irma and other women. Interestingly, Freud blurs what is in the dream and what is in the associations. He sees Irma's friend as in the dream when she clearly emerges only in the associations to how Irma appears to stand when next to the window.

It is apparent that the dream of Irma's injection is a counter-transference dream (Whitman, Kramer, & Baldridge, 1969) and is about a patient with whom Freud had a social relationship (Kramer, 1999). Tact may have necessitated some limitation on the interpretive process.

The seventh question about the Irma dream relates to the construction of the dream and is not really addressed. He does not describe how the manifest scenes are selected and tied together in an apparent sequence as the syntax of the dream is not directly his concern. He says that the dream is really the dream work mechanisms. No rules are given to explain how the process of selection and interconnection is done. He felt the interconnections were deceptive and not central to the process. Dreams need to be explored piecemeal in order to establish their latent content. Even establishing the interconnections of the latent content was attributed to experience and not methodologically described.

5. Are There Limits to Dream Interpretation?

Freud's recognition that a dream can have more than one meaning, overinterpretations, and his acknowledgement that the Irma dream was incompletely analyzed encouraged others to attempt to complete the analysis either by offering alternative day residues or the infantile source Freud did not provide (Kramer, 2000). Doctors take quite a beating in Freud's presentation of his consultants, particularly Dr. M. and Otto. Only Leopold was spared, perhaps because of his plodding conscientiousness. Bowler (Bowler, 1973) and van Velsen (van Velsen, 1984) both suggest that the Irma dream is a farce in that it condemns by ridicule what we consider important. Act I is the discovery of the infection. Act II is the diagnosis of a self-limiting disease (dysentery). And Act III is the discovery of the source of the infection. All problems are resolved. Dr. M. is asinine, Dr. L. is crude in his "feeling up" of Irma, and Otto was an irresponsible slob.

If the "Dream of Irma's Injection" was a Marx brother's film, the casting would be Groucho as Freud, Margaret Dumont as Irma, Harpo as Leopold, Chico as Otto, and Zeppo as Dr. M. Piotrowski (Piotrowski, 1973) felt it was not a farce because it wasn't humorous. Mautner (Mautner, 1991), acknowledging it as the observation of one of her students, refers to the "gang rape" tone of the consultation.

a. Additional Day Residues   We found in our literature review (Kramer, 2000) 11 additional or alternative day residues which illustrate the arbitrary nature of such speculations. They include the botched nasal surgery involving the turbinates and the sinuses of Emma Eckstein done by Dr. Wilhelm Fliess, Freud's personal intimate and mentor, which occurred, including complications, 2 months before the Irma dream (Schur, 1966). There is no evidence this was on Freud's mind or that Emma was Irma. The concern about his wife's pregnancy is offered by Elms (Elms, 1980) as a day residue. The interpretations are arbitrary starting with equating the "large hall" with his wife's pregnant abdomen or uterus. The most outlandish is the suggestion by Feldman (Feldman, 1984) that the dream is about Freud's wish to be rectally penetrated by Wilhelm Fliess. It bears no relationship to the dream and has been called irreverent although irrelevant is more to the point.

b. Possibly Determining Early Life Experiences   We have identified in our review (Kramer, 2000) seven early life experiences that have been suggested as the infantile source for the Irma dream. Erikson (Erickson, 1954) provides the most cited example of an infantile source for the Irma dream. It is of a urinary indiscretion by Freud as a child who urinated in a chamber pot in his parents' presence in their bedroom. His father said he wouldn't amount to much. Freud links the scene to dreams in which he enumerates his accomplishments, hardly the case in the Irma dream. Erikson does not deal with Freud's relationship to Irma or women. He speculates on what might have been on Freud's mind before going to bed the night of the Irma dream. At best a speculation, at worst a fictional historical reconstruction that enlivens but does not illuminate. Anderson (Anderson, 1986) speculates that the infantile base is the search for Freud's lost mother and the loss of his "wet nurse." It hinges, to a large degree, on children calling their mothers ma-ma in English, that Freud knew English, and that his mother's name was Amalie and that Irma was Emma Eckstein and that ma appears in both names. Credulity is stretched beyond recapture and Alice's experience with Humpty Dumpty is the guiding principle (Carroll & Gardner, 1960). Humpty says, "When I use a word... it means what I choose it to mean—neither more nor less."

F. Contributions of Textual Analysis to Dream Understanding

1. Dream Text

The dictionary definition of a text becomes a starting point, even if not a completely satisfactory one, to explore the possibility of whether the dream report may be considered a text (Rupprecht, 1993). If so it opens up a number of interpretive strategies that have been applied to texts. A text has been defined as "… the actual or original words of an author as distinguished from notes, commentary, paraphrases, and translation. It is the actual structure of words in a piece of writing or printing." In a logical positive sense, the report of a dream could be seen as a text.

Is everything that the dreamer reports to be regarded as the dream text, which could become the object of the search for meaning? If our interest in the dream is to elucidate the meaning of the dream experience, are repetitions, interpolations, clarifications, and associations to be considered part of the dream text or potentially part of the interpretive strategy? My own preference is to define the dream text narrowly as a recounting of the dream experience and exclude all elaborations as not part of the dream experience. The implicit communicative demands for clarification may be at the root of the dream reporters need to express elaborations.

Eagleton in his introduction to literary theory (Eagleton, 1983) describes a number of literary theorists who provide provocative ways to look at the dream text which may broaden our understanding of the interpretative process. Timothy Riess (Eagleton, 1983) has suggested that there are many discourses of which literature is one and it may be reasonable to consider that the dream report is another. He claims that the kind of reading that is applied to a literary text can be applied to any discourse. A discourse is a communication of thoughts by words and for some is the study of that communication. The dream may not be experienced with the intent to be communicated. However, once a dream report is created, the intent to communicate is implied if not explicit and the possibility of a discourse created.

It is not always clear as to what constitutes the text. Iser, of the "Reader Response School," has taken the position that the text is a consequence of the reader having read the text (Eagleton, 1983). Holland holds that the text is a subjective reaction of the reader (Eagleton, 1983). The views of reader response theoreticians speak to the interpretive process. They would deny the distinction between the text as object and the interpretation of the text. It is for them an indisolvable whole. No text can or does stand alone. This is a view also taken by Kristeva (Eagleton, 1983), who sees each text as echoing another text ad infinitum. A similar view is held by Derrida (Eagleton, 1983), each text holding the trace of another text and yet in some way each distinct from the others. Certainly what we report as a dream and how we report it may be influenced by its similarity to and difference from other dreams we have had.

2. Meaning: Literal or Figurative

If we are to reconstruct the meaning of the dream text, we must either implicitly or explicitly have some concept, more or less well developed, which captures the essence of what we are building, so we might know dream meaning when we see it. I have earlier given a dictionary definition of meaning essentially as that which is intended or in fact is conveyed, signified, or understood by language. Meaning is the sense, signification, import, or significance of words.

Meaning is by no means a settled issue. Ransom (Eagleton, 1983) has attacked the notion that language is purely denotative or referential, de Man has called attention to the difficulty in separating the literal from the figurative, and Miller has pointed out that basically all language is metaphorical (fictive).

It is apparent that the methodologies applied to the dream text treat the dream report as a figurative statement not as a literal description of a series of events. Rosenblatt takes the position that it is the subjective meaning of all experience one is trying to grasp. Our interest is in the connotative not the denotative, the figurative not the literal, the emotional more than the cognitive, and the irrational more than the rational. Derrida's decentering of logocentrism opens the way to the emotive. Richards recognized that "a theory of feeling, of emotion, of attributes and desires is required at all points in our analysis" (Eagleton, 1983, 45).

3. Contextual or Context Free

M. Bakhtin (Eagleton, 1983) has offered the position that meaning is completely contextual; Gadamer proposes that there are no context free universals of the history of the text or of the interpreter. In fact, for Gadamer the interpretation is never complete in time. Jamison, the sociocritical theorist (Marxist), implies a very broad cultural context for meaning and attempts to assess all the things and circumstances that contribute to the form and context of a human creation. The feminist critique is a social one that sees every cultural production in a social, historical and economic framework and postulates that action occurs in the context of power differences. In contrast, some schools attempt to deal with an absolute or relative detachment of the text from its context. The "New Critics" deal with the text, in their case poetry, context free. Richards saw meaning as largely noncontextual. Said has observed that Derrida's observations are intratextual and have no historical context.

My approach to the dream text in a dream translation is context free in the sense that it is divorced from any knowledge of the dreamer-author or the circumstances surrounding the dream being experienced or reported recognizing that it is not completely possible to be completely free of a context. The text, the dream report, has its own context that contributes to its meaning. This serves to help establish the meaning of the text. My approach does not deal initially with the author (the dreamer), his intent or action, with the circumstances of occurrence, nor with that the cultural, political, economic, or social surroundings. It does deal with the response of the reader, of the dream translator, who could be the dreamer or another person. This approach attempts to establish a *meaning* for the dream report. Help from the dreamer would be necessary to establish the *significance* of the dream. Moving from meaning to significance is going from the general to the specific. The import of the dream to the dreamer at the time the dream was experienced is the significance of the dream. The meaning and significance of the dream should be consonant with each other.

The initial confrontation in doing a dream translation in searching for the meaning of the dream is with the text in isolation like the approach of the "New Critics." However, this is part of an initial textual strategy and not an effort to always remain contextually isolated. The approach is not to establish the dream meaning equivalent of art for art's sake but to work from a meaning toward the significance of the dream which can be related to the subjective life of the dreamer.

4. Determinate or Indeterminate

There is deep concern about the determinate or indeterminate meaning of a text. Some have suggested that there is no one meaning, rather there is a pluralism of meanings. Not only is there not one meaning but also there is no unity or coherence in the text at all and meaning may be an infinite regress, an endless semiosis. However, Hartman (Eagleton, 1983) has suggested that it is this very indeterminacy that makes it possible, gives room, for a reader to interpret the text.

Alteri, a speech act theorist, takes the position that meaning is not indeterminate. The problem is the failure of the espousers of indeterminacy to see the difference between emotive and referential language. The bundled meanings take on a single communicative or expressive role in a particular situation. His focus is on language use. This seems to echo the focal conflict approach of French's (French, 1952) analysis of dream meaning. In searching for unity, for the wholeness of the text, one can choose between alternatives and counter the futility that deconstruction would offer. Eagleton (Eagleton, 1983) also rejects a plurality of meanings. The meaning of the dream of interest to the dream translator as well as the dreamer, of the many possible meanings, is the one most relevant at this particular time for this dreamer.

On what is one to base the establishment of the meaning of a text? Dilthey has suggested that the ground for understanding the text is "shared human experience." We start from "misunderstanding" and through dialogue we move toward "understanding" (Schliermacher). Each part depends for understanding on the whole and the whole is understood only through a grasp of its parts (the hermenutic circle) (Eagleton, 1983). The notion of shared "human experience" is the basis to begin to understand the text, empathy in Kohut's system (Kohut, 1971), and underpins the translator's associations in place of the dreamer's. The movement from beginning to end, from successive part to part, as recommended by the translation methodology, is analogous to the clarifying and correcting dialogue that Schliermacher describes as to how understanding is achieved. As many associations as possible are generated from each part of the text and in their interaction, a pattern begins to emerge. The selection from among alternatives assumes a textual coherence, unity and wholeness similar to the hermenutic methodology and the work of the "New Critics," but in contrast to the lack of unity and coherence found by Derrida. Gadamer leaves open the possibility that a text needs to be interpreted differently at a later time. For him, understanding is always an interpretation and interpretation is always a translation.

5. *Construction or Discovery of Meaning*

Meaning is found in the text, the dream report, and is extracted by reconstruction from it. Meaning is both constructed and discovered is the view described by Othman and Fish (Eagleton, 1983). One brings an interpretive system to the dream according to Iser. In literature, literary conventions determine the interpretation according to Mailloux as psychological ones do in dream interpretation. Language, the new semanticists point out, contains philosophical, moral, and psychological constructs.

The exploration of the text for meaning in a dream translation is psychological. Every psychological translator or interpreter brings to the text a set of psychological assumptions (theories) about the nature of man, particularly his inner life. It is these that we "find" in the dream and upon which we construct the meaning of the dream. It is certainly the case that, in Gadamer's view, there is no one system of interpretation or explanation. The explanatory system we adopt, according to Colomb, provides the "codes" and is a value generated choice. As we replace one text by another, we could be in an infinite regress as is found in the deconstructive approach to meaning. The particular situation and the interests of the participants, Colomb suggests, breaks the chain of regression.

Gadamer is deeply skeptical of context free universals. Searle also criticizes first principles. The only one he finds necessary for language is that language is useful. Postulating first principles such as the Feminist theorists do in seeing power, domination, and gender as inevitable determinants is not well supported. The reconstruction of understanding from a psychological approach, utilizing psychological theories suffers from there being indefensible first principles, although they may be useful.

The syntactic or pragmatic, not the semantic, is the concern of most schools of textual criticism. They are often more concerned with the syntactic aspects of the text, its internal structure and organization, its use (effects), or its pragmatics, than with its meaning, its semantics. The "New Critics," the formalists, the structuralists, and the deconstructionists are not centrally concerned with the semantic aspect of the text.

The translation methodology is concerned with the semantic aspect of the text. It is the meaning of the text, of the dream, not its internal structure or its potential or actual use that is the translator's immediate concern. However, my own interpretive assumption is of the conceptual nature of nonrational, emotional thought and that one thought, i.e., experience, with its accompanying affect, leads to another and stimulates the process as in an improvisation, i.e., without a beginning or end. I see the structure of the dream as being guided by a dialectic model, thesis-antithesis-synthesis, new thesis, and so on. It is an inherent effort at subjective problem solving. The problem solving effort has the effect of containing the emotional aspects of the dream experience and goes to the question of the potential pragmatic of the dream experience, i.e., maintaining the continuity of sleep.

6. Close Reading

The approach of close reading has been described as central to several schools of literary criticism (Eagleton, 1983). One of the hallmarks of the "New Critics" is their close reading of the text. The same has been said of I. A. Richards and the structuralists. The approach to the text in dream translation demands a close reading of the text in which each phrase, image, or concept is attended to individually and in its order of appearance in the text. The meaning derived from each part is related to what preceded and what follows, to other parts of the text and to the total text (the hermeneutic circle). It was striking in examining Freud's reading of the Irma dream that in his associations he left out some portions of the text and altered most of the rest. Though he claims his approach was *en detail* and not *en masse*, this was not completely the case.

7. The Author's Intention-Revelation

The dream translation method usually is concerned with utilizing the text to shed light first on the dream report and ultimately on the author, the dreamer. Leavis and I. A. Richards (Eagleton, 1983) were involved in trying to understand how the mind of the author worked from looking at his productions. One must recognize that the dream experience contains information about the dreamer, reveals various aspects of the dreamer's subjective-inner life, but is not necessarily intended, when experienced, as a communication. The dream experience does not occur in order to communicate anything to the dreamer and certainly not to others. Jung, many New Age theorists, and some Freudians would not accept this nonmessage view and do indeed see the dream as a message from one aspect of the self to another. The dream experience may become a communication when it becomes a dream report.

The textual critics take different positions about the examination of the text to re-create the author's intent. In a literary work, the author intended something in producing the work, e.g., the poem, story, or novel. The "New Critics" and the deconstructionists have no interest in the author's stated intent. The latter point out the difference that may exist between what the author intends and what he actually does. Hermeneutists' extreme interest is in the author's intent is seen especially in the work of E. A. Hirsch (Eagleton, 1983). He sees the reconstruction of the author's intent as the interpreter's task as the author, dreamer, is the final specifier of the meaning of the text. The social theorists are interested in the author's intent as part of their interest in all things that contribute to the form and content of a creation. The speech act theorists, especially Searle, are interested in the author's intent as are the semioticians. The problem, of course, is teasing out of the text, or in interaction with the text, what the author intended and if he did what he intended.

As we see it, the dream experience is not necessarily goal directed as there is no beginning or end. It's more like a happening than a story. At the so-called start of the dream the dreamer is in the midst of the dream. It evolves in a nongoal directed manner much like an improvisation and its apparent end is a point of interruption. Intentionality is "hard" to establish; linkages are not.

Conclusion

Our approach to the text is to examine the text in isolation from the author-dreamer, from its time/place of dreaming and from its historical, cultural, social, political, power, gender, and personal contexts except as directly revealed in the text. The only context is that internal to the dream.

The text in isolation is the position of the "New Critics," I. A. Richards to a large extent and, in a limited way, Derrida. Our examination of the text in isolation permits a focus on what is in the text before the text is "contaminated" by attention being paid to the author's intent and the broader cultural surround.

The text is not isolated from the response of the reader-translator. The task of the translator is to associate, to respond, to each part of the text in succession. In doing so, a dialogue with the text takes place as successive associations confirm, constrain, or clarify previous ones and a meaning is constructed. In this activity, the approach is similar to that of the reader-response theorists Othman and Fish. The self-correcting dialogue to achieve meaning is analogous to Schliermacher's observations about going from "misunderstanding" to "understanding" in a clarifying dialogue.

It is the reader-translator's role to construct the meaning of the text by interaction with it. The reader, Fish says, will "write" the text of what he has read according to the interpretive strategies of the interpretive community to which he belongs. Iser also recognizes the subjective nature of the reading (interpretation) process and its control by a prori interpretive conventions. And Holland points out that readers interpret a text depending on who they are (core identity themes) and are heavily influenced by their own unconscious emotional processes.

CHAPTER **11**

The Functions of Dreams

A. Dream Theory and Dream Function

Freud (Freud, 1955b) stated that the function of dreaming does not have to be part of a theory of dreaming. He took the position that any exposition on dreams that tries to encompass as many of the characteristics as possible of dreams from a particular point of view and that places the position of dreams in a broader area of phenomena deserves to be considered a theory of dreams. The many dream theories differ as they select one characteristic of dreams as the essence of the process and relate their explanations and correlations to this core or essential characteristic. A function may not be derivable from the espoused theory. Freud's preference is for theories that include a function for dreaming as part of the theory.

Freud suggests that dream theories may be categorized into three groups depending on their position in regard to the amount and nature of mental activity in the dream. The first category is theories in which all of mental life goes on in dreams. They offer no function for dreaming, as they offer no reason why dreaming even occurs. Second, there are dream theories that postulate a decrease of mental activity, a loosening of connections, and a decrease of material that can be found in dreams. Sleep intrudes on the mind beyond interrupting the connection to waking reality; it alters the functioning of the mind. Dreaming is seen as a partial awakening with only a fragment of mental functioning expressed and the quality of mental functioning improves as the sleeper becomes more awake and the senselessness of dreams diminishes. The causes of dreams are somatic not mental and therefore are incapable of interpretation. Dreams serve, through somatic processes, to relieve the brain of useless, either trivial or unresolved, thoughts and avoid overload. These theories posit an excretory function for dreaming. And third is a category that views the dreaming mind as capable of engaging in unique mental activities it could not do while awake. Dreaming is then useful. The mind has free run and rejuvenates itself through joyful imagination symbolically to create a world, a healing function. One of the benefits of sleep is dreaming as it refreshes the dreamer.

B. Constraints on Theories of Dream Function

There are a number of conditions (Freud, 1955b) that have been suggested that must be taken into account in approaching the establishment of a function for dreaming. Foulkes (Foulkes, 1993) has detailed those areas that he believes must be considered: (1) attention to the content and structure of dream reports under uniform collection procedures, (2) sampling of dreams from various states during sleep, (3) examination of changes in dream content and form at various ages throughout the life span, and (4) study of the relationships of dream variables to state and trait personality and demographic variables.

Foulkes notes two empirical observations that have not been adequately taken into account in theorizing about dream function: (1) that dreaming is not REM sleep locked and may not even be sleep bound, and (2) that dreaming has a developmental course different than that of REM sleep. Dreaming does not appear until certain cognitive skills have developed at between ages three and five, while REM sleep is present in the fetus. The central position in the brain of the anatomical initiator of REM sleep and the early evolutionary appearance of REM sleep suggest the secondary concomitance of dreaming with REM sleep rather than it being an intrinsic relationship. This does not preclude, contrary to what Foulkes suggests, that dreaming subserves directly or indirectly an adaptive function (Moffitt, Kramer, & Hoffmann, 1993). Further, contrary to Foulkes' view, aspects of visual imagery are predictable, i.e., correlated, so that there is regularity in dreaming (Kramer & Roth, 1979; Piccione, Thomas, Roth, & Kramer, 1976).

Foulkes points out that the waking consequences of dreaming may occur whether the dream is remembered or not. He raises question whether the evidence supports an information processing function during dreaming. The cognitive systems in dreaming, he suggests, may be the same as operate in wakefulness and may serve similar purposes. He sees dreaming as a primary state of existence in an imagined world but nevertheless a world. This is an existential view of dreaming (Boss, 1958).

C. The Functional Analysis of Dreaming

1. Introduction

It is essential to explore the general question of dream function (Kramer, 1981) in order to understand the problems involved before proceeding to particular theories of the function of dreaming. The issues related to the role of internal mental processes in a causal behavioral chain (Sternberg & Smith, 1988) are not generally explored in content based theories of dream function. The dominant, if not exclusive, position in the cognitive sciences is a monistic one in which the Hobbesian materialistic view has captured the day and the dualistic Cartesian position resides in the realm of mystical ideas (Delarosa, 1988). Unfortunately, the evidence for a holistic view in dream theories is not compelling (Hobson, 1988; Reiser, 1984). The cognitive sciences deal, little if at all, with nongoal directed, emotionally related, so-called nondetermined thinking (Smith, 1988). Issues related to mental causation need to be addressed in theories of dream function. The work on mirror neurons in which watching an activity stimulates neurons that are involved in the activity as if the observer undertakes a similar activity, including empathic and pornographic responses, may open a bridge across the mind-brain divide (Blakeslee, 2006; Carr, Iacobini, Dubeau, Mazziota, & Lenzi, 2003) and address the fundamental issue of what we mean by mental causation. Does the day residue, emotionally toned or related, serve as the stimulus to activate mirror neurons which underpin a similar emotional state which, through another mechanism, instantiate that state in a metaphorical image and narrative that we experience as a dream? Does figurative representation, e.g., metaphor, have a basis in mirror neurons or must we look elsewhere (Ramachandan, 2003)? These are questions to be answered.

2. The Functions of Dreaming: A Distinction

It is necessary to distinguish two senses in which the concept of function may be applied to psychological dreaming. The concept of function can be used either in the sense of *what* the dream does or *how* the dream is constructed (Breger, 1967) to exercise a function. If one explores the consequences of dreaming, its pragmatics, one is interested in what the dream does. What is the effect or result of dreaming? In this sense of function, one is concerned with the dream as independent variable and with subsequent waking thought or behavior as the dependent variable. Leveton (Leveton, 1961) has suggested that dreams can be viewed as the "night residue" that helps precipitate the subsequent waking behavior.

Function can be used in another sense to describe how things are made. In the case of psychological dreaming, the function of dreaming also relates to the construction and organization of the dream, the syntax of the dream. What contents are selected, by what rules and how are they melded together? These are the questions the *how* function of dreaming addresses. Studies that examine the mode by which pre-sleep elements and elements from memory are selected (Piccione, Jacobs, Kramer, & Roth, 1977) and enter directly or by transformation (Wikin, 1967) into the dream, which describe the interconnection of the parts of the dream (Klinger, 1971) and which delineate the sequential development of the dream across the REM period (Kramer, Roth, & Czaya, 1975) and across the night (Kramer, McQuarrie, & Bonnet, 1980; Kramer, Whitman, Baldridge, & Lansky, 1964) are all examples of the *how* function of dreaming. From the perspective of dream construction, the dream is the dependent measure.

The two aspects of dream function, what the dream achieves (i.e., its effects or consequences, its pragmatics), and how the dream is constructed and organized (i.e., its syntax) are often related. Freud (Freud, 1955b) clearly related the two. The dream for Freud was constructed in response to an awakened disturbing infantile wish to provide a disguised gratification of the wish that results in the protection of the continuity of sleep. This infantile wish may be seen as the independent variable and the disguised gratification as the dependent variable. The dream work was postulated by Freud as the mechanism for constructing the dream in which the disguised gratification occurred. The dream experience of disguised gratification becomes either a new independent variable or the intervening variable with sleep protection as the consequent dependent variable.

The distinction between the dream as independent and dependent variable has been explored by others as well (Cartwright, 1978; Fiss, 1979). Unfortunately, the distinction has not been consistently applied, and evidence for the *what* (i.e., the pragmatics) of dream function often has been confused with the evidence for the *how* (i.e., the syntax) of dream construction.

3. Adaptive Dream Function: An Overview

The concept of adaptation in biology focuses on the survival value of some aspect of a living organism's function and is a cornerstone of evolutionary theory. Fishbein (Fishbein, 1976) has suggested that characteristics (1) may have survival value at their time of occurrence, (2) may not have survival value at their time of occurrence but are needed to build or combine with another characteristic that will have survival value at a later time, (3) do not have survival value but are the result of characteristics that do, or (4) do not have survival value and are not the outcome of characteristics that do. Dynamic functional theories, e.g., anthropologic, developmental, personality, and clinical theories, fall under characteristics one or two. Cognitive and biological theories, e.g., the static functional theories, emphasize categories three and four.

Even apparently afunctional or antifunctional theories of dreaming such as the activation synthesis hypothesis (Hobson, 1988; Mamelak & Hobson, 1989) and various neural net theories (Crick & Mitchison, 1983; Hinton & Sejnowski, 1986) fall in the first two categories. The randomness of neural activity at the physiological level is neutral with respect to the functional significance of dreaming at the psychological level.

Dreaming may have an epiphenomenal or indexical function, level three, if it is regular and therefore a reliable index. It may then throw light on the possible significance of other systems. Dreaming has been shown, for example, to index and participate in the creative imagination of artists (Gaines & Price-Williams, 1990). And dreaming can index a self-regulatory process without participating in self-regulation.

Dream forgetting as Robert (Freud, 1955b) has suggested may be a necessary function to maintain the mental function of dreamers. A similar view is offered by Crick and Murchison (Crick & Mitchison, 1983) who attribute a regulatory function to dream forgetting, namely to maintain the stability of waking thought. My colleagues and I (Kramer, Schoen, & Kinney, 1984) have observed better waking functions associated with lower dream recall in Vietnam veterans who have had PTSD, and Lavie and Kaminer (Lavie & Kaminer, 1991) reported a similar finding of better long term adaptation in Holocaust survivors with a lower rate of dream recall.

A review of the chapters in *The Functions of Dreaming* (Moffitt, Kramer, & Hoffmann, 1993) shows (1) that because dreaming is regular it can be used to index other biological, psychological, and cultural processes; (2) that dreaming may be part of the organization and functioning of the self and be independent of the function of any particular sleep stage or interact with them in maintaining search, memory, signal detection, and problem solving functions; (3) that dreaming may be seen as being an adaptive response to stress and as adaptive problem solving in response to challenges to the integrity of the self; and (4) that when dreaming has effects upon wakefulness (Kramer, 1993; Purcell, Moffitt, & Hoffmann, 1993; Koulack, 1993; Kuiken & Sikora, 1993), we approach level one and two aspects of adaptation described by Fishbein (Fishbein, 1976).

4. Adaptive Dream Function: Assimilative and Accommodative

Those theories of psychological dreaming that specify a consequent function often are adaptive in nature. Such theories espouse either an assimilative or accommodative function for dreaming (Piaget, 1962). Theories of dreaming that view dream function as assimilative are more likely to be able to account for the totality of the dream experience. In these assimilative theories, the dreaming process functions automatically, outside of conscious awareness that is without recall and secondary reworking. These theories have the dream achieve some corrective (Kramer & Roth, 1973b) or reductive goal (French, 1952).

In the accommodative theories of dream function, the dreamer is altered as a result of the dream experience (Jung, 1974). The dream is a special experience that has the potential for a significant and often a decisive impact on the dreamer's life. In the accommodative theories of dream function, the dream must become conscious, enter awareness, and be "understood" to have its transforming effects (Glucksman & Kramer, 2004).

It is possible, if not probable, that the dream serves both an assimilative and accommodative function. It well may be that those dreams that are recalled and related to more significant events of the moment (Cohen, 1974; Trinder & Kramer, 1971) carry the potential for the transforming experience either in themselves or in conjunction with a waking exploration. Meanwhile, the bulk of dreaming would continue outside of awareness to achieve the more modest but necessary reductive assimilative goal.

5. Criteria for Demonstrating a Function for Dreams

To adequately pursue a function for psychological dreaming, one needs to pursue both the *how* of dream formation and the *what* of dream consequence. Either alone is half the story. Therefore, a complete theory of psychological dreaming needs to place the dream between the waking events that preceded it and the waking events that follow it. This wake-dream-wake paradigm needs to be the basis for exploring the function of dreaming.

If one can manipulate aspects of the pre-sleep experience and/or the dream experience itself, the possibility for demonstrating an effect on the dream and subsequent wakefulness becomes possible. It has been shown to a greater or lesser degree that the content of the dream can be directly manipulated (Tart, 1979). For example, a pre-sleep suggestion to dream about certain topics or to have specific dreams has been effective (Meier, 1966). Post-hypnotic suggestions to have certain kinds of dreams have also met with some success (Schrotter, 1959). Paradigms that have conditioned subjects to respond when a certain type of dream is occurring have also been accomplished (Cartwright & Lamberg, 1992). Further, dreams can be directly manipulated. Stimuli introduced concomitantly with REM sleep have been shown to effect dreaming systematically (Castaldo & Holzman, 1969; Kramer, Kinney, & Scharf, 1983). Also, dream content probably can be altered by prior REM deprivation with an intensity increase in the rebound condition (Firth, 1974). The systematic exploration of some, if not all, of these manipulations might well permit us to gain sufficient control over the dreaming process to manipulate it effectively either as a dependent or independent variable.

If one can alter various aspects of the dream experience, the possibility for demonstrating an effect on subsequent wakefulness then exists. However, one needs to have some idea in what aspect of subsequent wakefulness one might expect to see changes caused by the manipulation of the dream experience.

The variables to examine in wakefulness that are likely to be effective in influencing dream content or to be subsequently influenced by dream content are those of an affective rather than cognitive nature (Ekstrand, Barrett, West, & Maier, 1977). We found that the waking experiences most likely to appear in dreams are those with an affective charge (Piccione, Jacobs, Kramer, & Roth, 1977). And, the link of waking life to dreams is more likely, but not exclusively, to be an affective rather than cognitive one from both a state (Kramer, Roth, Arand, & Bonnet, 1981) and trait (Kramer, Roth, & Palmer, 1976) point of view. In examining the wake-sleep-wake continuum, we should look for the relationship between pre-sleep affective states, the consequent dream experience, and the relationship of dreaming to the affective state of the dreamer the next morning (Kramer & Brik, 2002). The consequence of affective change, if any, on adaptive function should be explored (Johnson, Spinweber, Gomez, & Matteson, 1990; Lutz, Kramer, & Roth, 1975).

D. The Selective Mood Regulatory Theory of Dreaming: An Adaptive Theory of Dreaming

1. The Core Observation

a. The Contribution of REM Physiology   Freud (Freud, 1955b) proposed that the function of dreaming was to preserve the continuity of sleep. Taking our lead from this proposal, the physiological study of REM sleep, the concomitant mental content of which will be taken as our paradigm for psychological dreaming, has contributed three observations that buttress this suggestion. First, if the dream is related to maintaining the continuity of sleep and as the longer one sleeps across the night the more likely one is to wake up, then the distribution of REM sleep across the usual sleep period is appropriate; it increases as the night goes on with more of it being in the second half of the night (Webb, 1969). The second observation about the role of dreaming in maintaining the continuity of sleep relates to the fact that a period of REM sleep often ends in a brief arousal. In research we conducted with 10 subjects studied one night each, 90% of the REM periods ended in a brief arousal of less than 15 seconds for which there was no memory. Third, it has been found (Solms, 1997) that those patients who have had a brain injury who report they no longer experience dreaming have an increased number of awakenings during the night indicating a difficulty maintaining the continuity of sleep. One is encouraged by these observations to explore a relationship between dreaming and the continuity of sleep.   Yet, some dreams appear to disturb rather than to protect the continuity of sleep. The following dream discussed in chapter 10 was reported by a 26-year-old man who was a patient in a VA hospital:

> I dreamed I was back in Vietnam and I had thrown a grenade into one of the Vietnamese huts. I went inside and there was one of the babies blown up all over the inside of the hut. I woke up and was terrified, nauseated and crying.

The dream was troubling and led to an awakening associated with negative affect and the clear recall of the troubling dream (Kramer & Roth, 1977). A dream such as this one that disturbs sleep tests Freud's proposal that the dream protects sleep and led to his postulation of the only exception to his wish fulfillment theory of dreams, a mastery function in which the repetition of disturbing dreams was an effort to master the anxiety associated with the dream. He hypothesized that the mastery function was a predecessor to the pleasure principle (Freud, 1955a). When the pleasure principle becomes dominant, the wish fulfilling and sleep protecting function of sleep emerges.

Many dreams have no feeling in them and in those that do, a negative feeling is more common than a positive one (Hall & Van de Castle, 1966). The romantic notion of the "land of dreamy dreams" (Gilchrist, 1981) is not borne out in our studies of the experience of dreaming. Taub (Taub, Kramer, Arand, & Jacobs, 1978) compared an individual's dream to that same individual's nightmare. In a similar group of people, he asked them to make up a nightmare, not one they had experienced. The subjects' dream experience was the least affect laden while the confabulated nightmare was the most emotionally intense. A successful dream, one that doesn't disturb sleep, appears to have muted feeling as its usual accompaniment.

b. The Intensity of Dreaming   The intensity of the dream experience has a developmental course across the REM period (Kramer, Roth, & Czaya, 1975; Kramer, Czaya, Arand, & Roth, 1974). We collected dream reports from the last 10 seconds at six time points into the REM period, and the reports were scored along a number of dimensions using a dream intensity questionnaire. The intensity increase in emotionality is essentially linear between 2.5 and 30 minutes with a plateau between 10 and 20 minutes, which fits the eye movement pattern (Aserinsky, 1971; Johnson, Kramer,

Bonnet, Roth, & Jansen, 1980). Aserinsky speculated that dream content might vary in the ebb and flow pattern of the REM sleep eye movements.

c. Dreaming and the Emotional Surge   The rise and fall in the intensity of content and affect across the dream period is in keeping with the possibility that during REM sleep there is a surge of emotion. We are of the opinion that a function of dreaming is to contain or attempt to contain that surge.

Several questions arise. Is the recallability of a dream influenced by the relative success of the dreaming process in containing the emotional surge occurring during REM sleep? Does the arousal after a dream period lead to the awakening of the "nightmare" because the "intensity" of the surge exceeds the integrative capacity of the dream experience? The variability and magnitude of alterations in heart rate, blood pressure, and respiration associated with REM sleep may also point to the affective nature of the REM experience (Freemon, 1972). Efforts to connect content with variability in autonomic function have been minimally successful, if at all (Pivik, 2000). Nevertheless, the autonomic functions during REM sleep are experiencing fluctuations in keeping with an emotional surge. It is possible that if the integrative sleep maintaining function of dreaming is successful, the dream does not enter awareness. The dream is encompassed in the amnesia that is sleep and the function of such a dream is subsumed under an assimilative function for dreaming.

d. Dream Function: Containment of the Emotional Surge   What factors might influence or determine the success of the dream experience to contain the emotional surge of the REM period and help keep the dreamer asleep, and without dream recall? Is the attempt to contain the emotional surge related to the content of the dream experience, to the preoccupation with the ability of the dreamer to recall dreams, to the emotional condition (psychopathology, predispositional states) of the dreamer, or to the responsivity of the dreamer to the dream experience (heightened arousal levels)?

We compared individuals who reported having at least two nightmares per week with a group of vivid dreamers (Kramer, Schoen & Kinney, 1984). The two groups had the same content categories at about the same frequency in their dreams. Apparently the integrative capacity of dreaming cannot be accounted for by the content of dreams. The ability to recall dreams does not reflect the capacity to integrate the emotional surge of dreaming as the vivid dreamers have a much higher dream recall of 89%, compared to 54% for the nightmare sufferers. We would expect higher recall in the nightmare subjects if dream recall occurs because the emotional surge is not contained, but this was not the case.

There does appear to be a predispositional factor which may be determining of the capacity of the dreamer to contain the REM sleep emotional surge. The nightmare subjects had higher scores on all the MMPI scales and on emotionally based scales of the Cornell Medical Index and had more psychiatric hospitalizations. They reported that the nightmare was related to current feelings, e.g., anger, sensitivity, and general emotion. The immediate emotional state of the person appears to be a determinant of the integrative capacity of their dreams on a given night.

The emotional responsivity of the dreamer to the dream experience is another factor reflecting the activity of the integrative function of dreaming. Those with nightmares are described by others as more responsive and frightened during sleep, apparently in reaction to the dream experience.

The integrative failure that is reflected in an increased responsivity in nightmare sufferers was confirmed in a study of Vietnam War veteran patients with Chronic Delayed Post Traumatic Stress Disorder (CDPTSD) who have frequent nightmares (Kinney & Kramer, 1985). When they were given an above threshold tone during sleep, they responded in 93% of trials while the control group responded only 52% of the time. They are more responsive and more emotionally troubled (Kramer, Kinney, & Schoen, 1983). Predispositional factors, such as existing psychopathology, alter responsiveness. This integrative failure may be due to an inability to contain "internal emotional forces." The CDPTSD patients had a higher awakening threshold than controls (Kramer & Kinney, 2003). If they were being vigilant, as they said they were, it was internally rather than externally directed. If it were externally directed, we would have expected lower rather than higher thresholds.

The CDPTSD subjects in the threshold study (Kinney & Kramer, 1985) failed to identify the external source of the awakening stimulus at a much higher rate than the control group, 92% compared to 60%. This supports the internal focus of attention in the CDPTSD patients.

There is evidence, both psychologically and physiologically, of an emotional surge that rises and falls across the REM period. If the dream functions successfully, a brief arousal occurs for which there is no memory. If the dreamer is emotionally troubled and therefore hyper-responsive on either a transient or chronic basis, this predisposition has as an associated feature a failure of the dream to contain the emotional surge and the likelihood of a dream recall or a frightening awakening is enhanced. The capacity to contain the emotional surge is determined by the "soil," the affective state of the dreamer that the dream falls on at the time of dreaming.

It appears that the emotional surge within a REM period is inextricably linked to the intensity of the dream experience (Kramer, Roth, & Czaya, 1975; Kramer, Czaya, Arand, & Roth, 1974) and probably to the intensity of the physiological variables such as eye movements (Aserinsky, 1971, Johnson, Kramer, Bonnet, Roth, & Jansen, 1980), heart rate, blood pressure, and respiration that occur during the dream period (Freemon, 1972). These observations suggest that an examination of both the waking affective and mental state as they relate to dreaming would be appropriate.

2. Mood Before and After Sleep

a. An Introduction   The core observation in approaching the function of dreaming led to a view that the dream, as Freud (Freud, 1955b) had suggested, serves to protect the continuity of sleep by containing the repeated disruptions and emotional surges that occur across the night regularly in REM sleep and perhaps irregularly from other sources. These observations draw our attention to the relationship of dreaming in particular and sleep in general to the emotional-affective state of the individual.

It is apparent that there is an intimate relationship between sleep and how one feels. The likelihood of obtaining a good night's sleep is generally credited to the subjective state of the person prior to going to sleep. How one feels in the morning is believed to be the consequence of the quality and quantity of the sleep that preceded it. Sleep, if one is trying to understand its function, is best seen as placed between two periods of wakefulness. Prior wakefulness impacts sleep and sleep impacts subsequent wakefulness.

How depressed or anxious a person is before going to sleep has been shown to alter how well one sleeps (Rimon, Fujita, & Takahata, 1986; Rosa, Bonnet, & Kramer, 1983). From a psychological perspective, the more intense the emotional experiences of the day (Piccione, Jacobs, Kramer, & Roth, 1977) and the thoughts a person has before going to sleep (Kramer, Moshiri, & Scharf, 1982; Piccione, Thomas, Roth, & Kramer, 1976; Kramer, Roth, Arand, & Bonnet, 1981), they are likely to appear in the dreams of the subsequent night's dreams. Sleep is clearly responsive to the experiences that precede it during the day.

The physiological and psychological aspects of sleep are also related to the waking activity of the next day. How well one performs on various psychomotor tasks following a night's sleep is influenced by even small alterations in the number of hours of prior sleep; for example, decrements in performance can be shown with even a one hour reduction in prior sleep (Wilkinson, 1968). Feeling states are predictive of performance (Lutz, Kramer, & Roth, 1975) and feeling states on arising are better predictors of performance during the day than the prior total hours of sleep (Johnson, Spinweber, Gomez, & Matteson, 1990). Mental activity in the morning is linked to the dreams of the prior night (Kramer, Moshiri, & Scharf, 1982).

There is a thematic continuity between the dreams of the night and the spontaneous verbal behavior of the following morning. Wakefulness is responsive to the experiences during sleep that preceded it. Sleep is linked both to prior and subsequent wakefulness in both its physiological and psychological aspects.

The possibility that sleep functions to alter the subjective state of the person seems plausible. An exploration of the sleep-mood interaction should look at the relationship of both the psychology and physiology of sleep to waking mood. A systematic study of the mood-sleep relationship will be described starting from relatively normal situations and extending them to more extreme circumstances. Mood appears to vary from day to day, across the day, and might well bear a relationship to both dreams and sleep physiology.

b. The Measurement of Mood   The mood measurement device used in our studies was the Clyde Mood Scale (Clyde, 1963), a 48-item adjective checklist which yields scores on six factors: friendly, aggressive, clear thinking, sleepy, unhappy, and dizzy (anxious). We established that the subscales were independent and that the scale was reliable (i.e., yielded scores that were similar to the published factor norms), sensitive to change from night to morning, and that repeated use did not lead to stereotype or adaptation (Kramer & Roth, 1973b).

c. Mood Difference Across the Night   The mood scale was administered to subjects sleeping in the laboratory generally for 15 to 20 consecutive nights. We found that the intensity and variability of mood subscale scores decreased from night to morning. This was true in the laboratory (Kramer & Roth, 1973b; Roehrs, Kramer, Lefton, Lutz, & Roth, 1973), at home (Lysaght, Kramer, & Roth, 1979) , across a wide age range (20–70) (Roth & Kramer, 1976), identically for both men and women (Lysaght, Kramer, & Roth, 1979; Kramer, Sepate & Leavengood, 1990), whether the subjects were in a hypnotic medication study (Schwartz, Kramer, & Roth, 1974) or had been awakened for dream collection. We had expected that the mood scale scores for men and women would be different as their affective state is different (Cattell, 1973) and as is their sleep physiology to some degree (Williams, Karacan, & Hursch, 1974), and their dream patterns (Winget & Kramer, 1979). If the night and morning mood differences can be related to the psychology and physiology of sleep, then sleep may play a role in mood regulation across the night.

d. Mood Predictability Across the Night   We were interested in how stable a person's mood might be. Do the various aspects of mood vary systematically from night to morning and from day to day as does dreaming for each individual? We studied night and morning mood scores from 52 people, 40 women and 12 men, for 17 to 21 days (Kramer, 1993). We did two correlations. In the first, to capture the trait aspect of mood, we did a between subject correlation of the averaged night score to the averaged morning score on each subscale. In the second, to capture the state aspect of mood, we did a within subject correlation of night to morning mood for each mood subscale and then averaged the subscale correlations across subjects. The trait aspects of mood mean correlations are quite high with four of six being above .88. Two correlations were low, sleepy $r = .26$, the only nonsignificant one, and dizzy (anxious) $r = .62$; friendly, aggressive, unhappy, and clear thinking had correlations between $r = .88$ and $r = .95$. The state aspects of mood mean correlations were all quite low between $r = .03$ and $r = .29$, none of which were significant. We clearly have evidence for a systematic night to morning mood relationship at the trait level for five of six aspects of mood, but at the individual level the variability is so high that none of the aspects of mood shows a systematic night morning relationship. If we look at the individual subscale correlations, we find 77, 25%, are significant when only 16 would be expected by chance (52 subjects × 6 subscales = 312 × .05 significance level = 15.6). We find that 42 of 52 subjects, 81%, have at least one significant correlation. The largest number of significant correlations is with the unhappy mood subscale in 22 of 52 subjects, 42%. The lowest number of significant correlations is with the sleepy subscale in 8 of 52 subjects, 15%.

The individual subscale scores showed a decline on 50% or more nights (64, 59, 62, and 56%) for friendly, aggressive, unhappy, and clear thinking; sleepy and anxious showed a decrease on just under 50% of the nights (49 and 47%). The number of subjects showing a 50% decline or more on the aggressive subscale was 76%, for unhappy 74%, for friendly 69%, for clear thinking 63%, for sleepy 46%, and for anxious 41%.

We found a series of systematic relationships between pre- and post-sleep mood both between and within subjects. The mood relationship is specific for an individual such that on average, for example, how friendly one is at night and in the morning is specific for that individual, different from others, and a trait aspect of the person. On a day-to-day basis, an individual may have a specific relationship on a particular mood subscale from night to morning, most commonly the unhappy subscale, a state aspect of the individual.

e. Mood Change and Sleep Deprivation   We did two sleep deprivation studies to establish whether the change in mood across the night was related to the intervening period of sleep. The first was one night of sleep deprivation done in a group (Roth, Kramer, & Lutz, 1976). We found that after the deprivation, the sleepy, aggressive, and friendly scores were increased, but recovered after one night of recovery sleep. The second sleep deprivation study was done in the laboratory with two consecutive nights of deprivation (Vaccarino, Rosa, Bonnet, & Kramer, 1981). With increasing deprivation, the subjects showed increased scores on the sleepy and anxious scales and decreased scores on the clear thinking scale. No changes were noted on the unhappy and aggressive scales. Pre- and post-sleep mood is sensitive to one night of sleep loss reflected in increased sleepy and anxious scores and decreased clear thinking scores. Changes in the friendly and aggressive scores may be more related to the social aspects of the experimental situation than the sleep loss (Kramer & Roth, 1973b; Roehrs, Kramer, Lefton, Lutz, & Roth, 1973; Roth, Kramer, & Lutz, 1976). The decrease in the unhappy scale score in normative studies remains to be explained (Lysaght, Kramer, & Roth, 1979; Roehrs, Kramer, Lefton, Lutz, & Roth, 1973; Roth & Kramer, 1976).

f. Mood Change Across the Day   Mood change occurs across the day as well (Lysaght, Roth, Kramer, & Salis, 1978) with the cheerful, energetic, and general activation scales being maximal at noon and minimal at bedtime and the reverse being true for the inert-fatigue and deactivation scales. The changes across the day of the activation/deactivation scales are phase advanced about 4 hours on the diurnal temperature curve. These changes in mood, with low activity maximal at bedtime and peaking at noon, support the findings that that the night-morning mood changes are different than those across the day although they are related. Most importantly, these mood patterns are not simple epiphenomenon of the diurnal temperature curve.

g. Mood and Daytime Performance   Does mood bear any relationship to significant daytime activity? In two studies we found that mood relates to daytime performance on psychomotor and cognitive tasks. In the first study (Lutz, Kramer, & Roth, 1975), at three time points, 3.5, 10, and 22.5 hours, after ingesting an hypnotic, five of six mood scales—sleepy (–.53), clear thinking (.38), friendly (.36), unhappy (.33), and aggressive (.18)—showed a significant correlation with performance scores. In a second study, subjects who were sleep deprived and had shown changes in mood also showed performance decrements (Rosa, Bonnet, Warm, & Kramer, 1981). Johnson (Johnson, Spinweber, Gomez, & Matteson, 1990) had also shown that post sleep performance correlated better with morning mood than hours of prior sleep.

h. Summary: Mood and Sleep
We have shown that

i. mood is different before and after sleep;

ii. the level and variability of mood decreases from night to morning;

iii. the change in mood from night to morning is due to the intervening sleep;

iv. the friendly, unhappy, and sleepy aspects of mood show the most systematic change across the night;

v. almost all of the aspects of mood, five of six, show a highly correlated relationship from night to morning;

vi. most subjects, 81%, have at least one significant mood subscale correlation from night to morning;

vii. mood subscale correlations from night to morning across days for an individual occur most often with the unhappy subscale (42% of subjects) and least often with the sleepy subscale (15% of subjects);

viii. a decrease in mood intensity occurs on the majority of days (63%);

ix. morning mood and daytime performance, both cognitive and psychomotor, are related.

3. Mental Content Before, After, and During Sleep

a. Introduction   As the dream is related to the affective state of the dreamer, does it show changes similar to what we found in our studies of mood? To test the suggestion that dreams vary similarly to mood, the dream content of a number of groups and individuals were explored.

b. Dream Differences Between Groups   Demographic variables such as sex, age, race, marital status, and social class are powerful psychological factors that may have important covariates both cognitive and affective. Does dream content reflect differences in demographic variables? In a representative sample of the adults in Cincinnati (Kramer, Winget, & Whitman, 1971; Winget, Kramer, & Whitman, 1972), we found the five demographic variables had different dream content associations. The sex of the dreamer had 10 content differences, social class had six, age had four, and race and marital status had three each. To illustrate, women had more characters and emotions in their dreams while men had more aggression and achievement striving with success. Younger adults had more guilt in their dreams while those over 65 had more death anxiety. Whites had more covert hostility than blacks. The widowed and divorced had more death concerns than single and married people. People in the lower social class had more characters in their dreams than those in the upper social class.

Demographic variables are associated with dream content differences. The dreamer's sex is the most important determiner of dream content with emotion being among the differences, yet we found no difference in mood change across the night related to the sex of the subject (Lysaght, Kramer, & Roth, 1979; Kramer, Sepate, & Leavengood, 1990). The limited differences between whites and blacks are surprising given the centrality of race in our public discourse. The importance of sex in determining dream content was supported by our finding a number of significant differences in a laboratory study (Kramer, Kinney, & Scharf, 1983) that compared the dreams of men and women and found that men dreamed more about other men and women about both men and women, men had more fullness references while women had more intensity and thinking references.

We have observed in both a laboratory (Kramer & Roth, 1973a) and nonlaboratory study (Kramer, Baldridge, Whitman, Ornstein, & Smith, 1969) that the dreams of schizophrenic and depressed patients are different. The schizophrenic patient has strangers as his unique character type and the depressed have family members as theirs. Patients with chronic delayed PTSD who served in the military in the Vietnam War have 50% of their laboratory collected dreams related to their military experience, while essentially none of the control group, who had also served in Vietnam, did (Kramer, Schoen, & Kinney, 1984).

The dream reflects psychological differences at the group level in both normal and psychopathological populations. The mood state of the individual may be found to relate to these dream content differences.

c. Dream Differences Between and Within Individuals   The central question in our current discussion is whether the dream is organized at the individual level such that differences between individuals can be identified as well as between nights of an individual as we found in our studies of the relationship between pre and post-sleep mood. We examined this question among dreams of normals and schizophrenics (Kramer, Hlasny, Jacobs, & Roth, 1976) and found that the dreams of individuals are distinguishable one from the other, whether the person is mentally healthy or psychiatrically ill, and the dreams of an individual are different night to night. However, dreams from night to night are linked (Kramer & Roth, 1979); across 20 nights, the correlative level increases so that nights one to two have a content correlation of .05 and nights 19 to 20 of .80.

d. Dream Differences Across the Night   Was the content of REM dreams across the night different from each other? This is what one would expect if some processing change was occurring. We found (Kramer, McQuarrie, & Bonnet, 1980) that the number of words differed between REM period reports so that the report from the first REM period was shorter than from the second and the third was shorter than the fourth, but two and three did not differ. Eight of 22 dream content categories showed a change across the night with word length held constant. We found word length and content changes across almost all REM report periods, four from one to two, five from two to three but none from three to four. The mean content score of three of the significant content categories (i.e., total characters, single characters, and female characters) show the inverted U shaped change across REM periods with a numerical but nonsignificant decrease in period four. This is the pattern that one might expect if a problem solving activity were occurring across the night in which there would be tension accumulation, discharge, and regression or relaxation. There is clear support for some type of systematic dream content change across the night (see the section on "The Sequential Dream Pattern" later in this chapter).

e. Dreaming and Waking Thought   Are dreaming and waking thought related? If so, then the possibility that the processing of content in dreams across the night might be relatable to subsequent waking thought. We were asking if the waking current concerns of the individual, that are reflected in his dreams, are linked to his waking thought. We compared (Kramer, Roth, & Palmer, 1976) the content of TAT stories to the content of REM dreams and found that the intensity of the content of the two fantasy productions was significantly correlated, .72. We felt this provided evidence for a trait relationship between waking and dreaming.   We next examined (Kramer, Roth, Arand, & Bonnet, 1981) the relationship of the verbalized mental content immediately before and after sleep to the content of the intervening REM dreams and found that nine of the 18 contents scored showed a significant correlation with a mean of the significant correlations of .38. This demonstrated a state relationship between waking and dreaming thought.

We explored the coherence within and connectedness between REM dreaming and waking (Kramer, Moshiri, & Scharf, 1982). We found the pre- and post-sleep verbalizations of subjects thematically connected in 95% of individuals but the themes of REM dreams were only relatable in 75% of people—a significant difference. Pre-sleep mentation was thematically connected to the subsequent night's dreams in 85% of individuals, post-sleep mentation was connected to the prior night's dreams in only 70% of people. Waking thought is more coherently organized than dreaming thought and dreams appear to be more reactive that proactive.

There is a thematic connection (Kramer, Moshiri, & Scharf, 1982; Kramer, Roth, Arand, & Bonnet, 1981; Kramer, Roth, & Palmer, 1976) across the wake-sleep-wake continuum. The possibility of a functional interrelationship remains to be demonstrated.

f. The Similarity of Change in Dream Content and Mood   Dreams vary in a manner analogous to, if not identical with, that of waking mood. Dreams reflect psychological differences in demographically and psycho-pathologically different populations in which affective differences may well exist. Dreams of individuals are different from each other and dreams of an individual are different night to night and analogously pre- and post-sleep mood are different among individuals and from day to day within an individual. Pre-sleep mental content is related to dream content and the dream content is also related to morning mental content. This makes the processing of dream content across the night a possibility. Dream content changes across the night as does mood. The change in dream content across the night might be responsible for the change in mood from night to morning.

4. The Dream's Responsiveness to the Emotional State of the Dreamer

a. Introduction   I have repeatedly called attention to the organized nature of the dream report. The dream is also a highly responsive experience especially to the emotional state of the dreamer. We have done a series of studies to explore this relationship.

b. Emotionally Significant Waking (Interpersonal) Experiences Influence Dream Content   We have earlier described a series of seven studies that demonstrate that the principal emotional concern of the dreamer influences the theme of the night's dreams. First, we have shown that the more emotionally intense experiences of the day are what appear in dreams (Piccione, Jacobs, Kramer, & Roth, 1977). Second, specific emotionally capturing experiences such as beginning and ending an involving activity can be distinguished from each other in dream reports (Kramer, Roth, & Cisco, 1977). Third, the pre-empting nature of the laboratory continues to be represented in dreams across time (Piccione, Thomas, Roth, & Kramer, 1976). Fourth, the interpersonal situation between dreamer and dream collector influences what is selected for reporting (Whitman, Kramer, & Baldridge, 1963b). Fifth, the emotional concern about who will observe and evaluate you can and does focus your dreams (Whitman, Kramer, & Baldridge, 1963a). Sixth, the sexual make-up of a dream collection pair, same or different, influences the content of the dream experience and report (Fox, Kramer, Baldridge, Whitman, & Ornstein, 1968). And seventh, emotionally meaningful names presented during REM sleep are more likely to be incorporated into the dream experience than meaningless names (Kramer, Kinney, & Scharf, 1983). The emotionally responsive nature of the dream experience has, I believe, been convincingly demonstrated.

c. Medication Treatment and Affective Change   We looked at an impersonal treatment that altered affect to see if dream content changed when affect changed (Kramer, Whitman, Baldridge, & Ornstein, 1968). We observed in depressed patients that after successful treatment with an anti-depressant medication, their REM dream content changed such that depression, hostility, anxiety, and intimacy in the dreams decreased and heterosexuality and motility increased. Medication that affects the emotional-affective dimension of the patient alters their dream content.

5. *The Relationship Between Mood and Dreams*

We have shown that mood and sleep are related and that dreams are related to the individual's waking affective state as well as being reactive to the emotional state of the dreamer. If dreams contain or alter affective state, dream content and mood change should be related.

a. The Mood Change-Dream Content Relationship   We studied two men in the lab for 20 consecutive nights collecting from them pre- and post-sleep mood scores and their REM dreams (Kramer & Roth, 1973b). We correlated 31 dream content categories with the mood subscale change scores across the night. We found a series of significant relationships with the largest number of correlations being between the change (decrease) in the unhappy subscale and an increase in characters in the dream. It was of considerable interest that the change that related most strongly to dream content change was the unhappy subscale. The unhappy subscale was one of three subscales, friendly and sleepy being the other two that showed the most consistent change in the sleep through studies. As discussed above, it was changes in the unhappy subscale that previously remained unexplained (Lysaght, Kramer, & Roth, 1979; Roehrs, Kramer, Lefton, Lutz, & Roth, 1973; Roth & Kramer, 1976). We repeated the study with 12 male subjects and found that mood change was significantly related to dream content (Kramer & Roth, 1980). A significant relationship to dream content was found for five of the six mood subscales with friendly being the exception. The distribution of correlations across the mood subscales was not random and the unhappy subscale had significantly more correlations than the others. A significant relationship was found between three groups of content scales, i.e., characters, descriptive elements and activities, and mood change. The greatest number of correlations was between the character scales and the change in the unhappy mood subscale. How happy you feel on awakening in the morning depends on who you spent the night with in your dreams.

Affect is not directly and simply processed across the night (Kramer & Brik, 2002). We looked at the relationship between pre- and post-sleep mood and dream content in 20 men who slept in the lab for 20 consecutive nights. We found 10 significant correlations between mood and dream content; two were with pre-sleep mood and eight with post-sleep mood. We found no direct pass-through relationship in which a pre-sleep aspect of mood correlated with an aspect of dream content and that content with the same aspect of mood post-sleep. Five of the 10 significant correlations were between aspects of pre- and post-sleep mood and affect in the dream. The two pre-sleep correlations were between the dizzy (anxious) aspect of mood and dream confusion and sexual social interactions. There were three correlations with the post-sleep unhappy score, namely dream sadness, confusion, and aggressive social interactions. The post-sleep friendly aspect of mood correlated with dream apprehension, anger, and aggressive social interactions. Post-sleep aggressive and clear thinking aspects of mood had one dream content correlation each. There was no relationship to total characters. Pre- and post-sleep mood is as connected to dream affect as it is to other dream contents. The connections were more proactive, eight of the significant correlations, than reactive, two of the significant correlations. How you feel in the morning is related to how you feel in your dreams and what transpires in them.

A serious question has been raised by Strauch and Meier (Strauch & Meier, 1996) about the central role of affect in dreaming as only 50.2% of dream reports contain a specific affect and an additional 23.4% a general feeling. In a study that tabulated the frequency of dream reporting in psychoanalytic treatment (Kramer & Glucksman, 2006), we found that only 58.3% of dreams had affect in their manifest content but 96% had affect if the associations were included. We found that within a dream across time, there was a systematic development of emotional intensity (Kramer, Czaya, Arand, & Roth, 1974; Kramer, Roth, & Czaya, 1975). It is apparent from our two studies that affect is universally connected to the dream experience and could play a central role.

b. Reprise of the Mood-Change Dream Content Relationship At this point, the evidence indicates that

    i. mood before and after sleep is different;
    ii. the level and variability of mood decreases from night to morning;
    iii. the change in mood is due to the intervening sleep;

iv. almost all aspects of mood (five of six) show a highly predictable relationship from night to morning;

v. it is the unhappy, friendly, and sleepy aspects of mood that show the most systematic change from night to morning;

vi. most subjects (81%) have at least one significant mood subscale correlation from night to morning;

vii. mood correlations from night to morning across days for an individual occur most frequently with the unhappy mood subscale;

viii. on the majority of days (63%), a decrease in mean mood intensity occurs across the night;

ix. the change in various aspects of mood across the night is related to the dream content of the night;

x. the change in the unhappy mood subscale across the night is related to the characters that appear in the night's dreams;

xi. dream characters distinguish the depressed from the schizophrenic and, with the lifting of a depression, dream content changes in the depressed.

6. The Relationship Between Mood and the Physiology of Sleep

a. Introduction   The possibility that similar mood changes would occur in relationship to the physiology of sleep, i.e., in sleep stages and total sleep time, invites an examination of their relationship. This would address the unlikely possibility that mood change is more related to the physiology than the psychology of sleep and would establish if mood change had any relationship to sleep physiology as well as dreams.

b. Sleep Deprivation and Mood Change   Total sleep deprivation studies were clearly linked to alterations in mood (Roth, Kramer, & Lutz, 1976; Vaccarino, Rosa, Bonnet, & Kramer, 1981). There was an increase in the sleepy and dizzy (anxious) subscale score and a decrease in clear thinking after one night of sleep loss, all of which was intensified after the second deprivation night but not the aspects of mood change (unhappy) most related to dreaming.

c. Mood Change and Sleep Physiology   We did two studies to examine the relationship between mood change and sleep physiology. In the first study (Kramer & Roth, 1973b), the change across the night in the six mood subscales in six male subjects who slept 15 consecutive nights were correlated with five sleep variables (i.e., total sleep time, REM time, stage three/four time, stage two time, and number of awakenings). The largest number of significant correlations was between the change in the sleepy mood subscale and total sleep time. Sleepy had not been found in previous studies

(Kramer & Roth, 1980) to be related to the content of dreaming. In the second replication study (Kramer, Roehrs, & Roth, 1976), 11 men slept for 15 consecutive nights in the lab. Their pre- and post-sleep moods were assessed and seven sleep variables were scored. Awakenings were not scored but stage one time, sleep latency, and REM latency were added to the variables in the first study. We did a regression analysis using the seven sleep variables to predict the six mood subscale score changes. Four of the six correlations were significant (sleepy and friendly at $r = .42$ and aggressive and clear thinking at $r = .24$, while unhappy and dizzy were not significant with an $r = .22$). The two highest correlations, sleepy and friendly, were significantly different than the two lowest, unhappy and dizzy. We also performed analyses to see which of the sleep variables were predictive of which aspects of mood. We found that it was the non-REM aspects of sleep (stage two time, stage three/four time, and sleep latency) that was predictive of the changes in the sleepy and friendly scores. The unhappy aspect of mood, the mood subscale most particularly related to dream content, was not related to the physiology of sleep.

We looked further at the relationship of the unhappy aspect of mood to REM sleep. We studied the relationship of scores on the D-scale of the MMPI and the pre-sleep unhappy mood subscale score in 11 men who slept in the lab for 15 consecutive nights (Kramer, Roehrs, & Roth, 1972). We found no relationship between their D-scale MMPI scores or their pre-sleep unhappy mood scores and the amount of REM sleep they had. Unhappy mood is related to the content of dreaming and not to the amount of REM sleep.

Dream content and sleep physiology are related to different aspects of mood change across the night. In two pilot studies (Kramer & Roth, 1973b), we found the distribution of significant correlations for dream content categories and sleep variables to aspects of mood change across the night to be different (see Table 8.1). The 54 significant mood-dream correlations are primarily to the unhappy and secondarily to the friendly and aggressive aspects of mood change. The 26 significant sleep variable mood change correlations are primarily to the sleepy, dizzy, and clear thinking aspects of mood.

d. The Mood Regulatory Function of Sleep   Sleep has a systematic relationship to mood change across the night. It appears that the physiology of sleep and the psychology of sleep may be differentially related to various aspects of mood change across the night. The change in the sleepy aspect of mood across the night relates to how much non-REM sleep one has had, while the change in the unhappy aspect of mood is a function of who one dreams about. People are important to us even in our dreams. The mood regulatory function of sleep is suggested by the fact that pre-sleep mood is different than post-sleep mood. Specifically, the mean level and variability of mood decreases across the night. It is as if a "funneling action" occurs which decreases the intensity and variability of various aspects of mood. The physiological and psychological activities during sleep appear to be "corrective" like a thermostat operating to move the mood level toward a central and lower point. The dream seems particularly involved with one aspect of mood (i.e., unhappy) and may be seen as a selective affective (mood) regulator, an "emotional thermostat," so to speak. Similarly, the physiological aspects of sleep, particularly non-REM sleep, are related to changes in the sleepy aspects of mood also acting as a selective mood regulator.

7. The Dream Mechanism for Mood Change: Emotional Problem Solving

a. Introduction   Dreaming should be related to the emotional state of the dreamer if dreaming is to protect sleep by absorbing the emotional surge that appears to accompany REM sleep as indeed it is as previously described in the discussion of the mood change-dream content relationship. The question remains as to how the dream might change the affective state of the dreamer from pre-sleep to post-sleep? We have established that pre- and post-sleep mood and the intervening dream content are related (Kramer & Brik, 2002) and that the change in mood across the night is also related to the intervening dreams (Kramer & Roth, 1980).We have further shown that the pre-sleep content of thought and the post-sleep thought content are also related to the intervening dream content (Kramer, Roth, Arand, & Bonnet, 1981). Waking thought pre- and post-sleep is related in both its affective and cognitive aspects to the intervening dream content. The mechanism for mood change is not a simple sequential alteration of affect through the REM dreams of the night (Kramer & Brik, 2002). The linear change in REM dream content across the REM period and the night is such that the processing of mental and emotional content could be occurring as previously suggested.

b. Patterns of Emotional Problem Solving   Two patterns of thematic dream development across the night are discernible (Kramer, Whitman, Baldridge, & Lansky, 1964), one of a progressive-sequential type in which a problem is stated, worked on, and resolved, and the other of a repetitive-traumatic type in which the problem is simply restated in different images or metaphors and no progress toward resolution occurs. The effectiveness of a night's dreaming in reducing the intensity and variability of dreaming occurs in about 60% of nights (Kramer, 1993). This variation for an individual in the effectiveness of a night's dreaming may be the result of the differential pattern of dreaming across the night. If one has experienced a progressive-sequential dream pattern, there may be a positive alteration in the emotional state of the dreamer. If the problem one goes to sleep with is simply restated and not solved, a traumatic-repetitive dream pattern, then a less successful night's dreaming has occurred. I am suggesting that it is through this mechanism of "emotional problem solving" or failure to "problem solve" that the affective alteration in dreaming takes place (French, 1952) or fails to occur. This thematic dream change may be concomitant with the change in the intensity of unhappiness across the night and the appearance of the appropriate number and types of characters in the dream. Dreamers show both patterns in approximately the same frequency (Kramer, Whitman, Baldridge, & Lansky, 1964), 60/40, as we noted for the effectiveness of a night's dreams in changing waking affect across the night. People show both patterns, which underscores that there is not universal success in altering the residual emotional problems of the day. This could account for some of the variability in how a person feels on awakening in the morning. Illustrations of the two dream patterns from the same person who slept in the lab may serve to capture more graphically what is meant by emotional problem solving.

c. The Progressive–Sequential Dream Pattern   The progressive-sequential pattern shows a metaphoric statement of the problem which is then worked on or explored and brought to some sort of figurative resolution, generally, by restating the problem in familiar, if inexact terms, and reducing it in solution to something familiar. The following series of dreams were collected from a woman subject from the sixth night she slept in the lab for REM dream collection (Kramer, Whitman, Baldridge, & Lansky, 1964).

1] Woman subject—dream night #6

(6-1): This little girl was asleep. She was being real cute, prolonging things for money or to stay in the hospital longer.

(6-2): I passed Frank's wife in a car. She saw me come...she pulled away. I got kind of mad. I decided it didn't make any difference....

(6-3): I was playing tennis. I hit it back real hard. We won the game.

(6-4): A patient didn't need the doctor after all. She started out thinking she needed a doctor but she didn't. She had a big bandage on her stomach.

(6-5): Doctor was not able to treat patient because he was not properly licensed. The patient is planning to use surgery against the doctor.

2] Thematic interpretation

(6-1): The thematic pattern seems to be that the subject wished to depend or cling to the doctor and hospital even if she had to claim illness, but the "cuteness" revealed a seductive motive as well.

(6-2): The subject, vis á vis the wife of a friend, experienced the feared and expected rejection that she tried to minimize.

(6-3): This dream can be seen as a turning point in that the victory in the tennis game appears to reduce effectively the tension generated by the conflict between a wish to be close to the doctor/experimenter for care and love and the feared rebuff of abandonment. She switches to successful competition with a partner. The inference was that whatever she was struggling with has been conquered.

(6-4): The victory with a partner in the previous dream permitted her to deny her need for the doctor that she admitted she once had, and there was evidence that the need continued (the bandage).

(6-5): The recognition of the continuing need for the doctor for care and love (6-4) caused her to intensify her rejection of him by being critical of his qualifications and expressing her wish to get even or hurt him. It is the familiar double assertion: "Not only do I not need you, you're no good anyway."

The pattern of movement has a clear progression from presenting as a dependent but manipulative child in order to hold on to help, followed by a rejection, leading to a triumph with someone, and then a rejection of the doctor who isn't desirable anyway.

d. The Repetitive-Traumatic Dream Pattern   The repetitive traumatic dream pattern involves a restatement of the conflict with different images and metaphors. Some interrelationship may be suggested but it is basically a figurative restatement within a narrow thematic range without the progression seen in the sequential pattern. The dreams that follow were collected from the same woman subject whose progressive-sequential pattern was reported above. This REM dream series was from her third night in the lab (Kramer, Whitman, Baldridge, & Lansky, 1964).

1] Woman subject—dream night #3

(3-1): Somebody was lost. It was a dog and they were trying to find out where it lived. A little kid or somebody couldn't tell where he lived. It wasn't my dog though. I wasn't lost. This person who was lost was always fumbling around leading everybody else around because he didn't know what he was doing. Some boy, I think. Somehow, we had telephone numbers trying to find the right one. It was supposed to be that little boy that was lost.

(3-2): They filled up the car. There wasn't enough room, unless I went back with the people we went back with before. I could go back with someone else. The place we were going was an orphanage some place, some house, a place like that.

(3-3): I was dreaming about visiting, I think it was some EEG laboratory or something like that where mothers could leave their children, and then could go shopping. I doubt whether they could, there wouldn't be enough room for all of these people.

2] Thematic interpretation

(3-1): The boy was seen as lost and misleading others. Not she, but the boy was lost. There was concern in the dream that she was going to be misled by the boy because of his inexperience so she tries to call home.

(3-2): In a setting of abandonment (orphanage) she hoped anxiously there would be room for her to return home. She had a ride home, but the car was crowded.

(3-3): She was in the laboratory temporarily and her mother was going to return for her (implied). There wasn't enough room.

The fear of being lost which is denied followed by being left because things are crowded, repeated in an orphanage and laboratory setting, shows no progress to solution but just a restatement of the abandonment fear.

e. Emotional Problem Solving: A Comment   These patterns are elaborations or specifications of the general thesis that dreams may subserve a problem solving function (French, 1952; French & Fromm, 1964). It may be that through this effort at emotional problem solving that the success or failure to contain the emotional surge occurs that leads to the arousal-awakening that is the hallmark of REM sleep. If successful, the arousal is for seconds and the dreamer returns to sleep with no memory of the arousal. If the problem is not solved, an awakening is more likely to occur. Difficulty in emotional problem solving in waking life is more associated with the psychopathologically troubled who have been found to be more responsive to the arousal-awakening after a REM period and who report more bad dreams and nightmares.

Sleep is generally a successful process, although there is great concern expressed about a disturbed night's sleep. Given that sleep is generally a successful process, one would expect to find that the progressive-sequential pattern would be more common than the repetitive-traumatic one. In the two subjects we studied in the laboratory, 50% of their nights had the sequential pattern, and 32% the repetitive pattern with the remainder a mixed pattern (Kramer, Whitman, Baldridge, & Lansky, 1964). It was in 63% of nights that the average mood intensity score decreased (Kramer, 1993). The current emotional and cognitive concerns of an individual are processed by a problem solving mechanism across the wake-sleep-wake continuum and the resultant state is a determinant of performance the next morning.

8. *The Concluding Summary*

Theories of dreaming need to address dreams that go on outside of awareness and those that enter awareness and potentially have the capacity for a more direct effect on the dreamer's consciousness (Kramer, 1981). One needs both an assimilative and accommodative theory of dreaming. The former is reductive and the latter is potentially transformative.

The selective mood regulatory theory of dreaming is an example of an assimilative theory of dream function. The dream functions to contain the affective surge that occurs during REM sleep. If successful, one has no memory of dreaming and sleep proceeds essentially undisturbed. If unsuccessful or partially so, a dream recall occurs that, if conditions are right, becomes a disturbing dream or nightmare with a troubled awakening.

The experience of the recalled dream, which depends to a degree on a troubled state in the dreamer, opens the possibility for an extension of the assimilative, reductive view to encompass some degree of transformation and of accommodation as well. States of disturbance increase the likelihood of change. Dreaming that enters awareness can become the object of attention for the dreamer and lead to change in the dreamer, to an enhancement of self-knowledge.

CHAPTER **12**
The Biology of Dream Formation

A. Introduction

Freud, in his introductory chapter to *The Interpretation of Dreams* (Freud, 1955b, 41-42) comments, "Even when investigation shows that the primary exciting cause of a phenomenon is psychical, deeper research will one day trace the path further and discover an organic base for the mental event." Freud rejected the speculative theories of his colleagues who wished to assign the dreaming process solely to demonstrable organic causes. The great psychologist of dreaming believed that his psychological descriptions of dream formation would at some time be related to organic (i.e., brain) activity. I believe it is the conviction that biology, the brain, is real and psychology, the dream, is ephemeral that supports the attraction of clinicians and researchers to biological explanations for experiential events.

B. Efforts to Bridge the Mind/Brain Divide

There has been an intense interest in brain activity (functioning) with the development of new techniques that can assess neuronal activity in various areas of the brain, functional MRIs, and relating the results correlatively to functions of the mind. Mental health professionals have gotten caught up in this biological fervor and see brain function and psychological experience as increasingly closely related. They have embraced the concept of the mind/brain to express this unification of the psychological and biological aspects of brain function. This is an effort to bridge the chasm that Descartes introduced some 500 years ago in his discussion of what came to be called the mind-body problem. Why this view, mind/brain, has been so vigorously and, I believe, unreflectively embraced by mental health professionals is part of the biological hegemony in present day mental health research and practice.

A review of the conceptual efforts that have been offered to bridge the mind-body divide may provide a helpful background for an examination of the suggested biological theories of the dreaming process. Kendler, a psychiatrist whose special expertise is in the genetic basis of the major psychiatric illnesses, has recently provided a sympathetic exploration of approaches to resolving the mind/brain problem (Kendler, 2001). He points out that it is a subject that psychiatrists need to engage and not avoid. He offers the following philosophical approaches to the problem:

  i. substance dualism in which there are two substances, material and mental;
 ii. property dualism in which mind and body are two distinct properties of the same substance (e.g., like color and mass);
iii. type identity in which the relationship is fundamentally the same, everywhere and always;
 iv. token identity in which the relationship between brain and mind is not universal; it is an identity at a point in time. Different brain states can yield the same mind state, sort of a common final pathway idea. No causal claims are made–just concomitance. Kendler could see type identity as one end of a continuum with token identity as the other;
  v. functionalism is any brain state that has some functional role, it offers functional and not biological equivalence;
 vi. eliminative materialism which is essentially epiphenomenalism; and
vii. explanatory dualism in which there are two aspects of a phenomena, these are complementary explanations, consistent with identity theories, and functionalism.

If we are to embrace the magic of neuroscience, we must confront the issue of how Qualia, the essence of what is experienced, is explained by biology. As minds appear to understand things, we must ask if biology can provide meaning, a concept central to the understanding of the mind? Further, behavior, even if not adaptive or problem solving, is goal directed and therefore purposeful, a teleologic concept that mechanistic biology has long abhorred. We are currently unable to traverse the divide from neurons firing in some part of the brain to the correlated mental experience. There is, as Levine (Levine, 1983) has pointed out, an explanatory gap and, as Chalmers (Chalmers, 1995) has said, the hard problem of consciousness will not simply go away using correlative explanations. McGuinn (McGuinn, 1999), a philosopher of science, doubts we have the intellectual tools to specify the transduction rules to go from the neurophysiology of brain to the psychology of mind.

Kendler (Kendler, 2001) has adopted explanatory dualism as his best take on the mind/brain problem. He points out that identity theorists who provide bottom up explanations are essentially reductionists. Kendler suggests that meaning, intentionality, *qualia*, and consciousness may be seen as emergent properties of brain function, an example of the whole being greater than the sum of the parts, and therefore not predictable from other aspects of brain activity, such as neuronal discharge patterns. He says mind is not like temperature, which is the index of the rate of molecular movement. He notes that evolution is another example of an emergent system. Evolution is not explained by the bottom up of traditional causality via DNA and RNA. Evolution works on the whole organism.

Antrobus, a noted dream researcher, takes a monist stance in that he studies the mind/brain (Antrobus, 1993). He states that the unity of body and mind is poorly understood. He concludes that he is a monist by faith but a dualist by practice. Perhaps this is a disappointing assessment of our success in bridging the gulf that Descartes described but a more realistic assessment of our current state of knowledge.

C. A Neurotransmitter Basis for Dreaming

Hartmann (Hartmann, 2003) has offered a view of dreaming that sees it on a consciousness continuum from focused waking to less structured thought to reverie, free association and daydreaming, to dreaming. He recognizes the central role of emotion in dreaming, if not in all conscious states, as he sees nightmares as a more emotionally intense form of dreaming.

We have reviewed aspects of the effect of various medications and neurotransmitters on dreaming (Kramer, Whitman, Baldridge, & Ornstein, 1966). Hartmann (Hartmann, 1984) provides a well reasoned pharmacological basis for the control of dreaming. He cites the literature that raphe cells in the brainstem contain neurons that release serotonin and serve to initiate or maintain sleep become inactive during dreaming. He points out the locus coeruleus nuclei in the pons which contain norepinephrine are also inactive during REM sleep, the dream state in his theorizing. The cholinergic neurons in the fronto-tegmental field (FTG cells) are active during REM sleep. He concludes that reciprocal interaction between the norepinephrine containing nuclei in the locus coeruleus and the serotonin containing raphe neurons and the cholinergic FTG neurons regulate the start and end of a REM period. He notes there is less evidence for dopamine in REM sleep control. The different patterns of release of these transmitters in the forebrain account for the differences in consciousness during wakefulness and REM dreaming. He reviews the pharmacologic evidence related to reserpine, L-dopa, beta adrenergic blockers, and cholinesterase inhibitors and particularly notes the increased reporting of nightmares in Parkinson patients given L-dopa. Hartmann concludes that decreased activity in norepinephrine and serotonin brain systems and an increase in acetylcholine and dopamine brain systems may account for dreaming and nightmares. He acknowledges that many brain regions are involved in sleep and the cortex is necessary for wake and dream consciousness.

Hartmann's equation of dreaming and REM sleep can only be maintained by rejecting non-REM dreaming. In his exposition on the nightmare, he has to create a special case for the nightmares in Post Traumatic Stress Disorder (PTSD) as they occur early in the night and can occur during non-REM sleep. He also recognizes that in some of the medications he discusses, the results are not consistent with his view as reserpine, which has nightmares as a side effect, would decrease dopamine not increase it. Beta blockers also have nightmares as a side effect but only decrease norepinephrine and do not affect acetylcholine or dopamine. Dopamine is associated with an increase in nightmares but does not reduce norepinephrine. The limitations in Hartmann's effort should not detract from the attention he has called to a possible neurotransmitter basis for dreaming and waking consciousness.

D. An Electrophysiologic Basis for Dreaming

Winson (Winson, 1985, 1990) has proposed a theory of dreaming from his studies of the relationship between the theta rhythm in the hippocampus and REM sleep in animals. Winson suggests that dreaming reflects a fundamental aspect of memory processing. He proposes that dreaming (REM sleep) in subprimate animals is the means by which animals form strategies for survival and evaluate current experience in light of those strategies. This may provide the basis for the meaning of dreams in humans. Brain stem neurons, in addition to generating the ponto-geniculate-occipital (PGO) neural pattern during REM sleep, also initiate a theta rhythm in the hippocampus, a part of the brain central to memory storage. There being no REM sleep in the echidna (an egg laying spiny anteater) indicates that REM sleep evolved 140 million years ago when marsupials and placentals diverged from monotremes like the echidna and suggests by evolutionary criteria that the survival of a complex neural process like REM sleep must have an important survival function. Understanding this function might help us understand the meaning of dreams.

Winson pointed out that the occurrence during wakefulness of the theta rhythm in the hippocampus happened when the animal was engaged in activities that required a response to changes in the environment essential to survival that was not genetically encoded. This waking information was then reprocessed into memory during REM sleep and indexed by the appearance of the theta rhythm in the hippocampus. Processing to and through the hippocampus occurs by sensory and associative area information from the neocortex going to the entorhinal cortex then to the hippocampus. The signal goes first to the granule cells of the dentate gyrus, then to CA3 pyramidal cells and lastly to the CA1 pyramidal cells. After completing its tour of the hippocampus, the neural signal returns to the cortex, first to the entorhinal, and then the neocortex. Theta rhythm has been demonstrated in the dentate gyrus, the CA1 neurons, and the entorhinal cortex. The brain stem initiator of the theta rhythm sends signals to the septum in the forebrain that initiates theta in the hippocampus and entorhinal cortex. He found that the theta rhythm was related to spatial memory. Foulkes (Foulkes, 1982) reported that as the spatial skills in children develop, they begin REM sleep reporting and in adults spatial skill ability is a predictor of dream recall. Solms (Solms, 1997) reports the loss of the spatial aspect of dreaming with right-sided injury to an area of the parieto-temporal-occipital area.

Long-term potentiation (LTP) may be the means by which long-term memory is encoded. The NMDA receptor in the dendrite and granule cells and CA1 cells of the hippocampus and throughout the neo-cortex are activated by glutamate. Occurrence of LTP in the hippocampus is linked to the theta rhythm which is activated by cells in the brain stem which in turn activate the NMDA cell receptors in the hippocampus. Sensory information, like place in space, arrive from the cortex to the hippocampus where, through the triggering by the theta rhythm, NMDA receptors enhance neuronal firing and LTP occurs that results in the information entering into long term memory. A similar process occurs during REM sleep without incoming information suggesting the reprocessing of information coded when the animal was awake. By this mechanism, Winson suggests each species could process information most important for its survival, e.g., location of food and means of predation or escape, activities present awake that occur with a theta rhythm. This information is accessed again in REM sleep and may then be integrated with past experience to provide an ongoing strategy for survival behavior. Dreams, he suggests, represent an individual's strategy for survival.

Winson presents an interesting and complex description of the concomitance of the hippocampal theta rhythm and memory consolidation during wakefulness and its reprocessing in REM sleep in animals. The absence of a hippocampal theta rhythm in humans or in primates regretfully leaves his thesis as simply a speculation. His equation of dreaming with REM sleep is an unfortunate equation but one that runs through most biological theories of dreaming. It would be appealing to those interested in dreaming to find that dreaming was problem solving and had survival value. But as Dr. Winson points out, theta rhythm may not even exist in humans as olfaction has been replaced by vision as the dominant sense.

E. An Anatomic Basis for Dreaming

From a neuroscience point of view, there are currently only two major competing theories of the functional anatomy of dreaming. One, the Activation-Synthesis theory of Hobson and his collaborators (Hobson, Pace-Schott, & Stickgold, 2000) has been extended into their AIM space state model, a bottom-up, subcortical brain stem view of the origin and content of dreaming. The source for the initiation of dreaming is in the pons, which send random signals to the cortex. The cortex responds passively to the pontine signals in that its response is determined by these random signals. The cortex elaborates the dream experience, making the best of a bad job. The content of the dream experience is shaped by affect in the dream (Hobson, 1999). The model for dreaming is the verbal output seen in the productions of delirious patients. The second, a competing view of a brain-based theory of dreaming, has been articulated by Solms (Solms, 1997). This theory is based on a clinico-anatomical approach, brain lesions, using neuropsychological techniques. It is allegedly a top-down, cortically based theory. Any stimulus that activates the brain can initiate the dreaming process. It requires engaging the ventral tegmental area of Tsai whose fibers pass through the ventromedial prefrontal area adjacent to the anterior horns of the ventricles.

In order to appreciate the value and, more importantly, the limitations of the neuroscience approach to dreaming, I will review the two theories (Hobson, 1999; Hobson, Pace-Schott, & Stickgold, 2000; Solms, 1997, 2003). They have major points of difference.

1. The Activation-Synthesis AIM Space Model of Dreaming

I will focus first on the older theory, the Activation-Synthesis (A-S) AIM space state model (Hobson, Pace-Schott, & Stickgold, 2000). The orientation in A-S toward dreaming is that

  i. dreaming is co-extensive with REM sleep;
  ii. the model for the experience of dreaming is delirium;

iii. the stimulus for cortical activation is random discharges from the pons in what has been described as PGO waves, ponto-geniculate-occipital waves;

iv. the cortical response to the PGO waves is a relatively passive one; and

v. the content of the dream is shaped by the affect in the dream.

Dreaming is defined in the A-S theory as "mental activity occurring in sleep which is characterized by vivid sensorimotor imagery, that is experienced as waking reality, despite such distinctly cognitive features as impossibility or improbability of time, place, person, and actions; emotions, especially fear, elation, and anger predominate over sadness, shame, and guilt and sometimes reach sufficient strength to cause awakening, memory for even vivid dreams is evanescent and tends to fade quickly unless special steps are taken to retain it" (Hobson, Pace-Schott, & Stickgold, 2000, 795). Hobson and colleagues believe that this definition captures what people mean by dreaming and serves both psychological and cognitive neuroscience.

In A-S, differences among REM, non-REM, and wake mentation will be explained by the distinctive physiology of REM sleep. REM sleep is related to dreaming.

1. Dream reports are obtainable twice as often from a REM sleep awakening (80%) than a non-REM sleep awakening (40%).
2. When the REM period ends, the retrieval of a dream report rapidly declines.
3. The length of the dream report correlates positively with the number of minutes of REM, and external stimuli can become part of dream narrative.
4. REM reports can be differentiated from non-REM reports.
5. There are qualitative differences between REM and non-REM reports. REM dream reports are longer, more intense, with more movement and emotion and are less related to waking life. Non-REM is more thought like.

The aspects of REM dreaming that are less common in non-REM include

1. The hallucinatory and delusional nature of the experience;
2. The quickly changing imagery that can be bizarre;
3. The decreased self-reflection and volitional control;
4. The creation of an unrealistic story; and,
5. That instinctual programs, such as fight/flight, organize thinking.

These features of dreaming, A-S theory holds, will be explained by the distinctive biology of REM sleep. The A-S theory postulates an isomorphism between the biology and psychology of dreaming that reflects either a similarity (biological meaning of isomorphism) or an identity (mathematical meaning) between the two. It is a highly reductionistic theory that explains the experience of dreaming by its biology.

The control of REM dreaming is described anatomically, physiologically, cellularly, and chemically. The anatomic control is in the pons; therefore, it is subcortical in the brainstem. Physiologically, it is represented by PGO waves from the pons to the lateral geniculate body to the occipital cortex. At the cellular level in the pons, the REM-on cells are in the mesopontine tegmentum. The REM-off cells are in the Nucleus Locus Coeruleus and Dorsal Raphe Nucleus. The chemical control of dreaming is a consequence of REM-on cells secreting acetylcholine while the REM-off cells secrete norepinephrine and serotonin.

In a three-dimensional model, the AIM space state model of the A-S hypothesis shows the change in activation during dreaming sleep from low to high; while the information source shifts from external to internal; and the modulation shifts from high norepinephrine and serotonin to high acetylcholine.

The activation of various brain areas in A-S theory is somewhat in this order. There is stimulus from the pontine and the midbrain reticular activating circuits and nuclei. This leads to an ascending arousal of multiple forebrain structures. The contribution to the dream experience is consciousness, eye movements, and motor pattern information via the PGO system.

i. Diencephalic structures, e.g., hypothalamus and basal forebrain, are activated involving autonomic and instinctual (fight/flight) functions, and cortical arousal. The contribution to dreaming is to further support consciousness and provide instinctual elements.

ii. Anterior limbic structures are active including the amygdala, anterior cingulate, parahippocampal cortex, hippocampus, and medial frontal areas. This contributes emotional labeling of stimuli, goal directed behavior, and movements. This activation contributes to the dreams emotionality, affective salience, and movement.

iii. The dorsolateral prefrontal cortex is inactive during dreaming. This area is involved with executive functions, logic and planning. This would explain in the dream the absence of volition, logic, orientation, and working memory.

iv. The basal ganglia become active. They are involved in the initiation of motor actions. In the dream, they may account for the initiation of fictive movement.

v. The thalamic nuclei become active, for example, the lateral geniculate nucleus that would be involved in the relay of sensory and pseudo-sensory information to the cortex. For the dream experience, it transmits PGO information to the cortex.

vi. Primary motor and sensory cortices and sensory cortices are blocked.

vii. The inferior parietal cortex is stimulated. It provides the spatial organization for the dream.

viii. The visual associational cortex becomes active and involves the integration of visual images.

ix. The cerebellum is activated and contributes imagined movement to the dream.

In the A-S theory, dreaming is generated by the random output of the brainstem and passively synthesized by the forebrain. The cortex, it is said, makes the best of a bad job. Delirium is the model for the dream.

2. The Cortical Theory of Dreaming

The forebrain, or cortical, theory of Solms (Solms, 1997, 2003) is based on a clinico-anatomical approach in patients with localized brain lesions, utilizing neuropsychological techniques to specify the functional deficiency, and CT scanning to confirm the lesion site. Dreaming is explained as a top-down process despite the nuclei of Tsai being subcortical. Solms observed there was a loss of the experience of dreaming in patients who had either (1) a bilateral mediobasal frontal cortex lesion involving fibers from the ventral tegmental area of Tsai, an appetitive center which is the source of seeking, wishing/desiring behavior; or (2) a lesion of the inferior parietal area of either side of the brain which on the right involves spatial orientation and on the left involves symbolic activity. Individuals who said they had lost the experience of dreaming were those who also reported poorer sleep. In those patients with a lesion in the parieto-temporo-occipital association region, the visual elements in dreaming are lost as well as the ability to create visual images from memory while awake.

Dreaming is not assumed to be REM sleep dependent in the cortical theory (Hobson, Pace-Schott, & Stickgold, 2000). Dreaming is initiated by an arousing stimulus, such as REM sleep, seizures, or noise.

1. This activation stimulates cells in the ventral tegmental area of Tsai, a dopaminergic system.
2. The ventral tegmental area of Tsai circuits are connected to frontal and limbic structures and instigate goal-seeking behavior. It is the wanting, wishing command system.
3. Anterior limbic structures block transmission, which interrupts goal directed behavior, e.g., voluntary motor activity, and facilitates "back projection" processes.
4. The dorso-lateral cortex (the voluntary executive center) and primary visual cortices (the site for perception) are inhibited.
5. The inferior parietal cortices become active and provide the spatial (right side) and symbolic (left side) aspects of dreaming.
6. And lastly, the occipital association areas provide memories of perceptions from which the imagery of dreaming is constructed.

For Solms (Solms, 1997, 2003), dreaming does not isomorphically reflect simple activation of perceptual and motor areas, as these are not activated during dreaming. The imagery of dreaming is not just reproduced it is constructed each time from memory.

3. *Limitations of Anatomic Theories of Dreaming*

a. Activation-Synthesis Hypothesis   Let me now address more particularly the limitations (Kramer, 2000; Kramer, 2002) I find in the A-S hypothesis (Hobson, Pace-Schott, & Stickgold, 2000). I would question whether the object of study as characterized in the A-S theorists' particular definition of the dream is representative of the dreaming process. Dreaming is defined in the A-S theory as "vivid, sensorimotor imagery, experienced as waking reality, despite it being improbable or impossible at times, and emotions are seen as prominent." This is a highly selective and arbitrary definition of dreaming. Nielsen (Nielsen, 2003) points out there is a continuum of cognitive experiences during sleep from so-called apex dreaming, to regular dreaming, to cognitive activity (often called sleep mentation), to cognitive processes. There is no generally accepted or standardized definition. The position put forth by the A-S theorists that their definition captures what people mean by dreaming and that it serves both psychology and cognitive neurosciences is questionable. Taub and colleagues (Taub, Kramer, Arand, & Jacobs, 1978) have shown that what people say they think a nightmare is like and what they report as a personal nightmare experience are clearly different. The concept of nightmare, i.e., what people think nightmares are like, is more intense, better constructed, and reported in fewer words than their own nightmare experience. A definition of dreaming needs to be made on an empirical basis rather than out of opinions about what it is or is not. Utilizing idealized versions of experience may be suitable for literary undertakings but not for scientific ones either in psychology or in the neurosciences.

Assumptions by the A-S hypothesis theorists (Hobson, Pace-Schott, & Stickgold, 2000) that dreaming is co-extensive with REM sleep has been widely challenged. Solms (Solms, 2003) has pointed out that dreaming and REM sleep are doubly dissociated, not all REM sleep yields a dream report, and dream reports can be recovered from non-REM sleep. Further, dreaming may not even be sleep bound as both Foulkes and Fleisher (Foulkes & Fleisher, 1975) and Kripke and Sonnenschein (Kripke & Sonnenshein, 1978) have collected dream reports from subjects who were awake.

That dreaming is the result of the activity of the pontine generator for REM sleep has been challenged by the clinico-anatomical studies of Solms (Solms, 1997). He reports that patients with core brainstem lesions, who are hypoaroused while awake, continued to report dreaming.

Conceptualizing that the model for the dream experience is the output of the delirious brain is related to the description of the physiologic processes that A-S theorists assume underpin dreaming. In their view, random discharges from the pons, so-called PGO waves, stimulate cortical structures that do the best they can to organize these chaotic stimuli and the results are hallucinations and narratives that are poorly organized, confabulated, and easily forgotten, allegedly like the experiences of the delirious person awake. The cortex makes the best of a bad job. However, Snyder (Snyder, 1970) has pointed out, based on his large series of laboratory collected dreams, that it is the dreams' mundane nature that best characterizes them, rather than their being impossible or improbable. Heynick (Heynick, 1993), in a systematic analysis of speech reported as part of the content of the dream experience, observes how well constructed the speech in dreams is from a grammatical and syntactical point of view. Apparently our linguistic capacity during dreaming operates with surprising efficiency and is capable of generating well-formed, often syntactically complex sentences. Kramer (Kramer, 1982) has shown that dream content is highly ordered and where we know there are psychological differences, there are dream content differences as well. This is true at the group level as demographic variables show dream content differences. Dream content is different by gender, age, race, marital status, and social class. And in psychopathologic groups, the dreams of schizophrenics are different than those of the depressed. At the individual level, dream content varies across the REM period and from REM period to REM period across the night. The dreams of one individual are different from those of another, different within an individual, and different night to night. However, there is a content correlation from night to night such that across 20 nights of laboratory collected dreams, the dream content of night 19 correlates 0.8 with that of night 20. Dreams are more predictive night to night than the physiology of sleep (Kramer & Roth, 1979). Dreaming is ordered, not chaotic, and certainly not random. The predictive ability of the A-S model has not been, nor is it likely to be, able to distinguish the dream differences that have been described.

Viewing the cortical response to PGO stimulation as a relatively passive one underpins the conviction that the form of the dream will be determined by the physiological stimulus and the dream will be isomorphic with the determining physiology, PGO waves. Pivik (Pivik, 2000, 495) has concluded from a review of the psycho-physiological studies of dreaming that there is a "general absence of robust psycho-physiological relationships between tonic levels of physiological activity and sleep mentation." And that "studies…were unable to demonstrate a consistent correlation of phasic activity with the qualitative aspects of sleep mentation." Pivik's conclusions contradict any suggestion of isomorphism, a central tenet of the A-S hypothesis. Further, as the sensorimotor cortices are not activated during dreaming while the association areas are activated, the images experienced during dreaming are constructed each time and are not the result of perception; thus decreasing the likelihood of an isomorphic relationship between the physiological and psychological aspects of dreaming.

Reiser (Reiser, 2001, 354) along with Hobson (Hobson, 1999) is of the opinion "that emotion is a prominent part of the dream experience and that it plays a role in generating and shaping both the process and the content of dreaming." Dream content studies (Hall & Van de Castle, 1966; Kramer & Brik, 2002; Strauch & Meier, 1996) have not found emotions to be an inevitable part of the dream experience. Hall and Van de Castle found emotions in at most 56% of spontaneously reported dreams of men and 84% of the dreams of women. Strauch and Meier noted that a specific emotion was present in about half of laboratory reported dream experience. Kramer and Brik found emotions reported in at almost 37% of the laboratory collected dreams of men. Kramer and Glucksman (Kramer & Glucksman, 2006) found that emotion was present in 58.3% of dreams reported in psychoanalytic therapy, but if the affect found in the associations was included, emotion was present in 96% of dreams. Kramer (Kramer, 1993) in his Selective Affective Theory of Dream Function suggests in addition that it is the change in emotion from pre-sleep to post-sleep that is related to dream content. However, the central role of emotion in dreaming is supported by our finding emotional intensity increasing across time in our study of dream development across a REM period (Kramer, Roth, & Czaya, 1974) and that five of the 10 significant correlations between pre- and post-sleep mood and dream content are to the affect in the dream (Kramer & Brik, 2002).

The story-like nature of the dream, its narrative structure, has not been addressed by A-S theory but is a central feature of dreaming. Foulkes (Foulkes, 1999) sees the narrative aspect of dreaming as the driving force in dreaming more so than dream affect. Freud (Freud, 1955) has described the narrative aspect of dreaming as secondary revision, an aspect of the concealing activity of dreaming and a response to the dream work output and not central to dream construction.

In summary, the specific critiques of the A-S theory of dreaming (Hobson, Pace-Schott, & Stickgold, 2000) include

    i. The recognition of the limited and arbitrary nature of their definition of dreaming;
    ii. The doubt cast on the idea that delirium is an appropriate model for dreaming;
    iii. The evidence that REM sleep and the dreaming experience are not co-extensive;
    iv. The work that shows that dreaming is not isomorphic with REM sleep;
    v. The work that shows that differences in dream content that have been demonstrated have not and are unlikely to be shown by neurochemical and neurophysiological strategies;
    vi. The fact that emotion is not an inevitable accompaniment of the dream experience; and
    vii. The narrative nature of the dream is not explained.

The anatomical cortical theory of Solms (Solms, 1997, 2003) is offered as a top-down theory. It, too, is not able to predict from the pattern of neuronal activation to the content of the dream. It may be helpful to review aspects of the theory to see how it compares to the A-S hypothesis and in what way it lends anatomic support to Freudian dream theory. Reiser (Reiser, 2001) however, has advised that we not look to the neurosciences to confirm or refute Freud.

b. The Cortical Theory:

    i. Places the initiation of the dreaming process in a subcortical area related to goal seeking behavior of an appetitive sort and not in the pons as in A-S theory (this suggests the Freudian wish fulfilling as a motivating force);
    ii. Calls attention to the blocking of access to the sensorimotor cortex by anterior limbic structures leading to a backward (regressive)

movement in dream formation (suggesting both the Freudian censor in the block and topographical regression);

iii. Points out that it is the visual association areas that are activated during dreaming not the primary visual cortex, and therefore images are constructed from memory and are not perceptions, making the isomorphism postulated by A-S theory less likely;

iv. Calls attention to the fact that both spatial and symbolic activity is involved in dreaming (A-S theory does not address this issue);

v. Identifies that the loss of dreaming occurs in those who complain of sleep problems (suggests the possible sleep protective function of dreaming); and

vi. Notes that dreaming is actively constructed and not passively elaborated (suggesting the dream work).

Hobson and colleagues (Hobson, Pace-Schott, & Stickgold, 2000) provide a telling and detailed critique of the anatomical cortical theory (Solms, 1997).

i. They point out the limitations of lesion studies, e.g., the recovery in time of the lost function raises question about the role of the damaged brain area as essential to the transiently lost function.

ii. They wonder if REM awakening studies are the basis for the claim of lost dreaming (which they are not), as spontaneous memory of dreaming would be an inadequate test.

iii. They question the support Solms seeks from the leucotomy literature for the role of the medio-basal prefrontal area in dream initiation. Not all leucotomy patients, for example, reported the loss of dreaming. The leucotomy surgery could well have interfered with the recovery of intra-psychic experiences. The surgery could well have destroyed connections to subcortical limbic structures as well as those from ventral tegmental area.

iv. They see the role of dopamine in dreaming as problematic. They point out that dopamine has been reported as both inhibiting dreaming and enhancing it.

The cortical theory is a reductive theory that also poses biology as explaining the psychological experiences of dreaming, but less so than A-S. It does not address, anymore than A-S does, the narrative or affective aspects of dreaming.

What we want to know about dreaming begins with our desire to know the content of the dream experience for dream content is basic to our search for what the dream experience means, what is it made of, how is it constructed, and what does it accomplish. The functional anatomical explanations or the descriptions of the secretions from various cells of neurotransmitters or neuromodulators do not contribute to answer questions about the content, meaning, construction, or function of the dream experience.

As McGuinn (McGuinn, 1999) has so elegantly pointed out, there are no transduction rules to go from the discharge of neurons in the central nervous system or from the secretions of neurons to the concomitant mental states. He is, as I noted earlier, so pessimistic as to doubt that we have the intellectual tools to develop such a system. The biological dream theories cannot provide us with the content of dreams, the meaning of dreams, the construction of dreams, or the function of dreaming. They cannot address the differences in the content of the dream experience among individuals or within an individual night to night. These theories do not address the semantics or pragmatics of dreaming; they limit themselves, at best, to the syntax of dreaming.

Where might we expect the search for a biological basis for dreaming to turn? I would speculate that the intriguing implications offered by the work on mirror neurons might begin to gather more attention from those dream researchers with biological interests. Carr and colleagues (Carr, Iacobini, Dubeau, Mazziota, & Lenzi, 2003) have shown that watching and imitating emotional facial expressions activated similar brain areas and may be the anatomical base for empathy. They note that the superior temporal and inferior frontal cortices are critical areas for action representation and are connected to the limbic system via the insula, which may be the critical tie to emotion. Will we be able to identify mirror neurons for action and emotion awake and during dreaming with sufficient specificity to predict the dream experience from the mirror neurons that may be active during dreaming? Will the mirror neurons allow us to see the reflection of ourselves that the dreaming experience offers? This is an intriguing question yet to be answered.

F. Concluding Remarks

I hope it is apparent that the mind/brain problem has not been resolved by the current biological approaches to dreaming. Even explanatory dualism serves to keep the two domains, biology and psychology, separate and noninteractive, as perhaps they should be at this point in time. Emergent functions are descriptive and not explanatory. Concomitance is not explanation. It is not that biology isn't interesting, but rather it simply does not answer the questions we ask. Biology does not address the meaning of behavior, the goal directed aspect of behavior, or explain the nature of experience (*qualia*). The problem of consciousness is not illuminated. The explanatory gap remains.

CHAPTER 13

Journey's End? No, a Time for Assessment

The dream experience does not have an end. We are at a stopping place, a place where we can consider where we have been and we can speculate on where we may be going. The "sentimental journey" through dream land on which we embarked in company with the Cincinnati Dream Team has covered many areas that have been of interest to dream clinicians and scientists through the ages. I could recapitulate the chapter descriptions I offered in the preface as a way to summarize where we have been, but I prefer to focus on what I think our journey has taught us and where it should take us in the future: the take home message that my students demand from every seminar, what is it?

I would offer that the central message of this exploration is that the dream report is a highly organized and well constructed rendering of an experience that occurred during sleep and that may be occurring during wakefulness as well. The dream is an orderly production and not the disorganized response of a sleep impaired brain to random signals from subcortical areas. The model for dreaming is not delirium with the cortex making the best of a bad job, but rather it is a short story. I would look to O'Henry rather than Oliver Sacks for guidance about the nature of the dream experience.

The experience of dreaming is perhaps even more like a happening than a story. The dream takes on its more explicit narrative form in the reporting, which gives the experience its appearance of having a rather clear beginning, middle, and end. The dream starts by the dreamer placing himself somewhere and the experience unfolds. In a sequential close reading, the outcome often seems implicit in the beginning but even in a happening the events are constrained by the physical and human surround.

The interpenetration of sleep and wakefulness has been well documented by my physiologically committed colleagues. Sleep walking during deep or delta sleep is one case in point. The same has been found in the case of dreaming. In circumstances of relaxed wakefulness during which arousal remains high but focused attention is low, individuals will report experiences indistinguishable from nocturnal dreaming. It is this same combination of increased arousal, e.g., REM sleep, and unfocused attention during sleep that permits the dream experience to occur. The removal of the foreground din of wakefulness permits the background dream experience to emerge.

The dream can be studied scientifically although it is a subjective report of an inner process. Under the impact of the cognitive sciences, we have begun to recognize that verbalized subjective or first person states can be studied with the tools used to study so-called objective third person states. Science, I would offer, is a method of study not determined by the object of study. Since the identification of the correlation of dreaming with REM sleep, we have been able to collect a larger number of dreams at a particular time so that experimental approaches to studying the dream experience were possible. The development of techniques to quantify verbal behavior such as dream reports were undertaken and developed so that the quantification necessary for the scientific study of dreams became possible. Collection and measurement permitted dream science to move from mysticism and anecdote to science.

The dream as reported is not an infinitely variable experience any more than is waking life. There are content regularities that permit us to describe the normative aspects of dreaming. The average dream is one which has about three people in it, with a little more than one social interaction, five activities, one emotion, and one negative comment; it has very few positive events with misfortunes occurring about half the time. The content is most influenced by the sex of the dreamer, so that Freud's epigram that "anatomy is destiny" is borne out by the male/female differences in dreaming. Other demographic variables such as social class, age, education, and marital status do influence dream content but to a lesser degree than the sex of the dreamer. The so-called typical dreams such as falling, being attacked, or having a loved one endangered occur in all cultures with similar frequencies, do not show sex differences, and may have fixed meanings representing common aspects of human concerns. Nightmares, also a universal experience, decrease in frequency with age, may be related to abuse early in life, and may be a response to the dream experience rather than intrinsic to dreaming and seem to occur at times of personal stress when coping capacity is decreased. The dream in psychopathologic states has clear content differences that reflect aspects of the pathology itself, i.e., schizophrenics dream about strangers, the depressed about family members, the mentally healthy about friends. The nonrecall of dreams found in the better adjusted Holocaust survivor and former PTSD patient may reflect an avoidance-adaptive strategy. However dreaming about behavior to be avoided decreases the likely of engaging in the behavior as is illustrated by alcoholics who dream about drinking staying dry longer.

The interest in dreaming has a long and interesting history. The assumption that this strange nocturnal experience must have some meaning if it could only be deciphered goes back to our earliest recorded history in Egypt and Mesopotamia. The source of the dream has moved from the deity to the body to the mind and currently to the brain. The dream report has the necessary regularity and orderliness to be signal and not noise. Among people where we have convincing evidence that psychological differences exist, e.g., between men and women, young and old, schizophrenic and depressed, we find there are systematic, understandable, and meaningful dream content differences. The fact that dreams of individuals are different from each other and that dreams are different night to night as well as related night to night for a particular individual enhances the likelihood that dreams have meaning and opens the possibility that meaning could be extracted or constructed from a study of the dream. That dreams are related to the mental and emotional state of the dreamer before and after sleep and that it is the more emotionally intense daytime experiences that appear in dreams justifies the effort of therapists to seek to establish the meaning of the dream report of patients and to link that report to the current life circumstances of the dreamer. There is the suggestion that the dream experience properly understood provides additional information about the psychology of the dreamer that is not readily available from other sources.

The linkage between waking and dreaming thought is affective, thematic, and figurative rather than concrete and literal. The dream experience is affectively determined and narratively and affectively driven. Dreaming is less constrained by reality considerations and more open to associative connections built more on connotative rather than denotative meanings. The imagination plays a greater role in the construction of dreaming than it manifestly plays in our waking verbalizations. The affective impact of interpersonal situations on the dreamer plays a central role in the experience of dreaming. The content of dreaming is a response to the emotional uncertainties of life situations and is an attempt to figuratively solve these emotional concerns.

Given the difficulty in agreeing on the meaning of an event and recognizing the multiple possibilities and overdetermination of human experience, how are we to establish the meaning of a particular experience? This indeterminate view of meaning with its inevitable but unfortunate consequence of endless regress is countered by the recognition that at any particular time only one of the many possible meanings is likely to be focal and it is the one that reflects or relates to the preempting immediate current concern of the dreamer. A close reading or listening to the dream report in which the reader/listener lets himself be transiently enveloped by the report of the dream experience allows the listener to empathetically enter the dreamer's world. It is our shared human experience that allows this entry to the world of the dreamer. The associations of the listener stirred by having entered the world of the dreamer's dream are constrained by the context of the unfolding dream experience, as if the listener were in dialogue with the dreamer, and provide the clues to extract or construct the thematic metaphorical meaning of the dream. It is this metaphorical theme that through the door of the day residue provides the path to the waking emotional world of the dreamer. This dream translation approach can connect the consciousness of sleep to the consciousness of wakefulness.

But does the dream experience subserve any functional and adaptive purpose? The answer I would offer is that, indeed, dreaming and, more generally, sleep is a regulator of our affective state. Our mood changes across the night so that on arising in the morning the intensity and variability of the components of our mood are decreased. The two aspects of sleep, psychological and physiological, are differential affective regulators, serving as emotional thermostats, to reset across the night the different aspects of our emotional condition. Each aspect of sleep changes different aspects of our overall mood.

The sleepy, clear thinking, and anxious aspects are related to the physiological aspects of sleep, particularly the non-REM aspects. The psychological aspect of sleep (i.e., dreaming) is related particularly to the change across the night in the unhappy dimension of mood and less so to the friendly and aggressive dimensions. It is particularly the characters in the dream that are related to the change in the unhappy aspect of mood. How do these changes come about? If the immediate affectively laden waking current concern of the dreamer metaphorically represented is effectively processed across the dreams of the night in a progressive-sequential manner then the unhappy aspect of mood is improved, the emotional disturbance that could interrupt sleep is prevented, and the continuity of sleep is maintained. However, if a traumatic repetitive pattern is experienced in which the concern is simply restated in various metaphorical forms and no progression occurs, then the change in the unhappy dimension of mood does not take place. The change in the sleepy and related aspects of mood depends on the amount of non-REM sleep the sleeper obtains. How you feel on awakening in the morning is a determinant of your psychomotor performance the next day. Sleep differentially and automatically alters how you feel which relates to how you perform and achieves an assimilative adaptive function.

The dream experience is dependent on a functioning brain. The observation that much of dreaming is associated with a particular brain state (i.e., REM sleep) does not permit the equating of dreaming with this physiological state. Dreaming has been seen as an expression of the mind while REM sleep is an expression of brain function. Mind function is not and may never be reducible to brain function and the isomorphism of biological reductionism is not well supported. Mind may be seen as an emergent function of brain but not reducible to it. The study of dreaming is of interest as it provides an opportunity to study mind in relatively pure culture without the intrusions and noise of waking consciousness. The study and explanation of consciousness asleep and awake is the next goal to be sought in our dream journey. Dreaming consciousness sets constraints on biological explanations of dreaming and consciousness. The biological explanations of dreaming cannot limit themselves to the syntax of dreaming but must engage the semantics (i.e., meaning) and pragmatics (i.e., function) of dreaming. The mind-body problem has not been solved by the study of dreaming, concomitance is not causation, and even in our description of dream content development across a REM period being consonant with the pattern of eye movements, we provide only parallelism not causation.

And indeed Shakespeare got it right again; it is "Sleep that knits up the raveled sleave of care… [and that through dreams sleep provides the] Balm of hurt minds." The personal motive that has sustained me on my journey over 40 years is captured in a bit of verse by Dr. Milton Miller (Kramer, 1969c):

> One mystery alone remains
> Of my beloved's sleep:
> We've solved the movement of her eyes
> And why they do repeat,
> We know what brings her breath in sighs,
> We've tracked her EEG;
> The haunting doubt that still remains
> Is does she dream of me?

Bibliography

Abraham, H., & Freud, E. (1965). *A psychoanalytic dialogue: The letters of Sigmund Freud and Karl Abraham, 1907–1926*. New York: Basic Books.

Adler, A. (1956). *The individual psychology of Alfred Adler; A systematic presentation in selections from his writings* (1st Ed.). New York: Basic Books.

Agnew, H., Webb, W., & Williams, R. (1966). The first night effect: an EEG study of sleep. *Psychophysiology, 2*(3), 263–266.

Altshuler, K., Barad, M., & Golfarb, A. (1963). A survey of dreams in the aged. II. Noninstitutionalized subjects. *Archives of General Psychiatry, 8*, 33–37.

Anderson, T. (1986). The specimen dream as a childhood trauma. *American Imago, 43*, 171–190.

Antrobus, J. (1993). Dreaming: Could we do without it. In A. Moffitt, M. Kramer, & R. Hoffmann (Eds.), *The functions of dreaming* (pp. 549–558). Albany: State University of New York Press.

Arand, D., Kramer, M., Czaya, J., & Roth, T. (1972). Attitudes toward sleep and dreams in good versus poor sleepers. *Sleep Research, 1*, 130.

Archibald, H., Long, D., Miller, C., & Tuddenham, R. (1962). Gross stress reaction in combat—a 15 year follow-up. *American Journal of Psychiatry, 119*, 317–322.

Aserinsky, E. (1971). Rapid eye movement density and pattern in the sleep of normal young adults. *Psychophysiology, 8*(3), 361–375.

Aserinsky, E., & Kleitman, N. (1953). Regularly occurring periods of eye motility and concomitant phenomena during sleep. *Science, 118*, 273–274.

Askenasy, J., Gruskiewicz, J., Braun, J., & Hackett, P. (1986). Repetitive visual images in severe war head injuries. *Resuscitation, 13*(3), 191–201.

Baldridge, B., Whitman, R., & Kramer, M. (1965). The concurrence of fine muscle activity and rapid eye movements during sleep. *Psychosomatic Medicine, 27*, 19–26.

Barad, M., Altshuler, K., & Goldfarb, A. (1961). A survey of dreams in aged persons. *Archives of General Psychiatry, 4*, 419–424.

Barber, B. (1969). Factors underlying individual differences in rate of dream reporting. *Psychophysiology, 6*, 247–248.

Barrett, D., & Loeffler, M. (1992). Comparison of dream content of depressed versus non-depressed dreamers. *Psychological Reports, 70*, 403–406.

Bartlett, J. (Ed.). (1980). *Bartlett's familiar quotations*. Boston: Little, Brown.

Bastide, R. (1966). The sociology of dreams. In G. Von Gruenbaum & R. Caillois (Eds.), *The dream and human societies* (pp. 199–221). Berkeley: University of California Press.

Beauchemin, K., & Hays, P. (1995). Prevailing mood, mood changes and dreams in bipolar disorder. *Journal of Affective Disorders, 35*(1-2), 41–49.

Beauchemin, K., & Hays, P. (1996). Dreaming away depression: the role of REM sleep and dreaming in affective disorders. *Journal of Affective Disorders, 41*(2), 125–133.

Beck, A. (1967). *Depression: Clinical, experimental and theoretical aspects.* New York: Hoeber Medical Division.

Beck, A. (1969). Discussion of Cartwright: Dreams compared to other forms of fantasy. In M. Kramer (Ed.), *Dream psychology and the new biology of dreaming* (pp. 373–376). Springfield, IL: Charles C. Thomas.

Belicki, D., & Belicki, K. (1982). Nightmares in a university population. *Sleep Research, 11,* 116.

Belicki, K. (1986). Recalling dreams: an examination of daily variations and individual differences. In J. Gackenbach (Ed.), *Sleep and dreams: A source book* (pp. 187–206). New York: Garland.

Belicki, K., & Cuddy, M. (1991). Nightmares: facts, fictions and future directions. In J. Gackenbach & A. Sheikh (Eds.), *Dream images: A call to mental arms* (pp. 99–113). Amityville, NY: Baywood Publishing Co.

Benyakar, M., Tadir, M., Groswasser, Z., & Stern, M. (1988). Dreams in head-injured patients. *Brain Injuries, 2*(4), 351–356.

Berger, R. (1963). Experimental modification of dream content by meaningful verbal stimuli. *British Journal of Psychiatry, 109,* 722–740.

Bixler, E., Kales, A., & Soldatos, C. (1979). Sleep disorders encountered in medical practice. *Behavioral Medicine,* 1–6.

Bixler, E., Kales, A., Soldatos, C., Kales, J., & Healey, S. (1979). Prevalence of sleep disorders in the Los Angeles metropolitan area. *American Journal of Psychiatry, 136*(10), 1257–1262.

Blackburn, S. (2001, December 24). To feel and feel not. *New Republic,* 134–138.

Blakeslee, S. (2006, January 10). Cells that read minds. *New York Times,* p. F1&F4.

Bonnet, M., Alter, J., & Kramer, M. (1981). Memory for events occurring during arousal from sleep. *Sleep Research, 10,* 124.

Bonnet, M., & Kramer, M. (1981). The interaction of age, performance and hypnotics in the sleep of insomniacs. *Journal of the American Geriatric Society, 29*(11), 508–512.

Bonnet, M., Kramer, M., & Roth, T. (1981). A dose response study of the hypnotic effectiveness of alprazolam and diazepam in normal subjects. *Psychopharmacology (Berl), 75*(3), 258–261.

Boss, M. (1958). *The analysis of dreams.* New York: Philosophical Library.

Bowler, J. (1973). Irma injection flops: A theatrical criticism of a play in three acts by Dr. Sigmund Freud entitled the Irma injection dream. *Psychiatric Quarterly, 47,* 604–608.

Breger, L. (1967). Function of dreams. *Journal of Abnormal Psychology, 72*(5)(Suppl.), 1–28.

Breger, L., Hunter, I., & Lane, R. (1971). *The effect of stress on dreams.* New York: International Universities Press.

Brenman, E. (1982). Separation: a clinical problem. *International Journal of Psychoanalysis, 63*(Pt. 3), 303–310.

Brett, E., & Ostroff, R. (1985). Imagery and posttraumatic stress disorder: an overview. *American Journal of Psychiatry, 142*(4), 417–424.

Brink, S., & Allan, J. (1992). Dreams of anorexic and bulimic women: a research study. *Journal of Analytical Psychology, 37*(3), 275–297.

Brockway, S. (1987). Group treatment of combat nightmares in Post Traumatic Stress Disorder. *Journal of Contemporary Psychotherapy, 17,* 270–284.

Broughton, R. (1968). Sleep disorders: disorders of arousal? Enuresis, somnambulism, and nightmares occur in confusional states of arousal, not in "dreaming sleep." *Science, 159*(819), 1070–1078.

Buckley, J. (1970). *The dreams of young adults: A sociological analysis of 1133 dreams of black and white students.* Phd Dissertation Wayne State, Detroit.

Burstein, A. (1984). Dream disturbances and flashbacks. Letter. *Journal of Clinical Psychiatry, 45,* 46.

Carr, L., Iacobini, M., Dubeau, M., Mazziota, J., & Lenzi, G. (2003). Neural mechanisms of empathy in humans: A relay from neural systems for imitation to limbic areas. *Proceedings National Academy of Sciences, 100,* 5497–5502.

Carroll, L., & Gardner, M. (1960). *The annotated Alice: Alice's adventures in Wonderland & through the looking glass* (1st ed.). New York: C. N. Potter.

Cartwright, R. (1969). Dreams compared to other forms of fantasy. In M. Kramer (Ed.), *Dream psychology and the new biology of dreaming* (pp. 361–372). Springfield, IL: Charles C. Thomas.

Cartwright, R. (1972). Dreams, dream content and their psychophysiological correlates. In M. Chase (Ed.), *The sleeping brain*. Los Angeles: Brain Information Service, Brain Research Institute.

Cartwright, R. (1978). *A primer on sleep and dreaming*. London: Addison-Wesley.

Cartwright, R. (1979). The nature and function of repetitive dreams: A survey and speculation. *Psychiatry, 42*(2), 131–137.

Cartwright, R. (1991). Dreams that work: the relationship of dream incorporation to adaptation to stressful events. *Dreaming, 1,* 3–9.

Cartwright, R., & Kasniak, A. (1991). The social psychology of dream reporting. In S. Ellman & J. Antrobus (Eds.), *The mind in sleep* (2nd ed., pp. 251–264). New York: Wiley.

Cartwright, R., & Lamberg, L. (1992). *Crisis dreaming: Using your dreams to solve your problems* (1st ed.). New York: HarperCollins Publishers.

Cartwright, R., Lloyd, S., Knight, S., & Trenholme, I. (1984). Broken dreams: A study of the effects of divorce and depression on dream content. *Psychiatry, 47*(3), 251–259.

Cartwright, R., & Romanek, I. (1978). Repetitive dreams of normal subjects. *Sleep Research, 7,* 174.

Cartwright, R., & Wood, E. (1993). The contribution of dream masochism to the sex ratio difference in major depression. *Psychiatry Research, 46*(2), 165–173.

Castaldo, V., & Holzman, P. (1967). The effects of hearing one's own voice on sleep mentation. *Journal of Nervous and Mental Disorders, 144*(1), 2–13.

Castaldo, V., & Holzman, P. (1969). The effects of hearing one's own voice on dream content: A replication. *Journal of Nervous and Mental Disorders, 148*(1), 74–82.

Cattell, R. (1973). *Personality and mood by questionnaire* (1st ed.). San Francisco: Jossey-Bass Publishers.

Cayce, E., & Cayce, H. (1971). *The outer limits of Edgar Cayce's power* (1st ed.). New York: Harper & Row.

Cernovsky, Z. (1985). MMPI and nightmares in male alcoholics. *Perceptual and Motor Skills, 61*(3 Pt 1), 841–842.

Cernovsky, Z. (1986). MMPI and nightmare reports in women addicted to alcohol and other drugs. *Perceptual and Motor Skills, 62*(3), 717–718.

Chalmers, D. (1995). Facing up to the problem of consciousness. *Journal of Consciousness Studies, 2,* 200–219.

Chomsky, N. (1968). *Language and mind*. New York: Harcourt.

Chomsky, N. (1980). *Rules and representations*. New York: Columbia University Press.

Christo, G., & Franey, C. (1996). Addicts' drug-related dreams: Their frequency and relationship to six-month outcomes. *Substance Use and Misuse, 31*(1), 1–15.

Churchland, P. (2002). *Brain-wise: Studies in neurophilosophy*. Cambridge, MA: MIT Press.

Clark, J., Trinder, J., Kramer, M., Roth, T., & Day, N. (1972). An approach to the content analysis of dream content scales. *Sleep Research, 1,* 118.

Clyde, D. (1963). *Manual for the Clyde-Mood scale*. Miami: Biometric Laboratory, University of Florida.

Cohen, D. (1969). Frequency of dream recall estimated by three methods and related to defense preference and anxiety. *Journal of Consulting and Clinical Psychology, 33*(6), 661–667.

Cohen, D. (1974). Toward a theory of dream recall. *Psychology Bulletin, 81*(2), 138–154.

Colby, K. (1958). *A skeptical psychoanalyst*. New York: Ronald Press Co.

Crick, F., & Mitchison, G. (1983). The function of dream sleep. *Nature, 304*(5922), 111–114.

Cuddy, M., & Belicki, K. (1992). Nightmare frequency and related sleep disturbances as indicators of a history of sexual abuse. *Dreaming, 2,* 15–22.

Dagan, Y., & Lavie, P. (1991). Subjective and objective characteristics of sleep and dreaming in war related PTSD patients. *Sleep Research, 20A,* 270.

Dagan, Y., Lavie, P., & Bleich, A. (1991). Elevated awakening thresholds in sleep stage 3-4 in war related post-traumatic stress disorder patients. *Biol. Psychiatry, 30,* 618–622.

Damascio, A. (1999). *The feeling of what happens: body and emotion in the making of consciousness*. New York: Harcourt Brace.

Darwin, C. (2003). *The origin of species by means of natural selection*. New York: Fine Creative Media.

Dashevsky, B., & Kramer, M. (1998). Behavioral treatment of chronic insomnia in psychiatrically ill patients. *Journal of Clinical Psychiatry, 59*(12), 693–699.

Dawood, N., & Wyatt, T. (1991). *The Koran: with parallel Arabic text*. New York: Penguin Classics.

Deekin, M., & Bridenbaugh, R. (1987). Depression and nightmares among Vietnam veterans in a military outpatient clinic. *Military Medicine, 152*, 590–591.

DeFazio, V., Rustin, S., & Diamond, A. (1975). Symptom development in Vietnam era veterans. *American Journal of Orthopsychiatry, 45*(1), 158–163.

Delarosa, D. (1988). A history of thinking. In R. Sternberg & E. Smith (Eds.), *The psychology of human thought* (pp. 1–18). Cambridge: Cambridge University Press.

DeMartino, M. (1953a). Sex differences in the dreams of southern college students. *Journal of Clinical Psychology, 9*, 199–201.

DeMartino, M. (1953b). Some characteristics of the manifest dream content of mental defectives. *Journal of Clinical Psychology, 10*, 175–178.

Dement, W. (1974). *Some must watch while some must sleep*. San Francisco: W. H. Freeman.

Dement, W., Kahn, E., & Roffwarg, H. (1965). The influence of the laboratory situation on the dreams of the experimental subject. *Journal of Nervous and Mental Disorders, 140*, 119–131.

Dement, W., & Wolpert, E. (1958). The relation of eye movements, body motility and external stimuli to dream content. *Journal of Experimental Psychology, 55*(6), 543–553.

Denizen, N. (1988). Alcoholic dreams. *Alcohol Treatment Quarterly, 5*, 133–139.

Dennett, D. (1977). Are dreams experiences? In C. Dunlop (Ed.), *Philosophical essays on dreaming* (pp. 227–250). Ithaca, NY: Cornell University Press.

Dennett, D. (2005). *Sweet dreams: philosophical obstacles to a science of consciousness*. Cambridge, MA: MIT Press.

deSaussure, J. (1982). Dreams and dreaming in relation to childhood trauma. *International Journal of Psychoanalysis, 63*, 167–175.

Descartes, R. (1912). *Philosophical works of Descartes* (E. Haldane & G. Ross, Trans. Vol. I). Cambridge, UK: Cambridge University Press.

Deutsch, H. (1985). A case that throws light on the mechanism of regression in schizophrenia. *Psychoanalytic Review, 72*(1), 1–8.

Dippel, B., Lauer, C., Riemann, D., Majer-Trendel, K., Krieg, J., & Berger, M. (1987). Sleep and dreams in eating disorders. *Psychotherapy and Psychosomatics, 48*(1-4), 165–169.

Domhoff, B. (1969). Home dreams versus laboratory dreams. In M. Kramer (Ed.), *Dream psychology and the new biology of dreaming* (pp. 199–217). Springfield, IL: Charles C. Thomas.

Domhoff, B. (1993). The repetition of dreams and dream elements. In A. Moffitt, M. Kramer & R. Hoffmann (Eds.), *The functions of dreams* (pp. 293–320). Albany: State University of New York Press.

Domhoff, B. (1996). *Finding meaning in dreams: A quantitative approach*. New York: Plenum Press.

Domhoff, B., & Kamiya, J. (1964a). Problems in dream content study with objective indicators. 3. Changes in dream content throughout the night. *Archives of General Psychiatry, 11*, 529–532.

Domhoff, B., & Kamiya, J. (1964b). Problems in dream content study with objective indicators. I. A comparison of home and laboratory dream reports. *Archives of General Psychiatry, 11*, 519–524.

Domhoff, B., & Kamiya, J. (1964c). Problems in dream content study with objective indicators. II. Appearance of experimental situation in laboratory dream narratives. *Archives of General Psychiatry, 11*, 525–528.

Dow, B., Kelsoe, J., & Gillin, J. (1996). Sleep and dreams in Vietnam PTSD and depression. *Biological Psychiatry, 39*(1), 42–50.

Dowling, S. (1982). Dreams and dreaming in relation to trauma in childhood. *International Journal of Psychoanalysis, 63*, 157–166.

Dunlop, C. (Ed.). (1977). *Philosophical essays on dreaming*. Ithaca, NY: Cornell University Press.

Eagleton, T. (1983). *Literary theory: An introduction.* Minneapolis University of Minnesota Press.

Edelson, M. (1972). Language and dreams: The interpretation of dreams revisited. *Psychoanalytic Study of the Child, 27,* 203–282.

Ekstrand, B., Barrett, T., West, J., & Maier, W. (1977). The effect of sleep on human long term memory. In R. Drucker-Colin & J. McGaugh (Eds.), *Neurobiology of sleep and memory* (pp. 419–438). New York: Academic Press.

Ellman, S., & Antrobus, J. (Eds.). (1991). *The mind in sleep: Psychology and psychophysiology.* (2nd ed.). New York: Wiley.

Elms, A. (1980). Freud, Irma, Martha: sex and marriage in the "dream of Irma's Injection." *Psychoanalytic Review, 67,* 834–909.

Erichson, J. (1882). *On concussion of the spine.* New York: Birmingham.

Erickson, E. (1954). The dream specimen of psychoanalysis. *Journal of the American Psychoanalytic Association, 2,* 5–56.

Feldman, B. (1984). Biographical roots. *American Imago, 41,* 295–307.

Feldman, M., & Hersen, M. (1967). Attitudes toward death in nightmare subjects. *Journal of Abnormal Psychology, 72*(5), 421–425.

Firth, H. (1974). Sleeping pills and dream content. *British Journal of Psychiatry, 124:* 547–553.

Firth, S., Blouin, J., Natarajan, C., & Blouin, A. (1986). A comparison of the manifest content in dreams of suicidal, depressed and violent patients. *Canadian Journal of Psychiatry, 31*(1), 48–53.

Fishbein, H. (1976). *Evolution, development and children's learning.* Pacific Palisades, CA: Goodyear Publishing Company.

Fisher, C. (1965a). Psychoanalytic implications of recent research on sleep and dreaming. I. Empirical findings. *Journal of the American Psychoanalytic Association, 13,* 197–270.

Fisher, C. (1965b). Psychoanalytic implications of recent research on sleep and dreaming. II. Implications for psychoanalytic theory. *Journal of the American Psychoanalytic Association, 13,* 271–303.

Fisher, C., Byrne, J., & Edwards, A. (1968). NREM and REM nightmares. *Psychophysiology, 5,* 221–222.

Fisher, C., Byrne, J., Edwards, A., & Kahn, E. (1970). A psychophysiological study of nightmares. *Journal of the American Psychoanalytic Association, 18*(4), 747–782.

Fisher, C., Kahn, E., Edwards, A., & Davis, D. (1973a). A psychophysiological study of nightmares and night terrors. I. Physiological aspects of the stage 4 night terror. *Journal of Nervous and Mental Disorders, 157*(2), 75–798.

Fisher, C., Kahn, E., Edwards, A., & Davis, D. (1973b). A psychophysiological study of nightmares and night terrors. The suppression of stage 4 night terrors with diazepam. *Archives of General Psychiatry, 28*(2), 252–259.

Fisher, S., & Greenberg, R. (1977). *The scientific credibility of Freud's theories and therapy.* Hassocks, NY: Harvester Press; Basic Books.

Fiss, H. (1979). Current dream research: a psychobiological perspective. In B. Wolman (Ed.), *Handbook of dreams* (pp. 20–75). New York: Van Nostrand Reinhold.

Fiss, H. (1980). Dream content and response to withdrawal from alcohol. *Sleep Research, 9,* 152.

Fiss, H., Klein, G., & Bokert, E. (1966). Waking fantasies following interruption of two types of sleep. *Archives of General Psychiatry, 14*(5), 543–551.

Fliess, R. (1953). *The revival of interest in the dream; a critical study of post-Freudian psychoanalytic contributions. With an article on the 'spoken word.'* New York: International University Press.

Foster, J., & Anderson, J. (1936). Unpleasant dreams in childhood. *Child Development, 7,* 77–84.

Foulkes, D. (1966). *The psychology of sleep.* New York: Scribner.

Foulkes, D. (1978). *A grammar of dreams.* New York: Basic Books.

Foulkes, D. (1982). *Children's dreams: Longitudinal studies.* New York: John Wiley.

Foulkes, D. (1993). Data constraints on theorizing about dream function. In A. Moffitt, M. Kramer & R. Hoffmann (Eds.), *The functions of dreaming* (pp. 11–20). Albany: State University of New York Press.

Foulkes, D. (1999). *Children's dreaming and the development of consciousness.* Cambridge, MA: Harvard University Press.

Foulkes, D., & Fleisher, S. (1975). Mental activity in relaxed wakefulness. *Journal of Abnormal Psychology, 84*(1), 66–75.

Fox, R., Kramer, M., Baldridge, B., Whitman, R., & Ornstein, P. (1968). The experimenter variable in dream research. *Diseases of the Nervous System, 29*(10), 698–701.

Frayn, D. (1991). The incidence and significance of perceptual qualities in the reported dreams of patients with anorexia nervosa. *Canadian Journal of Psychiatry, 36*(7), 517–520.

Freemon, F. (1972). *Sleep research: A critical review.* Springfield, IL: Charles C. Thomas.

French, T. (1952). *The integration of behavior.* Chicago: University of Chicago Press.

French, T., & Fromm, E. (1964). *Dream interpretation.* New York: Basic Books.

Freud, S. (1953). Fragment of a case of hysteria. In J. Srachey (Ed.), *Standard Edition* (pp. 3–122). London: Hogarth Press.

Freud, S. (1955a). *Beyond the pleasure principle* (Vol. XVIII). London: Hogarth Press.

Freud, S. (1955b). *The interpretation of dreams* (1st ed.). New York: Basic Books.

Freud, S. (1957). Mourning and melancholia. In J. Strachey (Ed.), *The Standard Edition of the complete psychological works of S. Freud* (Vol. XIV, pp. 237–258). London: Hogarth Press.

Fromm, E. (1951). *The forgotten language: An introduction to the understanding of dreams, fairy tales and myths.* New York: Rinehart.

Frosch, J. (1976). Psychoanalytic contributions to the relationship between dreams and psychosis—a critical survey. *International Journal of Psychoanalytic Psychotherapy, 5*, 39–63.

Gackenbach, J. (1984). An estimate of lucid dreaming incidence. *Lucidity Letter Back Issues, 3*, 81–83.

Gahagan, L. (1936). Sex differences in the recall of stereotyped dreams, sleep-talking and sleep-walking. *Journal of General Psychology, 48*, 227–236.

Gaines, R., & Price-Williams, D. (1990). Dreams and imaginative processes in American and Balinese artists. *Psychiatric Journal of the University of Ottawa, 15*(2), 107–110.

Gardner, H. (1985). *The mind's new science.* New York: Basic Books.

Garfield, P. (1984). *Your child's dreams.* New York: Ballantine.

Gilchrist, E. (1981). *In the land of dreamy dreams: Short fiction.* Boston: Little, Brown.

Globus, G. (1987). *Dream life, wake life: The human condition through dreams.* Albany: State University of New York Press.

Glucksman, M., & Kramer, M. (2004). Using dreams to assess clinical change during treatment. *Journal American Academy of Psychoanalysis and Dynamic Psychiatry, 32*(2), 345–358.

Goldstein, G., van Kammen, W., Shelly, C., Miller, D., & van Kammen, D. (1987). Survivors of imprisonment in the Pacific theater during World War II. *American Journal of Psychiatry, 144*(9), 1210–1213.

Goodenough, D. (1978). Dream recall: History and current status of the field. In A. Arkin, J. Antrobus, & S. Ellman (Eds.), *The mind in sleep* (pp. 113–140). Hillside, NJ: Erlbaum.

Goodenough, D., & Koulack, D. (1976). Dream recall and dream recall failure: an arousal-retrieval model. *Psychological Bulletin., 83*, 975–984.

Goodenough, D., Lewis, H., Shapiro, A., Jaret, L., & Sleser, I. (1965). Dream reporting following abrupt and gradual awakenings from different types of sleep. *Journal of Personality and Social Psychology, 56*, 170–179.

Gottschalk, L. (1999). The application of a computerized measurement of the content analysis of natural language to the assessment of the effects of psychoactive drugs. *Methods and Findings in Experimental Clinical Pharmacology, 21*(2), 133–138.

Gottschalk, L., Winget, C., & Gleser, G. (1969). *Manual of instructions for using the Gottschalk-Gleser content analysis scales: anxiety, hostility, and social alienation—personal disorganization.* Berkeley: University of California Press.

Gottschlich, M., Jenkins, M., Mayes, T., Khoury, J., Kramer, M., Warden, G., et al. (1994). The 1994 Clinical Research Award. A prospective clinical study of the polysomnographic stages of sleep after burn injury. *Journal of Burn Care Rehabilitation, 15*(6), 486–492.

Green, B., Lindy, J., & Grace, M. (1985). Posttraumatic stress disorder. Toward DSM-IV. *Journal of Nervous and Mental Disorders, 173*(7), 406–411.

Greenberg, R., Pearlman, C., Blacher, R., Katz, H., Sashin, J., & Gottlieb, P. (1990). Depression: Variability of intrapsychic and sleep parameters. *Journal of the American Academy of Psychoanalyis, 18*(2), 233–246.

Griffith, R. (1950). *Typical dreams, a statistical study of personality correlates.*, Lexington: University of Kentucky.

Griffith, R. (1958). The universality of typical dreams: Japanese versus Americans. *American Anthropologist, 60,* 1173–1179.

Hall, C. (1953). *The meaning of dreams* (1st ed.). New York: Harper.

Hall, C. (1955). The dream of being attacked. *Journal of Personality, 24,* 168–189.

Hall, C., & Domhoff, B. (1963a). Aggression in dreams. *International Journal of Social Psychiatry, 10,* 259–267.

Hall, C., & Domhoff, B. (1963b). A ubiquitous sex difference in dreams. *Journal of Abnormal Social Psychology, 66,* 278–280.

Hall, C., & Domhoff, B. (1964). Friendliness in dreams. *Journal of Social Psychology, 62,* 309–314.

Hall, C., Domhoff, B., Blick, K., & Weesner, K. (1982). The dreams of college age men and women in 1950 and 1980: A comparison of dream content and sex differences. *Sleep, 5,* 188–194.

Hall, C., & Raskin, R. (1980). Do we dream during sleep? (pp. 1–46). Unpublished.

Hall, C., & Van de Castle, R. (1966). *The content analysis of dreams.* New York: Appleton-Century-Crofts.

Halliday, G. (1987). Direct psychological therapies for nightmares: A review. *Clinical Psychology Review, 7,* 501–523.

Harris, I. (1948). Observations concerning typical anxiety dreams. *Psychiatry, 11,* 301–309.

Harris, I. (1951). Characterological significance of the typical anxiety dreams. *Psychiatry, 14*(3), 279–294.

Harris, I. (1957). The dream of the object endangered. *Psychiatry, 20*(2), 151–161.

Hartmann, E. (1984). *The nightmare: The psychology and biology of terrifying dreams.* New York: Basic Books.

Hartmann, E. (1989). Boundaries of dreams, boundaries of dreamers: Thin and thick boundaries as a new personality measure. *Psychiatric Journal of the University of Ottawa, 14,* 557–560.

Hartmann, E. (2003). The waking to dreaming continuum and the effects of emotion. In E. Pace-Schott, M. Solms, M. Blagrove, & S. Harnad (Eds.), *Sleep and dreaming: Scientific advancements and reconsiderations* (pp. 158–161). Cambridge: Cambridge University Press.

Hartmann, E., Rosen, R., & Rand, W. (1998). Personality and dreaming: Boundary structure and dream content. *Dreaming, 8,* 31–39.

Hathaway, S., & McKinley, J. (1943). *The Minnesota multiphasic personality inventory* (Rev. ed.). Minneapolis: The University of Minnesota Press.

Hauri, P. (1975). Categorization of sleep mental activity for psychophysiologic studies. In G. Lairy & P. Salzarullo (Eds.), *The experimental study of human sleep* (pp. 271–281). New York: Elsevier.

Hauri, P. (1976). Dreams in patients remitted from reactive depression. *Journal of Abnormal Psychology, 85*(1), 1–10.

Hefez, A., Metz, L., & Lavie, P. (1987). Long-term effects of extreme situational stress on sleep and dreaming. *American Journal of Psychiatry, 144*(3), 344–347.

Helzer, J., Robins, L., & McEvoy, L. (1987). Post-traumatic stress disorder in the general population. Findings of the epidemiologic catchment area survey. *New England Journal of Medicine, 317*(26), 1630–1634.

Herman, J., Ellman, S., & Roffwarg, H. (1978). The problem of NREM recall re-examined. In A. Arkin, J. Antrobus & S. Ellman (Eds.), *The mind in sleep: psychology and psychophysiology* (1st ed., pp. 59–92). Hillside, NJ: Erlbaum.

Hertz, J. (Ed.). (1976). *The Pentateuch and Haftorahs.* London: Soncino Press.

Herzen, M. (1972). Nightmare behavior: A review. *Psychology Bulletin, 73,* 37–48.

Heynick, F. (1993). *Language and its disturbances in dreams: The pioneering work of Freud and Kraepelin updated.* New York: Wiley.

Hinton, G., & Sejnowski, T. (1986). Learning and re-learning in Boltzman machines. In D. Rummelhart & J. McClelland (Eds.), *Parallel distributed processing* (pp. 282–317). Cambridge, MA: MIT Press.

Hobson, J. (1988). *The dreaming brain.* New York: Basic Books.

Hobson, J. (1999). The new neuropsychology of sleep implications for psychoanalysis. Commentaries Solms, Braun, Reiser. *Neuropsychoanalysis, 1*, 157–224.

Hobson, J., Pace-Schott, E., & Stickgold, R. (2000). Dreaming and the brain: Toward a cognitive neuroscience of conscious states. *Behavior and Brain Science 23*(6), 793–842; discussion 904–1121.

Hollender, M., & Kramer, M. (1977). Another way of thinking about dreams. *American Journal of Psychiatry, 134*(1), 95–96.

Horney, K. (1945). *Our inner conflicts.* New York: Norton.

Horowitz, M., Wilner, N., Kaltreider, N., & Alvarez, W. (1980). Signs and symptoms of posttraumatic stress disorder. *Archives of General Psychiatry, 37*(1), 85–92.

Hudson, J., Bruch, H., DeTrinis, J., Ware, J., & Karacan, I. (1978). Content analysis of dreams of anorexia nervosa patients. *Sleep Research, 7,* 176.

Hughes, J. (1984). The dreams of Alexander the Great. *Journal of Psychohistory, 12*(2), 168–192.

Hurwitz, T., Mahwold, M., Kuskowski, M., & Engdahl, B. (1988). Polysomnographic sleep is not clinically impaired in Vietnam veterans with chronic post traumatic stress disorder. *Biological Psychiatry, 44*(1066–1073).

Jackson, C., Beumont, P., Thornton, C., & Lennerts, W. (1993). Dreams of death: Von Weizsacker's dreams in so-called endogenic anorexia: A research note. *International Journal of Eating Disorders, 13*(3), 329–332.

Jackson, C., Tabin, J., Russell, J., & Touyz, S. (1993). Themes of death: Helmut Thoma's "Anorexia nervosa" (1967)—a research note. *International Journal of Eating Disorders, 14*(4), 433–437.

Jackson, J. (1958). *Selected writings* (Vol. 2). New York: Basic Books.

Jersild, A. (1931). Memory for the pleasant compared to the unpleasant. *Journal of Experimental Psychology, 14,* 284–288.

Jersild, A., Markey, F., & Jersild, C. (1933). Children's fears, dreams, wishes, daydreams, likes, dislikes, pleasant and unpleasant memories. *Child Development Monograph, 12.*

Johnson, B., Kramer, M., Bonnet, M., Roth, T., & Jansen, T. (1980). The effect of Ketazolam on ocular motility during sleep. *Current Therapeutic Research, 28,* 792–799.

Johnson, L., Spinweber, C., Gomez, S., & Matteson, L. (1990). Daytime sleepiness, performance, mood, nocturnal sleep: The effect of benzodiazepine and caffeine on their relationship. *Sleep, 13*(2), 121–135.

Jones, E. (1959). *On the nightmare.* New York: Grove Press.

Jones, R. (1962). *The ego synthesis in dreams.* Cambridge, MA: Schenkman Publishing.

Jones, R. (1970). *The new psychology of dreaming.* New York: Grune & Stratton.

Jung, C. (1956). *Two essays in analytical psychology.* New York: Meridian Books.

Jung, C. (1960). *The psychology of dementia praecox.* London: Princeton University Press.

Jung, C. (1964a). Approaching the unconscious. In C. Jung (Ed.), *Man and his symbols.* New York: Doubleday. 18-103.

Jung, C. (1964b). *Man and his symbols.* New York: Doubleday.

Jung, C. (1974). *Dreams.* Princeton, NJ: Princeton University Press.

Jung, C. (1984). *Dream analysis: notes of the seminar of 1928–30.* Princeton, NJ: Princeton University Press.

Jus, A., Jus, K., Villeneuve, A., Pires, A., Lachance, R., Fortier, J., et al. (1973). Studies on dream recall in chronic schizophrenic patients after prefrontal lobotomy. *Biological Psychiatry, 6*(3), 275–293.

Kahn, E., & Fisher, C. (1969). The sleep characteristics of the normal aged male. *Journal of Nervous and Mental Disorders, 148*(5), 477–494.

Kaminer, H., & Lavie, P. (1991). Sleep and dreaming in Holocaust survivors. Dramatic decrease in dream recall in well-adjusted survivors. *Journal of Nervous and Mental Disorders, 179*(11), 664–669.

Kellett, S., & Beail, N. (1997). The treatment of chronic post-traumatic nightmares using psychodynamic-interpersonal psychotherapy: A single-case study. *British Journal of Medical Psychology, 70*(Pt. 1), 35–49.

Kellner, R., Neidhardt, J., Krakow, B., & Pathak, D. (1992). Changes in chronic nightmares after one session of desensitization or rehearsal instructions. *American Journal of Psychiatry, 149*(5), 659–663.

Kelsey, M. (1968). *Dreams: The dark speech of the spirit.* New York: Doubleday.

Kendler, K. (2001). A psychiatric dialogue on the mind-body problem. *American Journal of Psychiatry, 158*, 989–1000.

Kimmins, C. (1920). *Children's dreams*. London: Longman's Green.

Kinney, L., & Kramer, M. (1985). Sleep and sleep responsivity in disturbed dreamers. *Sleep Research, 14*, 178.

Kinney, L., Kramer, M., & Bonnet, M. (1981). Dream incorporation of meaningful names. *Sleep Research, 10*, 157.

Kinney, L., Schoen, L., & Kramer, M. (1983). Responsivity of night terror patients in sleep. *Sleep Research, 12*, 193.

Kinzie, J., Sack, R., & Riley, C. (1994). The polysomnographic effects of clonidine on sleep disorders in posttraumatic stress disorder: A pilot study with Cambodian patients. *Journal of Nervous and Mental Disorders, 182*(10), 585–587.

Kleitman, N. (1963). *Sleep and wakefulness*. Chicago: University of Chicago Press.

Klinger, E. (1971). *Structure and functions of fantasy*. New York: Wiley-Interscience.

Kohut, H. (1971). *The analysis of the sel: A systematic approach to the psychoanalytic treatment of narcissistic personality disorders*. New York: International Universities Press.

Koranyi, E., & Lehmann, H. (1960). Experimental sleep deprivation in schizophrenic patients. *Archives of General Psychiatry, 2*, 534–544.

Kosslyn, S. (1980). *Image and mind*. Cambridge, MA: Harvard University Press.

Koukkou, M., & Lehman, D. (1993). A model of dreaming and its functional significance: the shift state hypothesis. In A. Moffitt, M. Kramer & R. Hoffmann (Eds.), *The functions of dreaming* (pp. 51–118). Albany: State University of New York Press.

Koulack, D. (1991). *To catch a dream: Explorations of dreaming*. Albany: State University of New York Press.

Koulack, D. (1993). Dreams and adaptation to contemporary stress. In A. Moffitt, M. Kramer & R. Hoffmann (Eds.), *The functions of dreaming* (pp. 321–340). Albany: State University of New York Press.

Krakow, B. (1992). *Conquering bad dreams and nightmares: A guide to understanding, interpretation and cure*. New York: Berkley.

Krakow, B., Lowry, C., Germain, A., Gaddy, L., Hollifield, M., Koss, M., et al. (2000). A retrospective study on improvements in nightmares and post-traumatic stress disorder following treatment for co-morbid sleep-disordered breathing. *Journal of Psychosomatic Research, 49*(5), 291–298.

Kramer, M. (1966a). Drugs, depression, and dream sequences. *Ohio State Medical Journal, 62*(11), 1277–1280.

Kramer, M. (1966b). More on depression and dreams. *American Journal of Psychiatry, 123*(2), 232–233.

Kramer, M. (1966c). Psychiatric transactions and the use of the experimental dream. *Journal of the National Medical Association, 58*(3), 185–190.

Kramer, M. (1969a). Manifest dream content in psychopathological states. In M. Kramer (Ed.), *Dream psychology and the new biology of dreaming* (pp. 377–396). Springfield, IL: Charles C Thomas.

Kramer, M. (1969b). Paradoxical sleep. *Postgraduate Medicine, 45*(4), 157–161.

Kramer, M. (1969c). Preface. In M. Kramer (Ed.), *Dream Psychology and the New Biology of Dreaming* (pp. xiii). Springfield, IL: Charles C Thomas.

Kramer, M. (1970). Manifest dream content in normal and psychopathologic states. *Archives of General Psychiatry, 22*(2), 149–159.

Kramer, M. (1979). Dream disturbances. *Psychiatric Annals, 9*, 50–68.

Kramer, M. (1981a). Dream content in psychiatric conditions. In C. Perris, G. Struwe & B. Jansson (Eds.), *Biological psychiatry 1981* (pp. 306–309). New York: Elsevier.

Kramer, M. (1981b). The function of psychological dreaming. In W. Koella . (Ed.), *Sleep 1980* (pp. 182–185). Basel: S. Karger.

Kramer, M. (1982). The psychology of the dream: Art or science? *Psychiatric Journal University of Ottawa, 6*, 87–100.

Kramer, M. (1991a). Dream translation: A non-associative method for understanding the dream. *Dreaming, 1*, 147–159.

Kramer, M. (1991b). The nightmare: A failure in dream function. *Dreaming, 1*, 277–285.

Kramer, M. (1993a). Dream translation: An approach to understanding dreams. In G. Delaney (Ed.), *New directions in dream interpretation* (pp. 155–194). Albany: State University of New York Press.

Kramer, M. (1993b). The selective mood regulatory function of dreaming: an update and revision. In A. Moffitt, M. Kramer & R. Hoffmann (Eds.), *The functions of dreaming* (pp. 139–196). Albany: State University of New York Press.

Kramer, M. (1994). Freud's "The interpretation of Dreams": The initial response. *Dreaming, 4,* 47–52.

Kramer, M. (1999a). The role of dreaming in post traumatic stress disorder. *Sleep*(Suppl., 22), S253.

Kramer, M. (1999b). Unresolved problems in the dream of Irma's injection. *Journal of the American Academy of Psychoanalysis, 27*(2), 253–263.

Kramer, M. (2000a). Does dream interpretation have any limits? An evaluation of interpretations of the dream of Irma's injection. *Dreaming, 10,* 161–178.

Kramer, M. (2000). Dreaming has content and meaning not just form. *Behavioral and Brain Sciences, 23,* 959–961.

Kramer, M. (2000b). Hypnotic medication in the treatment of chronic insomnia: non nocere! Doesn't anyone care? *Sleep Medicine Reviews, 4*(6), 529–541.

Kramer, M. (2002). The biology of dream formation: a review and critique. *Journal of the American Academy of Psychoanalysis, 30*(4), 657–671.

Kramer, M. (2003). The biology of dream formation: a review and critique. *J. American Academy of Psychoanalysis and Dynamic Psychotherapy, 30,* 657–671.

Kramer, M. (2004). Hypnotic medication: shed light not heat! *Sleep, 27*(5), 1021.

Kramer, M., Baldridge, B. J., Whitman, R. M., Ornstein, P. H., & Smith, P. C. (1969). An exploration of the manifest dream in schizophrenic and depressed patients. *Diseases of the Nervous System, 30*(2), Suppl: 126–130.

Kramer, M., & Brik, I. (2002). Affective processing by dreams across the night by dreams. *Sleep* (Suppl. 25), A180–A181.

Kramer, M., Brunner, R., & Trinder, J. (1971). Discussion of Miller, J., Buckley, P. Dream changes in a manic depressive cycle. In J. Masserman (Ed.), *Science and psychoanalysis* (pp. 148–151). New York: Grune and Stratton.

Kramer, M., Clark, J., & Day, N. (1973). Dreaming in schizophrenia. In V. Zikmund (Ed.), *The occulomotor system and brain function* (pp. 439–452). London: Butterworths.

Kramer, M., Czaya, J., Arand, D., & Roth, T. (1974). The development of psychological content across the REM period. *Sleep Research, 3,* 121.

Kramer, M., & Glucksman, M. (2005). Affect frequency and valence in manifest dream reports and associations in psychoanalytic therapy. *Sleep* (Suppl. 28), A51.

Kramer, M., & Glucksman, M. (2006). Changes in dream affect during psychoanalytic therapy. *Journal of the American Academy of Psychoanalysis and Dynamic Psychotherapy, 34,* 249-260.

Kramer, M., Hlasny, R., Jacobs, G., & Roth, T. (1976). Do dreams have meaning? An empirical inquiry. *American Journal of Psychiatry, 133*(7), 778–781.

Kramer, M., & Kinney, L. (1985). Vulnerability to developing delayed post traumatic stress disorder: combat experience and psychological status. *Sleep Research, 14,* 131.

Kramer, M., & Kinney, L. (1988). Sleep patterns in trauma victims with disturbed dreaming. *Psychiatric Journal of the University of Ottawa, 13*(1), 12–16.

Kramer, M., & Kinney, L. (2003). Vigilance and avoidance during sleep in US Vietnam War veterans with posttraumatic stress disorder. *Journal of Nervous and Mental Disorders, 191*(10), 685–687.

Kramer, M., Kinney, L., & Scharf, M. (1983). Dream incorporation and dream function. In W. Koella (Ed.), *Sleep 1982* (pp. 369–371). Basel: S. Karger.

Kramer, M., Kinney, L., & Scharf, M. (1983). Sex differences in dreams. *Psychiatric Journal of the University of Ottawa, 8*(1), 1–4.

Kramer, M., Kinney, L., & Schoen, L. (1983). Personality measures in dream disturbed PTSD veterans. *Sleep Research, 12,* 206.

Kramer, M., Kinney. (1985). Is sleep a marker of vulnerability to delayed post traumatic sleep disorder? *Sleep Research, 14,* 181.

Kramer, M., McQuarrie, E., & Bonnet, M. (1980). Dream differences as a function of REM period. *Sleep Research, 9*, 155.

Kramer, M., McQuarrie, E., & Bonnet, M. (1981). Problem solving in dreaming: an empirical test. In W. Koella (Ed.), *Sleep 1980* (pp. 357-360). Basel: S. Karger.

Kramer, M., Moshiri, A., & Scharf, L. (1982). The organization of mental content in and between the waking and dreaming state. *Sleep Research, 11*, 106.

Kramer, M., Ornstein, P., Whitman, R., & Baldridge, B. (1967). The contribution of early memories and dreams to the diagnostic process. *Comprehensive Psychiatry, 8*(5), 344–374.

Kramer, M., Roehrs, T., & Roth, T. (1972). The relationship between sleep and mood. *Sleep Research, 1*, 193.

Kramer, M., Roehrs, T., & Roth, T. (1976). Mood change and the physiology of sleep. *Comprehensive Psychiatry, 17*(1), 161–165.

Kramer, M., & Roth, T. (1973a). A comparison of dream content in laboratory dream reports of schizophrenic and depressive patient groups. *Comprehensive Psychiatry, 14*(4), 325–329.

Kramer, M., & Roth, T. (1973b). The mood-regulating function of sleep. In W. Koella & P. Levin (Eds.), *Sleep 1972* (536-571) Basel: S. Karger.

Kramer, M., & Roth, T. (1975). Dreams and dementia: A laboratory exploration of dream recall and dream content in chronic brain syndrome patients.International Journal of Aging and Human Development, *6*(2), 179–182.

Kramer, M., & Roth, T. (1977). Dream translation. *Israel Annals of Psychiatry and Related Disciplines, 15*(4), 336–351.

Kramer, M., & Roth, T. (1978). Dreams in psychopathological groups: A critical review. In R. Williams & I. Karacan (Eds.), *Sleep disorders: diagnosis and treatment* (pp. 323–349). New York: Wiley.

Kramer, M., & Roth, T. (1979). The stability and variability of dreaming. *Sleep, 1*(3), 319–325.

Kramer, M., & Roth, T. (1980). The relationship of dream content to night-morning mood change. In L. Popoviciu, B. Asigian, and G. Bain,. (Eds.), *Sleep 1978* (621- 624). Basel: S. Karger.

Kramer, M., Roth, T., Arand, D., & Bonnet, M. (1981). Waking and dreaming mentation: A test of their interrelationship. *Neuroscience Letters, 22*(1), 83–86.

Kramer, M., Roth, T., Clark, J., & Trinder, J. (1972). The use of the dream in drawing clinical inferences. *Psychophysiology, 9*, 148.

Kramer, M., Roth, T., & Czaya, J.,(1975). *Dream development within a REM period.* In W. Koella and P.Levin (Eds) Sleep 1974 (406-408), Basel: S. Karger.

Kramer, M., Roth, T., & Palmer, T. (1976). The psychological nature of the REM dream report and T.A.T. stories. *Psychiatric Journal University of Ottawa, 1*, 128–135.

Kramer, M., Roth T. . (1979). Dreams in psychopathology. In B. Wolman (Ed.), *Handbook of dreams: Research, theories and applications* (pp. 361–387). New York: Von Norstrand Reinhold.

Kramer, M., Roth, T, & Cisco, J. (1977). The meaningfulness of dreams. In W. Koella and P. Levin,. (Eds.), *Sleep 1976* (324–326). Basel: S. Karger.

Kramer, M., & Schoen, L. (1984). Problems in the use of long-acting hypnotics in older patients. *Journal of Clinical Psychiatry, 45*(4), 176–177.

Kramer, M., Schoen, L., & Kinney, L. (1984). The dream experience in dream disturbed Vietnam veterans. In B. Van der Kolk (Ed.), *Post traumatic stress disorders: Psychological and biological sequellae* (pp. 81–95). Washington D.C.: American Psychiatric Press.

Kramer, M., Schoen, L., & Kinney, L. (1984). Psychological and behavioral features of disturbed dreamers. *Psychiatric Journal of the University of Ottawa, 9*(3), 102–106.

Kramer, M., Schoen, L., & Kinney, L. (1987). Nightmares in Vietnam veterans. *Journal of the American Academy of Psychoanalysis, 15*(1), 67–81.

Kramer, M., Sepate, M., & Leavengood, B. (1990). The relationship of pre-sleep mood to post-sleep mood. *Sleep Research, 19*, 136.

Kramer, M., Trinder, J., & Roth, T. (1972). Dream content analysis of male schizophrenic patients. *Canadian Psychiatric Association Journal, 17*(2), Suppl. 2:S.S.251–257.

Kramer, M., Trinder, J., Whitman, R., & Baldridge, B. (1969). The incidence of masochistic dreams in the night collected dreams of depressed subjects. *Psychophysiology, 6*, 250.

Kramer, M., Whitman, R., Baldridge, B., & Lansky, L. (1964). Patterns of dreaming: the inter-relationship of the dreams of a night. *Journal of Nervous and Mental Disorders, 139*, 426–439.

Kramer, M., Whitman, R., Baldridge, B., & Lansky, L. (1965). Depression: dreams and defenses. *American Journal of Psychiatry, 122*(4), 411–419.

Kramer, M., Whitman, R., Baldridge, B., & Lansky, L. (1966). Dreaming in the depressed. *Canadian Psychiatric Association Journal, 11*, Suppl.:178–192.

Kramer, M., Whitman, R., Baldridge, B., & Ornstein, P. (1966). The pharmacology of dreaming: A review. In G. Martin & B. Kisch (Eds.), *Enzymes in mental health* (pp. 102–116). Philadelphia: J. B. Lippincott.

Kramer, M., Whitman, R., Baldridge, B., & Ornstein, P. (1968). Drugs and dreams III. The effects of imipramine on the dreams of depressed patients. *American Journal of Psychiatry, 124*(10), 1385–1392.

Kramer, M., Whitman, R., Baldridge, B., & Ornstein, P. (1969). Dream content in male schizophrenic patients. *Diseases of the Nervous System, 31*, 51–58.

Kramer, M., Whitman, R., Baldridge, B., & Ornstein, P. (1970). Dream content in male schizophrenic patients. *Diseases of the Nervous System, 31*, (Suppl.): 51–58.

Kramer, M., Winget, C., & Roth, T. (1975). Problems in the definition of the REM dream. In W. Koella & P. Levin (Eds.), *Sleep 1972* (pp. 149–156). Basel: S. Karger.

Kramer, M., Winget, C., & Whitman, R. (1971). A city dreams: a survey approach to normative dream content. *American Journal of Psychiatry, 127*(10), 1350–1356.

Kripke, D., & Sonnenshein, D. (1978). A biologic rhythm in waking fantasy. In K. Pope & J. Singer (Eds.), *The stream of consciousness* (pp. 321–332). New York: Plenum.

Kuch, K., & Cox, B. (1992). Symptoms of PTSD in 124 survivors of the Holocaust. *American Journal of Psychiatry, 149*(3), 337–340.

Kuiken, D., & Sikora, S. (1993). The impact of dreams on waking thoughts and feelings. In A. Moffitt, M. Kramer, & R. Hoffmann (Eds.), *The functions of dreams* (pp. 419–476). Albany: State University of New York Press.

LaBerge, S. (1985). *Lucid dreaming.* Los Angeles: Jeremy Tracher.

LaBerge, S., Nagel, L., Taylor, W., Dement, W., & Zarcone, V. (1981). Evidence for lucid dreaming during REM sleep. *Sleep Research, 10*, 148.

LaBerge, S., Nagel, L., Taylor, W., Dement, W., & Zarcone, V. (1981). Psychophysiological correlates of the initiation of lucid dreaming. *Sleep Research, 10*, 149.

LaBerge, S., & Rheingold, H. (1990). *Exploring the world of lucid dreaming* (1st ed.). New York: Ballantine Books.

Lakoff, G., & Johnson, M. (2003). *Metaphors we live by.* Chicago: University of Chicago Press.

Langs, R. (1965). Earliest memories. *Archives of General Psychiatry, 12*, 379–390.

Langs, R. (1966). Manifest dreams from three clinical groups. *Archives of General Psychiatry, 14*(6), 634–643.

Lansky, M. (1991). The transformation of affect in posttraumatic nightmares. *Bulletin of the Menninger Clinic, 55*(4), 470–490.

Lansky, M. (1995). Nightmares of a hospitalized rape victim. *Bulletin of the Menninger Clinic, 59*(1), 4–14.

Lavie, P., & Hertz, G. (1979). Increased sleep motility and respiration rates in combat neurotic patients. *Biological Psychiatry, 14*(6), 983–987.

Lavie, P., & Kaminer, H. (1991). Dreams that poison sleep; dreaming in holocaust survivors. *Dreaming, 1*, 11–22.

Lavie, P., Katz, N., Pillar, G., & Zinger, Y. (1998). Elevated awaking thresholds during sleep: Characteristics of chronic war-related posttraumatic stress disorder patients. *Biological Psychiatry, 44*(10), 1060–1065.

LeDoux, J. (2002). *Synaptic self.* New York: Penguin Putnam.

Leveton, A. (1961). The night residue. *International Journal of Psychoanalysis, 42*, 506–516.

Levine, J. (1983). Materialism and qualia: The explanatory gap. *Pacific Philosophical Quarterly, 64*, 354–361.

Levitan, H. (1977). The relationship between mania and the memory of pain. A hypothesis. *Bulletin of the Menninger Clinic, 41*(2), 145–161.

Levitan, H. (1981). Implications of certain dreams reported by patients in a bulimic phase of anorexia nervosa. *Canadian Journal of Psychiatry, 26*, 228–231.

Lewis, H., Goodenough, D., Shapiro, A., & Sleser, I. (1966). Individual differences in dream recall. *Journal of Abnormal Psycholy, 71*(1), 52–59.

Lincoln, J. (1935). *The dream in primitive cultures.* London: The Cresset Press.

Lutz, T., Kramer, M., & Roth, T. (1975). The relationship between mood and performance. *Sleep Research, 4,* 152.

Lysaght, R., Kramer, M., & Roth, T. (1979). Mood differences before and after sleep: a test of its generalizability. *Sleep Research, 8,* 168.

Lysaght, R., Roth, T., Kramer, M., & Salis, P. (1978). Variations in subjective state and body temperature across the day. *Sleep Research, 7,* 308.

Mack, J. (1989). *Nightmares & human conflict.* New York: Columbia University Press.

Mahowald, M., & Schenck, C. (2000). REM sleep parasomnias. In M. Kryger, T. Roth & W. Dement (Eds.), *Principles and practice of sleep medicine* (3rd ed., pp. 724–741). Philadelphia: W. B. Saunders.

Malcolm, N. (1959). *Dreaming.* New York: Humanities Press.

Mamelak, A., & Hobson, J. (1989). Dream bizarreness as the cognitive correlate of altered neuronal behavior in REM sleep. *Journal of Cognitive Neuroscience, 1,* 201–222.

Mathew, R., Largen, J., & Claghorn, J. (1979). Biological symptoms of depression. *Psychosomatic Medicine, 41*(6), 439–443.

Mautner, B. (1991). Freud's Irma dream: a psychoanalytic interpretation. *International Journal of Psychoanalysis, 72* (Pt 2), 275–286.

McGuinn, C. (1999). *The mysterious flame.* New York: Basic Books.

Meier, C. (1966). The dream in ancient Greece and its use in temple cures (incubation). In G. von Gruenbaum & R. Caillois (Eds.), *The dream in human societies* (pp. 303–318). Los Angeles: University of California Press.

Mellman, T., Kulick-Bell, R., Ashlock, L., & Nolan, B. (1995). Sleep events among veterans with combat-related posttraumatic stress disorder. *American Journal of Psychiatry, 152*(1), 110–115.

Meloy, J. (1984). Thought organization and primary process in the parents of schizophrenics. *British Journal of Medical Psychology, 57* (Pt 3), 279–281.

Millon, T. (2004). *Masters of mind.* Hoboken, NJ: Wiley.

Modlin, H. (1985). Is there an assault syndrome? *Bulletin of the American Academy of Psychiatry and the Law, 13*(2), 139–145.

Moffitt, A., Hoffmann, R., & Galloway, S. (1990). Dream recall: imagination, illusion and tough-mindedness. *Psychiatric Journal of the University of Ottawa, 15*(2), 66–72.

Moffitt, A., Kramer, M., & Hoffmann, R. (1993). *The functions of dreaming.* Albany: State University of New York Press.

Molinari, S., & Foulkes, D. (1969). Tonic and phasic events during sleep: Psychological correlates and implications. *Perceptual and Motor Skills, 29*(2), 343–368.

Mollica, R., Wyshak, G., & Lavelle, J. (1987). The psychosocial impact of war trauma and torture on Southeast Asian refugees. *American Journal of Psychiatry, 144*(12), 1567–1572.

Moore, S., Walsh, J., Keenan, W., Farrell, M., Wolske, S., & Kramer, M. (1981). Periodic breathing in infants with histories of prolonged apnea. *American Journal of Diseases of Children, 135*(11), 1029–1031.

Moss, C. (1967). *The hypnotic investigation of dreams.* New York: Wiley.

Nagel, T. (2002, April 11). In the stream of consciousness. Review of consciousness in the world by Brian O'Shaughnessy. *New York Review of Books,* 75–76.

Nathan, R., Rose-Itkoff, C., & Lord, G. (1981). Dreams, first memories and brain atrophy in the elderly. *Hillside Journal of Clinical Psychiatry, 3*(2), 139–148.

New Yorker. (1964, October 31). Sleepy social climbers. *New Yorker,* 130.

Neylan, T., Lenoci, M., Maglione, M., Rosenlicht, N., Metzler, T., Otte, C., et al. (2003). Delta sleep response to metyrapone in post-traumatic stress disorder. *Neuropsychopharmacology, 28*(9), 1666–1676.

Neylan, T., Marmar, C., Metzler, T., Weiss, D., Zatzick, D., Delucchi, K., et al. (1998). Sleep disturbances in the Vietnam generation: findings from a nationally representative sample of male Vietnam veterans. *American Journal of Psychiatry, 155*(7), 929–933.

Nielsen, T. (2003). A review of mentation in REM and NREM sleep: "covert" REM sleep as a possible reconciliation of two opposing models. In E. Pace-Schott, M. Solms, M. Blagrove & S. Harnad (Eds.), *Sleep and dreaming: scientific advances and reconsiderations.* (pp. 59–74). Cambridge: Cambridge University Press.

Nowlis, V. (1970). Behavior and experience. In M. Arnold (Ed.), *Feelings and emotions.* New York: Academic Press.

Nussbaum, M. (2001). *Upheavals of thought: the intelligence of emotions.* Cambridge: Cambridge University Press.

O'Shaughnessy, B. (2002). *Consciousness and the world.* New York: Oxford University Press.

Old Testament. (1976). Genesis XLI. In J. Hertz (Ed.), *The Pentateuch and Haftorahs* (pp. 16–57) London: Soncino Press.

Ogden, C., & Richards, I. (1989). *The meaning of meaning: A study of the influence of language upon thought and of the science of symbolism.* San Diego, CA: Harcourt Brace Jovanovich.

Ohira, K., Kato, N., Namura, I., & Ishikawa, B. (1979). A psychopathology of schizophrenic dreaming: a feeling of passivity. *Sleep Research, 8,* 170.

Ornstein, P., Whitman, R., Kramer, M., & Baldridge, B. (1969). Drugs and dreams. IV. Tranquilizers and their effects upon dreams and dreaming in schizophrenic patients. *Experimental Medicine and Surgery, 27*(1-2), 145–156.

Osgood, C., Succi, G., & Tannenbaum, P. (1978). *The measurement of meaning.* Champaign: University of Illinois Press.

Overton, D. (1973). State-dependent retention of learned responses produced by drugs. Its relevance to sleep learning and recall. In W. Koella & P. Levine (Eds.), *Sleep 1972,48-53.* Basel: S. Karger.

Palmer, R. (1969). *Hermenutics: Interpretation theory in Schliermacher, Dilthey, Heidiegger and Gadamer.* Evanston, IL: Northwestern University Press.

Piaget, P. (1962). *Play, dreams and imitation in childhood.* New York: W. W. Norton.

Piccione, P., Jacobs, G., Kramer, M., & Roth, T. (1977). The relationship between daily activities, emotions and dream content. *Sleep Research, 6,* 133.

Piccione, P., Thomas, S., Roth, T., & Kramer, M. (1976). Incorporation of the laboratory situation in dreams. *Sleep Research, 5,* 120.

Piccione, P., Zorick, F., Lutz, T., Grissom, T., Kramer, M., & Roth, T. (1980). The efficacy of triazolam and chloral hydrate in geriatric insomniacs. *Journal of International Medical Research, 8*(5), 361–367.

Piotrowski, Z. (1973). The Piotrowski dream interpretation system. *Psychiatric Quarterly, 47,* 609–622.

Pivik, T. (2000). Psychophysiology of dreams. In M. Kryger, T. Roth & W. Dement (Eds.), *Principles and practice of sleep medicine* (3rd ed., pp. 491–501). Philadelphia: W. B. Saunders.

Polster, E. (1970). *An investigation of ego functioning in dreams.* Cleveland, OH: Case Western Reserve.

Puk, G. (1991). Treating traumatic memories: a case report on the eye movement desensitization procedure. *Journal of Behavior Therapy and Experimental Psychiatry, 22*(2), 149–151.

Purcell, S., Moffitt, A., & Hoffmann, R. (1993). Waking, dreaming and self-regulation. In A. Moffitt, M. Kramer & R. Hoffmann (Eds.), *The functions of dreams* (pp. 197–260). Albany: State University of New York Press.

Ramsey, G. (1953). Studies of dreaming. *Psychological Bulletin, 50*(6), 432–455.

Rank, O. (1952). *The myth of the birth of the hero: A psychological interpretation of mythology.* New York: R. Brunner.

Rechtschaffen, A., & Kales, A. (Eds.). (1968). *A manual of standardized terminology, techniques and scoring system for sleep stages of human subjects. Public Health Service.* Washington DC: US Government Printing Office.

Reiser, M. (1984). *Mind, brain, body: Toward a convergence of psychoanalysis and neurobiology.* New York: Basic Books.

Reiser, M. (2001). The dream in contemporary psychiatry. *American Journal of Psychiatry, 158*(3), 351–359.

Reynolds, C. (1989). Sleep disturbance in posttraumatic stress disorder: pathogenetic or epiphenomenal? *American Journal of Psychiatry, 146*(6), 695–696.

Riechers, M., Kramer, M., & Trinder, J. (1970). A replication of the Hall-Van de Castle character scale norms. *Psychophysiology, 7,* 328.

Riemann, D., Low, H., Schredl, M., Wiegand, M., Dippel, B., & Berger, M. (1990). Investigations of morning and laboratory dream recall and content in depressive patients during baseline conditions and under antidepressive treatment with trimipramine. *Psychiatric Journal of the University of Ottawa, 15*(2), 93–99.

Rimon, R., Fujita, M., & Takahata, N. (1986). Mood alterations and sleep. *Japanese Journal of Psychiatry and Neurology, 40*(2), 153–159.

Roehrs, T., Kramer, M., Lefton, W., Lutz, T., & Roth, T. (1973). Mood before and after sleep. *Sleep Research, 2,* 95.

Roffwarg, H., Dement, W., Muzio, J., & Fisher, C. (1962). Dream imagery: relationship to rapid eye movements of sleep. *Archives of General Psychiatry, 7,* 235–258.

Rosa, R., Bonnet, M., & Kramer, M. (1983). The relationship of sleep and anxiety in anxious subjects. *Biol Psychol, 16*(1-2), 119–126.

Rosa, R., Bonnet, M., Warm, J., & Kramer, M. (1981). The recovery of performance during sleep following sleep deprivation. *Sleep Research, 10,* 264.

Ross, J. (1965). Neurological findings after prolonged sleep deprivation. *Archives of Neurology, 12,* 399–403.

Ross, R., Ball, W., Dinges, D., Kribbs, N., Morrison, A., Silver, S., et al. (1994). Rapid eye movement sleep disturbance in posttraumatic stress disorder. *Biological Psychiatry, 35*(3), 195–202.

Ross, R., Ball, W., Sullivan, K., & Caroff, S. (1989). Sleep disturbance as the hallmark of posttraumatic stress disorder. *American Journal of Psychiatry, 146*(6), 697–707.

Ross, R., Ball, W., Sullivan, K., & Caroff, S. (1990). Letter: Sleep disturbance in post traumatic stress disorder. *American Journal of Psychiatry, 147,* 374.

Roth, T., Hartse, K., Saab, P., Piccione, P., & Kramer, M. (1980). The effects of flurazepam, lorazepam, and triazolam on sleep and memory. *Psychopharmacology (Berlin), 70*(3), 231-237.

Roth, T., & Kramer, M. (1976). Mood before and after sleep. *Psychiatric Journal of the University of Ottawa, 1,* 123–127.

Roth, T., Kramer, M., & Lutz, T. (1976). The effects of sleep deprivation on mood. *Psychiatric Journal of the University of Ottawa, 1,* 136–139.

Roth, T., Kramer, M., & Lutz, T. (1976a). Intermediate use of triazolam: A sleep laboratory study. *Journal of International Medical Research, 4*(1), 59–63.

Roth, T., Kramer, M., & Lutz, T. (1976b). The nature of insomnia: A descriptive summary of a sleep clinic population. *Comprehensive Psychiatry, 17*(1), 217–220.

Roth, T., Kramer, M., & Roehrs, T. (1977). The consistency of sleep measures. In W. Koella & P. Levin (Eds.), *Sleep 1976* (pp. 286–288). Basel: S. Karger.

Roth, T., Kramer, M., & Schwartz, J. (1974). Triazolam: A sleep laboratory study of a new benzodiazepine hypnotic. *Current Therapeutic Research, Clinical and Experimental, 16*(2), 117–123.

Roth, T., Kramer, M., & Trinder, J. (1972a). The effect of noise during sleep on the sleep patterns of different age groups. *Canadian Psychiatric Association Journal, 17*(2), Suppl. 2: SS197-201.

Roth, T., Kramer, M., & Trinder, J. (1972b). Volunteers versus non-volunteers in dream research. *Psychophysiology, 9,* 116.

Roth, T., Piccione, P., Salis, P., Kramer, M., & Kaffeman, M. (1979). Effects of temazepam, flurazepam and quinalbarbitone on sleep: Psychomotor and cognitive function. *British Journal of Clinical Pharmacology, 8*(1), 47S–54S.

Roth, T., Tietz, E., Kramer, M., & Kaffeman, M. (1979). The effect of a single dose of quazepam (Sch-16134) on the sleep of chronic insomniacs. *Journal of International Medical Research, 7*(6), 583–587.

Rupprecht, C. (1993). *The Dream and the text: essays on literature and language.* Albany: State University of New York Press.

Rychlak, J. (1960). Recalled dream themes and personality. *Journal of Abnormal and Social Psychology, 60,* 140–143.

Rychlak, J., & Brams, J. (1963). Personality dimensions in recalled dream content. *Journal of Projective Techniques, 27,* 226–234.

Sandler, L., Kramer, M., Fishbein, H., & Trinder, J. (1969). Interlaboratory reliability of the Hall-Van de Castle character scale. *Psychophysiology, 6,* 248.

Sandler, L., Kramer, M., Trinder, J., & Fishbein, H. (1970). Interlaboratory reliability of the Hall-Van de Castle characters, social interactions, activities, and emotions scales. *Psychophysiology, 7,* 333.

Sanford, J. (1968). *God's forgotten language.* New York: J. B. Lippincott.

Saul, L., Snyder, T., & Sheppard, E. (1956). On reading manifest dreams and other unconscious material. *Journal of American Psychoanalytic Association, 4,* 122–137.

Schacter, D. (2001). *The seven sins of memory: How the mind forgets and remembers.* Boston: Houghton Mifflin.

Schlosberg, A., & Benjamin, M. (1978). Sleep patterns in three acute combat fatigue cases. *Journal of Clinical Psychiatry, 39*(6), 546–549.

Schoen, L., Kramer, M., & Kinney, L. (1984). Auditory thresholds in the dream disturbed. *Sleep Research, 13,* 102.

Schoen, L., Kramer, M., & Kinney, L. (1985). Arousal patterns in NREM dream disturbed veterans. *Sleep Research, 12,* 315.

Schredl, M., Ciric, P., Gotz, S., & Wittmann, L. (2004). Typical dreams: stability and gender differences. *Journal of Psychology, 138*(6), 485–494.

Schreuder, J. (1996). Posttraumatic re-experiencing in older people: working through or covering up? *American Journal of Psychotherapy, 50*(2), 231–242.

Schrotter, K. (1959). Experimental dreams. In D. Rappaport (Ed.), *Organization and pathology of thought* (pp. 234–248). New York: Columbia University Press.

Schulman, B. (1969). An Adlerian view. In M. Kramer (Ed.), *Dream psychology and the new biology of dreaming* (117–131). Springfield, IL: Charles C. Thomas.

Schur, M. (1966). Some additional "day residues" of the "specimen dream of psychoanalysis." In R. Lowenstein, I. Newman, M. Schur, & A. Solnit (Eds.), *Psychoanalysis: A general psychology* (45-85). New York: International Universities Press.

Schwartz, D. (1939). *In dreams begins responsibilities.* New York: W. W. Norton.

Schwartz, J., Kramer, M., Palmer, T., & Roth, T. (1973). The relationship of personality factors to REM interruption and diary recall of dreams. *Sleep Research, 2,* 113.

Schwartz, J., Kramer, M., & Roth, T. (1974). Triazolam: a new benzodiazepine hypnotic and its effect on mood. *Current Therapeutic Research, Clinical and Experimental, 16*(9), 964–970.

Searles, J. (1992). *The rediscovery of mind.* Cambridge, MA: MIT Press.

Shafton, A. (1995). *Dream reader: Contemporary approaches to the understanding of dreams.* Albany: State University of New York Press.

Sharpe, E. (1951). *Dream analysis.* London: Hogarth Press.

Shrestha, N., Sharma, B., Van Ommeren, M., Regmi, S., Makaju, R., Komproe, I., et al. (1998). Impact of torture on refugees displaced within the developing world: Symptomatology among Bhutanese refugees in Nepal. *Journal of the American Medical Association, 280*(5), 443–448.

Siegel, L. (1980). Holocaust survivors in Hasidic and ultra-orthodox Jewish populations. *Journal of Contemporary Psychotherapy, 11,* 5–31.

Silberer, H. (1951). Report on a method of eliciting and observing certain hallucination phenomena (195-207). In D. Rappaport (Ed.), *Organization and pathology of thought.* New York: Columbia University Press.

Silvan-Adams, A., & Adams, M. (1990). "A dream is the fulfillment of a wish": traumatic dream, repetition compulsion and the pleasure principle. *International Journal of Psychoanalysis, 71,* 513–552.

Skinner, B. (1974). *About behaviorism* (1st ed.). New York: Knopf.

Smith, E. (1988). Concepts and thought. In R. Sternberg & E. Smith (Eds.), *The psychology of human thought* (pp. 19–49). Cambridge: Cambridge University Press.

Snyder, F. (1963). The new biology of dreaming. *Archives of General Psychiatry, 8,* 381–391.

Snyder, F. (1969). The physiology of dreaming. In M. Kramer (Ed.), *Dream psychology and the new biology of dreaming* (pp. 7–31). Springfield, IL: Charles C. Thomas.

Snyder, F. (1970). The phenomenology of dreaming. In L. Meadow & L. Stone (Eds.), *The psychodynamic complications of the physiological studies on dreams* (pp. 124–151). Springfield, IL: Charles C. Thomas.

Solms, M. (1997). *The neuropsychology of dreams: A clinico-anatomical study.* Mahwah, NJ: Erlbaum.

Solms, M. (2003). Dreaming and REM sleep are controlled by different mechanisms. In E. Pace-Schot, M. Solms, M. Blagrove & S. Harnad (Eds.), *Sleep and dreaming: Scientific advances and reconsiderations* (pp. 51–58). Cambridge: Cambridge University Press.

Spanjaard, J. (1969). The manifest dream content and its significance for the interpretation of dreams. *International Journal of Psychoanalysis, 50*(2), 221–235.

Sprince, M. (1984). Early psychic disturbances in anorexic and bulimic patients as reflected in psychoanalytic process. *International Journal of Child Psychotherapy*, 199–215.

Stern, B., & Stern, J. (1985). On the use of dreams as a means of diagnosis of brain-injured patients. *Scandanavian Jornal of Rehabilitation Medicine (Suppl), 12*, 44–46.

Stern, M., & Stern, B. (1990). Psychotherapy in cases of brain damage: A possible mission. *Brain Injury, 4*(3), 297–304.

Sternberg, R., & Smith, E. (1988). *The psychology of human thought*. Cambridge: Cambridge University Press.

Stickgold, R., Scott, L., Rittenhouse, C., & Hobson, J. (1999). Sleep-induced changes in associative memory. *Journal of Cognitive Neuroscience, 11*(2), 182–193.

Straker, G. (1994). Integrating African and Western healing practices in South Africa. *American Journal of Psychothery, 48*(3), 455–467.

Strauch, I., & Meier, B. (1996). *In search of dreams: results of experimental dream research*. Albany: State University of New York Press.

Strauss, M. (1968). *Familiar medical quotations* (1st ed.). Boston: Little.

Talmud. Haro'eh-chapter nine-Bearachos 55b.

Tart, C. (1979). From spontaneous event to lucidity: A review of attempts to consciously control nocturnal dreaming. In B. Wolman (Ed.), *Handbook of dreams* (226-288). New York: Van Norstrand Reinhold.

Taub, J., Kramer, M., Arand, D., & Jacobs, G. (1978). Nightmare dreams and nightmare confabulations. *Comprehensive Psychiatry, 19*(3), 285–291.

Tedlock, B. (1987). *Dreaming: Anthropological and psychological interpretations*. Cambridge: Cambridge University Press.

Terr, L. (1979). Children of Chowchilla. In *The psychoanalytic study of the child* (pp. 547–623). New Haven, CT: Yale University Press.

Terr, L. (1983a). Chowchilla revisited: The effects of psychic trauma four years after a school-bus kidnapping. *American Journal of Psychiatry, 140*(12), 1543–1550.

Terr, L. (1983b). Life attitudes, dreams and psychic trauma in a group of "normal" children. *Journal of the American Academy of Child Psychiatry, 22*(3), 221–230.

Titchener, J., & Kapp, F. (1976). Disaster at Buffalo Creek: Family and character change at Buffalo Creek. *American Journal of Psychiatry, 133*(3), 295–299.

Trenholme, I., Cartwright, R., & Greenberg, G. (1984). Dream dimension differences during a life change. *Psychiatry Research, 12*(1), 35–45.

Trinder, J., & Kramer, M. (1971). Dream recall. *American Journal of Psychiatry, 128*(3), 296–301.

Trinder, J., Kramer, M., Riechers, M., & Fishbein, H. (1970). The effect of dream length on dream content. *Psychophysiology, 7*, 333.

Ullman, M. (1969a). Discussion of Bonime, W. A culturist view. In M. Kramer (Ed.), *Dream psychology and the new biology of dreaming* (pp. 199–211). Springfield, IL: Charles C. Thomas.

Ullman, M. (1969b). Dreaming as metaphor in motion. *Archives of General Psychiatry, 21*(6), 696–703.

Ullman, M., & Zimmerman, N. (1979). *Working with dreams*. New York: Dellacorte Press.

Ushijima, S. (1988). On recovery from the postpsychotic collapse in schizophrenia. *Japanese Journal of Psychiatry and Neurology, 42*(2), 199–207.

Vaccarino, P., Rosa, R., Bonnet, M., & Kramer, M. (1981). The effect of 40 and 64 hours of sleep deprivation on mood. *Sleep Research, 10*, 269.

Van de Castle, R. (1974). Manifest content of schizophrenic dreams. *Sleep Research, 3*, 126.

Van de Castle, R. (1994). *Our dreaming mind*. New York: Ballantine Books.

van der Kolk, B., Blitz, R., Burr, W., Sherry, S., & Hartmann, E. (1984). Nightmares and trauma: A comparison of nightmares after combat with lifelong nightmares in veterans. *American Journal of Psychiatry, 141*(2), 187–190.

Van Dyke, C., Zilberg, N., & McKinnon, J. (1985). Post traumatic stress disorder: A thirty year delay in a world war II veteran. *American Journal of Psychiatry, 142*, 1070–1073.

van Velsen, T. (1984). Freud's specimen dream. Irma at the window: The fourth script of Freud's specimen dream. *American Imago, 41*, 245–293.

Verdone, P. (1965). Temporal reference of manifest dream content. *Perceptual and Motor Skills, 20*,(Suppl.),1253–1268.

Vogel, G., Foulkes, D., & Trosman, H. (1966). Ego functions and dreaming during sleep onset. *Archives of General Psychiatry, 14*(3), 238–248.

Von Grunebaum, G., & Caillois, R. (1966). *The dream and human societies*. Berkeley: University of California Press.

Ward, C., Beck, A., & Rascoe, E. (1961). Typical dreams. Incidence among psychiatric patients. *Archives of General Psychiatry, 5*, 606–615.

Watson, I. (1993). Post-traumatic stress disorder in Australian prisoners of the Japanese: a clinical study. *Australian and New Zealand Journal of Psychiatry, 27*(1), 20–29.

Webb, W. (1969). Partial and differential sleep deprivation. In A. Kales (Ed.), *Sleep physiology and pathology: A symposium* (pp. 221–231). Philadelphia: Lippincott.

Webb, W., & Kersey, J. (1967). Recall of dreams and the probability of stage 1-REM sleep. *Perceptual and Motor Skills, 24*(2), 627–630.

Weisz, R., & Foulkes, D. (1970). Home and laboratory dreams collected under uniform sampling conditions. *Psychophysiology, 6*(5), 588–596.

Wells, B., Chu, C., Johnson, R., Nasdahl, C., Ayubi, M., Sewell, E., et al. (1991). Buspirone in the treatment of posttraumatic stress disorder. *Pharmacotherapy, 11*(4), 340–343.

Wells, L. (1980). Anorexia nervosa: an illness of young adults. *Psychiatric Quarterly, 52*(4), 270–282.

White, R. (1990). *The interpretation of dreams: Oneirocritica by Artemidorus*. Torrance, CA: Original Books Inc.

Whitman, R. (1963). Remembering and forgetting dreams in psychoanalysis. *Journal of the American Psychoanalytic Association, 11*, 752–74.

Whitman, R., Kramer, M., & Baldridge, B. (1963a). Experimental study of supervision of psychotherapy. *Archives of General Psychiatry, 106*, 529–535.

Whitman, R., Kramer, M., & Baldridge, B. (1963b). Which dream does the patient tell? *Archives of General Psychiatry, 8*, 277–282.

Whitman, R., Kramer, M., & Baldridge, B. (1969). Dreams about the patient. An approach to the problem of countertransference. *Journal of the American Psychoanalytic Association, 17*(3), 702–727.

Whitman, R., Kramer, M., Ornstein, P., & Baldridge, B. (1967). The physiology, psychology and utilization of dreams. *American Journal of Psychiatry, 124*(3), 287–302.

Whitman, R., Kramer, M., Ornstein, P., & Baldridge, B. (1969). Drugs and dream content. *Experimental Medicine and Surgery, 27*(1-2), 210-223.

Whitman, R., Kramer, M., Ornstein, P., & Baldridge, B. (1970). The varying uses of the dream in clinical psychiatry. In L. Madow & L. Stone (Eds.), *The psychodynamic implications of the physiological studies on dreams* (pp. 24–46). Springfield, IL: Charles C. Thomas.

Whitman, R., Ornstein, P., & Baldridge, B. (1964). An experimental approach to the psychoanalytic theory of dreams and conflicts. *Comprehensive Psychiatry, 5*, 349–361.

Whitman, R., Pierce, C., & Maas, J. (1960). Drugs and dreams. In L. Uhr & J. Miller (Eds.), *Drugs and behavior* (pp. 591–595). New York: Wiley.

Whitman, R., Pierce, C., Maas, J., & Baldridge, B. (1962). The dreams of the experimental subject. *Journal of Nervous and Mental Disorders, 134*, 431–439.

Wilkinson, C. (1983). Aftermath of a disaster: the collapse of the Hyatt Regency Hotel skywalks. *American Journal of Psychiatry, 140*(9), 1134–1139.

Wilkinson, W. (1968). Sleep deprivation: performance tests for partial and selective sleep deprivation. In I. Abt & B. Reis (Eds.), *Progress in clinical psychology* (Vol. 17, pp. 28–43). New York: Grune and Stratton.

Williams, R., Karacan, I., & Hursch, C. (1974). *Electroencephalography (EEG) of human sleep: Clinical applications*. New York: Wiley.

Wilmer, H. (1982). Dream seminar for chronic schizophrenic patients. *Psychiatry, 45*(4), 351-360.

Wilmer, H. (1996). The healing nightmare: war dreams of Vietnam veterans. In D. Barrettt (Ed.), *Trauma and dreams* (pp. 88–99). Cambridge, MA: Harvard University Press.

Wilson, C. (1982). The fear of being fat and anorexia nervosa. *International Journal of Psychoanalysis and Psychotherapy, 9*, 233–255.

Wilson, C. (1983). Dream interpretation. In C. Wilson (Ed.), *Fear of being fat: The treatment of anorexia nervosa* (pp. 245–254). New York: Jason Aronson.

Winget, C., & Kramer, M. (1979). *Dimensions of dreams.* Gainesville: University Presses of Florida.

Winget, C., Kramer, M., & Whitman, R. (1972). Dreams and demography. *Canadian Psychiatric Association Journal, 17*(2)(Suppl. 2), SS203–SS208.

Winson, J. (1985). *Brain and psyche: The biology of the unconscious* (1st ed.). Garden City, NY: Anchor Press/Doubleday.

Winson, J. (1990). The meaning of dreams. *Scientific American, 263*(5), 86–88, 90-92, 94-96.

Witkin, H., & Lewis, H. (1967a). *Experimental studies of dreaming.* New York: Random House.

Witkin, H., & Lewis, H. (1967b). Pre-sleep experiences and dreams. In H. Witkin & H. Lewis (Eds.), *Experimental studies in dreaming* (pp. 148–201). New York: Random House.

Witkin, H., Oltman, P., Raskin, E., & Karp, S. (1971). *Group embedded figures test manual.* Palo Alto, CA: Consulting Psychological Press.

Wood, J., & Bootzin, R. (1990). The prevalence of nightmares and their independence from anxiety. *Journal of Abnormal Psychology, 99*, 64–68.

Woodward, S., Arsenault, E., Bliwise, D., & Gusman, F. (1991a). Physical symptoms accompanying dream reports in combat veterans. *Sleep Research, 20*, 153.

Woodward, S., Arsenault, E., Bliwise, D., & Gusman, F. (1991b). The temporal distribution of combat nightmares in Vietnam combat veterans. *Sleep Research, 20*, 152.

Yronwode, C. (2003). *Aunt Sally's policy players dream book.* Reprinted in *"Hoodo in theory and practice."* Forrestville, CA: Lucky Mojo Curio Co.

Index